ADVANCES IN MOTOR DEVELOPMENT RESEARCH

ADVANCES IN MOTOR DEVELOPMENT RESEARCH

Volume Two

Edited by

Jane E. Clark

and

James H. Humphrey

AMS PRESS
New York

Advances in Motor Development Research, 2

ISSN 0888-2990

International Standard Book Number
Series: 0-404-63450-8
Vol. 2: 0-404-63452-4
Library of Congress Catalog Card Number: 86-47829

AMS Press, Inc.
56 East 13th Street
New York, N.Y. 10003

MANUFACTURED IN THE UNITED STATES OF AMERICA

About the Editors

Jane E. Clark, Associate Professor of Physical Education at the University of Maryland, conducts and directs research in motor development. Her major research interest is in the area of motor control and coordination. Currently she is focusing on the development of locomotor skills.

James H. Humphrey, Professor Emeritus at the University of Maryland, is perhaps best known for his work in child learning through motor activity. In recent years he has been exploring the area of stress in childhood with reference to its influence on child development.

CONTENTS

Board of Reviewers   ix

Contributors   xi

Preface   xv

1. **Temporal Parameters in Jumping as Performed by Adults and Children**
   Beth E. Barnett 1

2. **Postural Support and Fine Motor Control in Children with Normal and Slow Motor Development**
   Donna Adams Johnson and *Harriet G. Williams* 23

3. **Development of Postural Control in Children: Effects of Gymnastics Training**
   Bettina Debu, Marjorie Woollacott, and *Marilyn Mowatt* 41

4. **The Effects of Age on Unresisted and Resisted Fractionated Reaction Time**
   Nancy C. Rich 71

5. **Perceptual Development and its Differential Influence on Limb Positioning Under Two Movement Conditions in Children**
   Katherine T. Thomas and *Jerry R. Thomas* 83

6. **The Effects of Controlled Videogame Playing on the Eye-Hand Coordination and Reaction Time of Children**
   Patricia J. McSwegin, Cynthia Pemberton, and *Nancy O'Banion* 97

7. **The Interaction of Conceptual Tempo and Modeling on the Motor Performance of 10- and 11-year-old Children**
   Shirley DeVard Brown and *Amelia M. Lee* 103

8. **Contributions of Motor, Concept, and Communication Skills to Preschool Learning**
   Geoffrey D. Broadhead and *Gabie E. Church* 115

Review Section

9. **The Weaver's Loom: A Developmental Metaphor**
   Mary Ann Roberton 129

10. **The Development of Visually Directed Reaching: From Description to Explanation**
    Jill Whitall 143

11. **Prehensile Development: A Contrast of Mature and Immature Patterns**
    Diane Manchester 165

12. **Development of Object Interception**
    Kathleen Williams 201

13. **Facilitating Aquatic Motor Development: A Review of Developmental and Environmental Variables**
    Stephen Langendorfer, Lawrence D. Bruya, and *Amy Reid* 219

Index 237

ix

Esther Thelen
Indiana University

Beverly Ulrich
Indiana University

Ann Van Sant
Medical College of Virginia

Michael G. Wade
University of Minnesota

Maureen Weiss
University of Oregon

Jill Whitall
University of Maryland

Harriet G. Williams
University of South Carolina

Kathleen Williams
Kansas State University

Marjorie Woollacott
University of Oregon

Craig Wrisberg
University of Tennessee

Judith Young
University of Maryland

X

CONTRIBUTORS

Beth E. Barnett,
Department of Physical Education,
Manhattan College, New York, NY

Geoffrey D. Broadhead,
School of Health, Physical Education, Recreation & Dance,
Louisiana State University, Baton Rouge, LA

Shirley DeVard Brown,
Department of Health, Physical Education, Recreation and Dance,
Southern University, Baton Rouge, LA

Lawrence D. Bruya,
Department of Physical Education,
North Texas State University, Denton, TX

Gabie E. Church,
Department of Experimental Statistics,
Louisiana State University, Baton Rouge, LA

Bettina Debu,
Department of Physical Education & Human Movement Studies,
University of Oregon, Eugene, OR

Donna Adams Johnson,
Department of Physical Therapy,
St. Louis School, Tyler, TX

Stephen Langendorfer,
School of Physical Education, Recreation & Dance,
Kent State University, Kent, OH

Amelia M. Lee,
School of Health, Physical Education, Recreation & Dance,
Louisiana State University, Baton Rouge, LA

Patricia J. McSwegin,
Division of Health, Physical Education, Recreation & Athletics,
Emporia State University, Emporia, KS

Diane Manchester,
Department of Physical Education & Human Movement Studies,
University of Oregon, Eugene, OR

Marilyn Mowatt,
Department of Physical Education & Human Movement Studies,
University of Oregon, Eugene, OR

Nancy O'Banion,
Division of Health, Physical Education, Recreation & Athletics,
Emporia State University, Emporia, KS

Cynthia Pemberton,
Department of Physical Education,
University of North Dakota, Grand Forks, ND

Amy Reid,
Department of Physical Education,
North Texas State University, Denton, TX

Nancy C. Rich,
Department of Health, Physical Education & Recreation,
Miami University, Oxford, OH

Mary Ann Roberton,
Department of Physical Education & Dance,
University of Wisconsin, Madison, WI

Jerry R. Thomas,
School of Health, Physical Education, Recreation & Dance,
Louisiana State University, Baton Rouge, LA

Katherine T. Thomas,
Department of Physical Education,
Southeastern Louisiana University, Hammond, LA

Harriet G. Williams,
Department of Physical Education,
University of South Carolina, Columbia, SC

Kathleen Williams,
Department of Physical Education, Dance & Leisure Studies,
Kansas State University, Manhattan, KS

Jill Whitall,
Department of Physical Education,
University of Maryland, College Park, MD

Marjorie Woollacott,
Department of Physical Education & Human Movement Studies,
University of Oregon, Eugene, OR

PREFACE

This second volume of *Advances in Motor Development Research* presents a variety of papers that are concerned with various aspects of motor development. Criteria for the consideration of papers for publication consisted of (1) original manuscripts of significant research topics in which valid research techniques were applied in the collection of data, with appropriate statistical treatment of the data, (2) state-of-the-art reviews on topics of current interest with a substantial research literature base and (3) theoretical papers presenting well formulated but as yet untested models. All papers were evaluated by the editors and at least two scholars with expertise in the particular topical area in question.

It is the intention of the editors and AMS Press, Inc. to provide a periodic series that reports original research and review papers that contribute to our understanding of motor development. The volumes should supplement and support journals and annual reviews reporting on similar topics. However, to the best knowledge of the editors, *Advances in Motor Development Research* is the only current series or periodical publication devoted specifically to research in motor development.

Motor development continues to evolve into a complicated and complex subject and involves, among others, biological, behavioral and biomechanical considerations. The scholarly researchers who have contributed to this second volume represent the field well, and we wish to extend our gratitude to them for their contributions. In addition, we wish to thank the members of the distinguished board of reviewers for giving their time and talent in evaluating the papers.

A volume of this nature could serve as a basic and/or supplementary text in motor development courses, as well as a reference for motor development specialists and for scientists investigating similar topics.

TEMPORAL PARAMETERS IN JUMPING AS PERFORMED BY ADULTS AND CHILDREN

Beth E. Barnett

Manhattan College

ABSTRACT

This study examined the effects of age (four-, six-, and eight-year-old children, and adults) and of preview (116, 181, and 260 ms) on possible temporal parameters used to organize a jump over a moving object. Cinematographic analysis yielded duration measures for the preparation, the action, and the flight phases, as well as for the movement time of the jump. Results indicated that all durations measures, except those of the flight phase, varied significantly across preview distances. Further analysis indicated decreasing variability in phase duration as the subject moved closer, in time, to passing over the moving object for the eight-year-old and the adult groups only. Relative timing of jump phases (phase durations divided by the movement time) as well as relative phasings (duration of one phase divided by the duration of another phase) varied significantly across preview distances. Both of these temporal characteristics were rejected as possible invariant features of the jump. Age-related differences in the temporal organization of the jump were discussed.

Research indicates developmental differences in the timing of motor skills (Hoffman, Imwold, & Koller, 1983; Stadulis, 1985; Williams, 1985). Some investigators have used age-related improvements in accuracy as indicators of these differences (Ball & Glencross, 1985; Williams, 1973). Variations in error scores have been used to observe accuracy changes across task conditions (Gallagher & Thomas, 1980). Few researchers have attempted to chart changes in movement characteristics which allow the age-related improvements or the task-related changes in accuracy. The present study represents such an attempt.

The ability to adapt a motor skill to changes in the temporal (such as target speed) or spatial (such as target size) characteristics of the performance environment has long been recognized (Bernstein, 1967). However, the manner in which these adaptations are made is not as clear. Several researchers have proposed possible means whereby the characteristics of a movement are adapted to changes within the performance environment. Two such proposals are discussed below.

Schmidt (1976, 1982) suggested that variation within the overall duration, the overall force and, possibly, the overall response size of a movement allows the execution of that movement under different environmental and task demands. Characteristics like relative phasing and relative force have been suggested as nonvarying movement characteristics (Pew, 1974; Schmidt, 1976; Shapiro & Schmidt, 1982). Schmidt applied the term "invariant features" to the nonvarying characteristics of a movement.

Several researchers have supported the use of invariant features and parameters in the organization of motor skills. An initial investigation in this area was undertaken by Armstrong (1970) who trained subjects to perform a sequence of arm movements at a set speed. When the task demands were changed so that a different performance speed was required, the movement time of the sequence varied. However, the relative timing of the different movement components (or phases) remained the same. Similar findings have been reported for handwheel cranking (Glencross, 1973), lever rotations (Shapiro, 1976), walking and jogging on a treadmill (Shapiro, Zernicke, Gregor, & Diestal, 1981), serial key pressing (Summers, 1975), and typing and handwriting (Viviani & Terzuolo, 1980).

A different perspective on the adaptation of movement characteristics to variations within the performance environment has resulted from investigations by several researchers (Gentile, Higgins, Miller, & Rosen, 1975; Higgins & Spaeth, 1972; Spaeth, 1973). Using a dart-throwing task, these investigators observed changes in movement characteristics which appeared to 'match' (Gentile et al., 1975; Higgins, 1972) changes in the spatial (position) or temporal (speed) characteristics of the target at which the darts were thrown. Results of these studies indicated that changes in the spatial or temporal characteristics of the target resulted in changes in the duration of the preparation phase (drawing the wrist of the throwing hand back toward the body) of the movement. In contrast to these duration changes within the preparation phase, Spaeth (1973) reported an apparent attempt by her subjects to maintain a constant duration for the action phase of the dart-throwing movement.

A comparison of the results of the Spaeth study with those of the Armstrong study indicated an incongruence. Armstrong reported an invariant relative phasing within the sequences of an arm movement. Spaeth reported a constant absolute duration of the action phase coupled with a variable duration of the preparation phase. Therefore, the relative timing of these phases was not consistent across changes in the speed characteristics of the target.

A similar conflict has appeared within a single investigation by Moxley and Moxley (1976). Their task, which involved knocking over three barriers while maintaining a constant movement time, allowed these researchers to compare consistencies in the absolute durations of each phase of this movement. They reported two response strategies. One strategy involved the maintenance of a consistent relative relationship among the durations of the movement phases, even at the cost of a variable movement time. The second strategy produced a variable relative timing of movement phases but maintained a constant movement time. While preliminary in nature, this investigation further illustrates the conflict between findings of variant and invariant relative timing in the organization of movement. Further investigation of movement timing is necessary before this conflict in results may be resolved.

The present study attempted to observe change and invariance in the absolute durations of movement phases and/or the relative timings of movement phases across changes in the performance environment. Additionally, developmental changes in the temporal characteristics of a movement were observed. Indications of age-related differences in movement organization were noted.

METHODS

Subjects

Four adults and 12 children, with 4 children in each of three age groups, participated in this study. Children were selected for inclusion within the 4-year-old group (in years and months, $M = 3:10$), the 6-year-old group ($M = 6:1$), or the 8-year-old group ($M = 7:11$). The adult group had a mean age of 21:3. Children were obtained through faculty and students at Manhattan College. Adults were selected from students currently in attendance at Manhattan College.

Apparatus

A wooden stick (38.10 × 3.81 cm) was released from the top of an inclined ramp (182.88 × 30.48 cm; slope = 45°). To obscure the subject's view of all but the final 5 cm of the ramp a black curtain (171.6 × 105.6 cm) was suspended from a wooden frame. A black carpet, placed under the performance area, aided in the reduction of sound from the rolling stick and provided better contrast between the white stick and the performance surface.

Cinematography and Cinematographic Analysis

A motor driven Red Lakes Laboratories Lo-Cam camera, fitted with a 25 mm lens and operating at 100 frames per sec, was positioned orthogonal to the black carpet covering the performance surface. The lens-to-subject distance was 2.44 m. The camera held in view the right side of the subject, the white marker designating the preview distance for the trial, and the visible 5 cm of the inclined ramp.

Film records were analyzed using a Lafayette film-analyzing projector and a rear projection system. Frame-by-frame analysis involved the use of a sonic digitizer (Science Accessories, graph pen series 6, model 30) to determine the x,y coordinates for the hip, knee, and ankle joints. A reliability coefficient of 0.98 was obtained based on the redigitizing of three trials per subject for a total of 48 trials. Angles at the knee joint were derived from the x,y coordinates and plotted against time.

Jump phases were defined by transitional changes in the direction of knee motion. The preparation phase was defined as beginning at the frame containing the first reduction in the angle at the knee and terminating at the frame before the first increase in knee angle. The action phase was defined as beginning with the frame in which the first increase in angle at the knee occurred and terminating with the last frame before the subject lost contact with the support surface. Finally, the frame in which the subject was no longer in contact with the support surface of the frame in which contact was regained was defined as the flight phase. Movement time was defined as the combined durations of the preparation, action, and flight phases.

The distance covered by each jump was obtained by calculating the change in the x coordinate of the ankle joint from the initiation of the preparation phase to the termination of the flight phase. Preresponse time was calculated as the time from when the stick first became visible until the initiation of the preparation phase of the jump.

Procedures

Subjects were instructed to assume one of three distances relative to the end of the inclined ramp.[1] Each distance represented a different preview condition. The distance of 4 ft (121.92 cm, producing an average stick velocity of 120.0 cm/sec and an average preview time of 116 ms) represented "limited" preview. "Moderated" preview was represented by a distance of 7 ft (213.36 cm, producing an average stick velocity of 118.0 cm/sec and an average preview time of 181 ms). Finally, 10 ft (304.8 cm, producing an average stick velocity of 117.0 cm/sec and producing an average preview time of 260 ms) represented the "extended" preview condition. A moveable white marker (1 × 36 in; 2.54

× 91.44 cm) was used to indicate to the subjects which relative distance they were to assume on each trial.

Subjects were told to initiate their jumps from a position directly behind the white marker. Periodic reminders of these instructions were given as necessary throughout the testing session. Prior to the release of the stick down the inclined ramp, the verbal signal of "ready" was issued. Subjects were instructed in the meaning of this signal and were told that no response to the signal was necessary. No feedback concerning the jump was given. Following each trial, the white marker was removed and replaced at the preview distance required for the next trial.

The three preview conditions were randomly presented within a block of three trials. A total of five blocks of trials were presented. Thus, each subject received a total of 15 trials.

Scores were represented by the mean of three successful trials analyzed under one preview condition. Success was defined as passing over the stick without contact. All subjects within the adult group and 2 of the 4 subjects within the 8-year-old group were able to complete this task successfully on all trials. All subjects were successful on at least three trials at each preview condition.[2] In order to insure that the analyzed responses were comparable across age groups, only the first three successful trials were analyzed at any one preview condition.

Statistical Analyses

The absolute duration of the preparation (ADP), the action (ADA), and the flight (ADF) phases, as well as the movement time of the jump were each analyzed separately. A simple main effects, 4 × 3 (age by preview condition) ANOVA was used for each duration analysis. The same statistical design was also used to analyze the distance jumped and the preresponse time.

To further investigate variability across preview in the absolute duration of each jump phase, a variability score was calculated. Coefficients of variation (standard deviation divided by the mean) were calculated, trial by trial, for all phases of the jump. Scores consisted of the mean of the three trials analyzed at each of the three preview conditions. A 4 × 3 (age by phase) simple main effects ANOVA was used for the analysis of this variable.

To assess the relative relationship within the temporal organization of the jump, both relative timing and relative phasing were analyzed.[3] The relative timing of the phases of the jump were calculated by dividing the absolute duration of each phase by the movement time. Relative timings were calculated trial by trial, with subjects' scores represented by the mean of the three ratios under each preview condition. These ratios were calculated for the preparation, the action, and the flight phases.

Relative phasings also were calculated trial by trial with subjects' scores consisting of the mean of the three ratios under each preview condition. Three ratios were obtained from these calculations. The first ratio represented the absolute duration of the action divided by the absolute duration of the preparation phase. The second ratio represented the absolute duration of the flight phase divided by the absolute duration of the preparation phase. Finally, the third ratio represented the absolute duration of the action phase divided by the absolute duration of the flight phase.

Individual 4 × 3 (age by preview condition) simple main effects ANOVAs were used to evaluate the relative timing and the relative phasing ratios. Each ratio was analyzed separately.

Tests of simple main effects were undertaken for all analyses. Significance levels were set at $p < .0125$ for group effects and at $p < .017$ for treatment effects. Newman-Keuls tests, with $p < .05$, were used for all post hoc analyses.

RESULTS

Absolute Duration Analyses

Movement time

The analysis of movement time revealed significant main effects of preview condition ($F(2, 24) = 70.44, p < .01$) and a significant age by preview condition interaction ($F(6, 24) = 2.76, p < .05$). Significant simple main effects of preview condition were found for all age groups ($F(2, 24) = 37.97, 22.58, 7.32,$ and 10.84 for the 4-, 6-, and 8-year-old, and adult groups, respectively). Post hoc analysis indicated significantly shorter movement times at the limited preview when compared to the extended and moderate conditions for the adult and the 8-year-old groups. All pairwise comparisons were significant for the younger subject groups. Subjects lengthened their movement time as preview was increased (Fig. 1).

Absolute duration of the preparation phase (ADP)

Main effects of preview condition ($F(2, 24) = 76.03, p < .01$) were significant for the ADP (Fig. 1). Simple main effects of preview condition were present within all age groups ($F(2, 24) = 16.54; 19.57, 15.05,$ and 28.16 for the 4-, 6-, and 8-year-old, and the adult groups, respectively). Post hoc analysis indicated a significantly smaller ADP at limited preview for the 4- and the 8-year-old groups. All pairwise comparisons were significant for the 6-year-old and the adult groups. As with movement time, subjects lengthened their ADP as preview was increased.

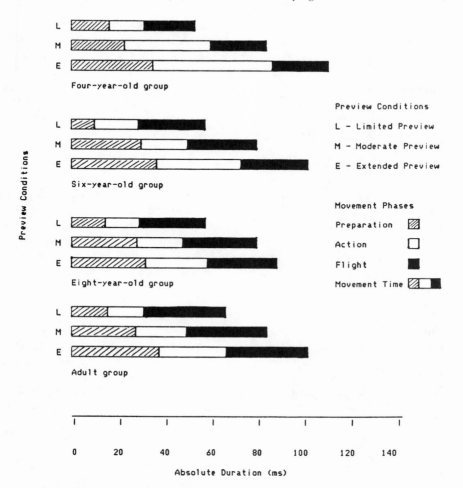

FIG. 1. Movement time and absolute durations for the preparation phase (ADP), the action phase (ADA), and the flight phase (ADF) at limited, moderate, and extended preview conditions

Absolute duration of the action phase (ADA)

Main effects of preview condition ($F(2, 24) = 60.79$, $p < .01$) and the interaction of age with preview condition ($F(6, 24) = 7.91$, $p < .01$) were significant for the ADA (Fig. 1). Simple main effects of age were present at the extended preview condition only ($F(3, 36) = 11.49$). This effect was attributed to the significantly longer ADA produced by the 4-year-old and the 6-year-old groups when compared to the 8-year-old and the adult groups at the extended preview condition. Simple main effects of preview condition were present within the 4-, 6-, and 8-year-old groups ($F(2, 24)$ = 55.09, 22.16, and 5.01, respectively). Post hoc analysis indicated significant differences within all pairwise comparisons for the 4- and the 6-year-old groups. The trend toward longer durations in response to increased preview continued within these age groups. The two older age groups demonstrated significant differences between the mean ADA at the limited and the extended previews only.

Absolute duration of the flight phase (ADF).

Main effects of age were present in the analysis of ADF ($F(3, 12)$ = 6.25, $p < .01$). Simple main effects of age were present for all preview conditions ($F(3, 36)$ = 9.94, 4.44, and 5.52 for limited, moderate, and extended preview conditions, respectively). The 4-year-old group demonstrated the shortest ADF at all preview conditions. The adult group had significantly longer means in all comparisons except with the 8-year-old group at the moderate preview condition.

Distance jumped

The shorter ADF demonstrated by the youngest subjects did not indicate that they covered less distance with their jumps. The ANOVA for distance jumped indicated main effects of age ($F(3, 12)$ = 48.15, $p < .01$) and preview condition ($F(2, 24)$ = 12.80, $p < .01$). Post hoc analysis revealed a significantly longer mean distance covered by the 4-year-old group when compared to the 8-year-old and the adult groups at the limited preview condition. At the moderate condition, both the 4- and the 6-year-old groups showed significantly longer mean distance covered when compared to the two oldest groups. Finally, the adult group demonstrated a significantly shorter mean distance when compared to all other age groups at the extended preview condition.

From subjective observation of the film records, it appeared that older subjects waited until the stick approached their starting position behind the white line. These subjects jumped vertically into the air, allowing the stick to roll beneath them. Younger children were more likely to jump out to meet the rolling stick. This strategy resulted in the younger subjects covering more distance with their jumps. Children in the 6- and 8-year-old groups appeared to jump out toward the stick under the extended preview condition (Fig. 2).

Preresp-time

Prerespose time

To further explore this phenomenon, prerespose time was analyzed. The interaction of age with preview condition ($F(6, 24)$ = 3.42, $p < .05$) was

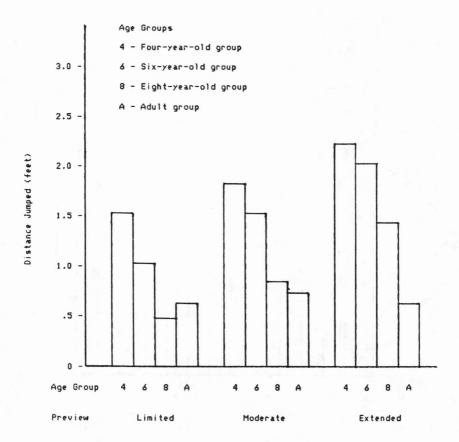

FIG. 2. Mean distance jumped at limited, moderate, and extended preview

significant. Simple main effects of preview condition were present within all age groups ($F(2, 24)$ = 26.42, 42.85, 85.19, and 63.11 for the 4-, 6-, and 8-year-old, and the adult groups, respectively). Each age group demonstrated a significantly longer preresponse time as preview was increased (Fig. 3). Of greater interest to the present discussion was the finding of simple main effects of age at the extended preview condition ($F(3, 36)$ = 8.36). This finding was due, in part, to the significantly shorter preresponse time of the 4-year-old group when compared to the preresponse time of the other age groups. Additionally, the 8-year-old group demonstrated a significantly longer preresponse time when compared to all other age groups at this preview condition.

The finding of an early response by younger children is congruent with the findings of other researchers (Rothstein, 1970; Shea, Krampitz, Northam, &

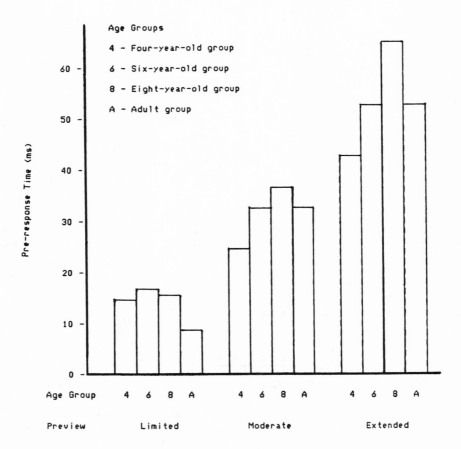

FIG. 3. Preresponse time (time from first view of block until initiation of the preparation phase) at the limited, moderate, and extended preview conditions

Ashby, 1982; Stadulis, 1972; Williams, 1985). These studies found that, with slow moving objects (which produce longer previews), young children appear to have difficulty waiting for the stimulus to reach an optimal position for response. As a result, they tended to respond early. As in the above mentioned studies, the younger children within this investigation tended to respond early in situations where a longer preresponse time might be expected. However, these children still experienced success in the execution of this task, in spite of their early responses.

The success of older children and younger subjects, despite the differences in the duration characteristics of their jumps, suggests the use of different approaches or strategies in the organization and execution of this movement. Older subjects apparently tried to ''use up'' extra time provided by the increased preview early in the organization and execution of their jumps. These subjects showed large increases in their preresponse times, smaller increases in the duration of their preparation phases, and little or no increase in the durations of their action and flight phases as preview was increased. This approach allowed the subjects to execute a jump in which they waited for the moving stick to come to them rather than jumping out to meet it.

Younger children demonstrated less of a change in their preresponse time across preview conditions. Therefore, under conditions of increased preview, they still had time to be ''used up'' before they could jump over the stick by allowing it to roll beneath their feet during the flight phase of the jump. The use of a shorter preresponse time led to a situation in which the stick was further away from the subject during all movement phases. The younger subjects could choose to lengthen the durations of their early movement phases, allowing the stick more travel time under conditions of increased preview. Or, the subjects could jump out to meet the stick rather than waiting for the stick to roll to them. Within this investigation, the younger subjects did lengthen the durations of their preparation and action phases. However, they also tended to jump further when preview was increased. From the information at hand, it is impossible to conclude whether their longer jumps were a product of their shorter preresponse times, or if some other parameter has influenced this characteristic of the jump. Further study of other movement parameters is necessary.

Summary of the absolute duration analyses

The results of the absolute duration analyses indicated a significant effect of preview condition on movement time and on ADP for all age groups. This effect also was seen in the ADA for the two younger age groups. Similar to the findings of Spaeth (1973) in her analysis of the dart throw, the 8-year-old and adult groups exhibited a variable duration for the preparation phase and no significant difference in the mean durations of the action phase between the moderate and extended preview conditions. Finally, no significant effect of preview condition was seen in the analysis of the ADF. It was concluded that adaptation within the temporal characteristics of the jump to available (preview) time occurred within the early (preparation and action phases) portions of the jump. The durations of the later jump phases (flight and, for the adult group, action) showed little effect of change in preview condition.

While the results of the analysis of the ADF would allow acceptance of this characteristic as an invariant feature, several aspects of the experimental task make it impossible to generalize this finding. Within this study, size characteristics of the stick were held constant across preview conditions. Because of this, the time needed to remain in the air in order to avoid contact with the stick did not vary across preview conditions. Had size characteristics been varied, the duration of the flight phase also may have varied. In light of the previous discussion, acceptance of the ADF as an invariant feature of the jump must await further investigation of the effects of covariation of spatial and temporal characteristics of the environment on this phase of the jump.

Analysis of the Coefficients of Variation (COV)

The main effects of age ($F(3, 12) = 5.45$, $p < .05$) and of phase ($F(2, 24) = 52.26$, $p < .01$), as well as the interaction of age with phase ($F(6, 24) = 3.50$, $p < .05$) were significant in the analysis of COV (Fig. 4). Significant simple main effects of age were present for the action ($F(3, 36) = 4.25$) and

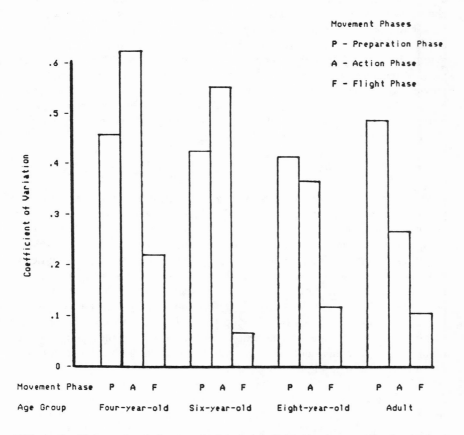

FIG. 4. Coefficients of variation (standard deviation divided by the mean) for the absolute durations of the preparation, action, and flight phases

flight phases ($F(3, 36) = 10.56$). The 4-year-old group had a significantly greater mean COV at the flight phase when compared to all other age groups. Both the 4- and 6-year-old groups demonstrated larger means for the action phase when compared to those of the two older age groups.

Significant simple main effects of phase were present for all age groups ($F(2, 24) = 15.50$, 23.56, 9.56, and 13.51 for 4-, 6-, and 8-year-old, and adult groups, respectively). However, the relationship between the mean COV at the preparation and action phases changed from one age group to another. The two younger groups demonstrated a significantly higher mean COV for the action phase when compared to the preparation and flight phases and a larger mean at the preparation phase when compared to the flight phase. The two older groups demonstrated a significantly lower mean COV for the flight phase when compared to the action and preparation phases. The adult group also demonstrated a significantly larger mean at the preparation phase when compared to the action phase.

The results of this analysis indicated that the duration of the later portion of the jump (flight) was less variable than the earlier portions (action and preparation) for all age groups. As indicated by this analysis and the analysis of ADF, variation in preview conditions had little effect on the duration of the flight phase. Age became a factor in determining the most variable phase. As reflected in this and the analysis of ADA, the adults and, to a lesser extent, children within the 8-year-old group, demonstrated less variability in ADA when compared to ADP. However, children in the younger groups were less variable in their ADP.

The results of the analysis of COV also support the use of different strategies for the organization of the jump by older and younger subjects. Subjects within the 8-year-old and the adult groups demonstrated greater variability within the ADP. They appear to adapt to changes in preview during this early phase of their movement. Lesser adaptations were made during the action phases and even fewer during the flight phase.

Younger children appear to make similar types of adaptations during the preparation phase of their jump. However, variation within their ADA is much larger than that exhibited by older children and adults. Perhaps this variation reflects an attempt by the younger subjects to "use up" the progressively greater amounts of time provided by their shorter preresponse times under conditions of increased preview. While a cause and effect relationship cannot be established from the data at hand, results do suggest a need for further investigation of the strategies used by the different age groups within this study.

Analyses of the Relative Timing of Each Phase

Relative timing of the preparation phase

Significant main effects of preview condition ($F(2, 24) = 16.84$, $p < .01$) were present in the relative timing of the preparation phase (Fig. 5). Simple main

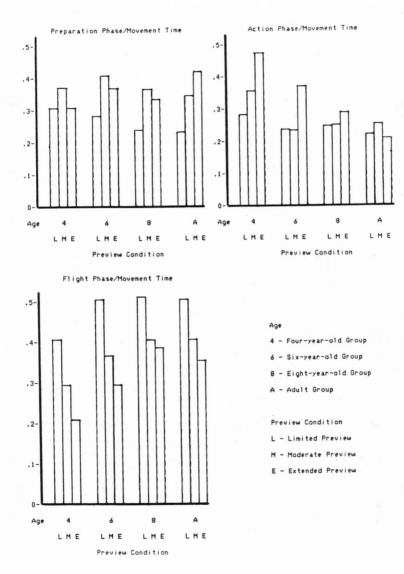

FIG. 5. Relative timing (phase absolute duration divided by movement time) at the limited, moderate, and extended preview conditions for the preparation, action, and flight phases

effects of preview were present within the six- ($F(2, 24) = 5.67$) and the 8-year-old ($F(2, 24) = 5.43$), and the adult ($F(2, 24) = 10.67$) groups. Post hoc analysis indicated a significantly lower ratio at the limited preview when compared to the moderate and extended conditions for the 6- and 8-year-old, and the adult groups. Additionally, the ratio for the moderate condition was significantly less than the ratio at the extended preview for the adult group.

Relative timing of the action phase.

Main effects of age ($F(3, 12) = 3.75, p < .05$) and preview condition ($F(2, 24) = 14.74, p < .01$), as well as the interaction of age with preview condition ($F(6, 24) = 4.66, p < .01$), were significant in the analysis of the relative timing of the action phase (Fig. 5). Significant simple main effects of age were present at the extended preview condition only ($F(3, 36) = 9.64$). Post hoc analysis indicated significantly larger ratios for the 4- and 6-year-old groups when compared to the 8-year-old and adult groups. Similar to the results of the analysis of ADA, these findings appear due to the longer mean ADA produced by the 4- and the 6-year-old groups at the extended preview condition. Significant simple main effects of preview condition were present for the 4-year-old ($F(2, 24) = 17.67$) and the 6-year-old ($F(2, 24) = 8.13$) groups. The ratio at extended preview was significantly larger than the ratios at the moderate and limited conditions for these age groups in the post hoc analysis.

Relative timing of the flight phase

Main effects of age ($F(3, 24) = 4.65, p < .05$) and preview condition ($F(2, 24) = 83.47, p < .01$) were significant in the analysis of the relative timing of the flight phase. Simple main effects of age were significant for the extended preview condition ($F(3, 36) = 5.50$) only. Post hoc analysis indicated that the ratios for both the 4- and the 6-year-old groups were significantly smaller than the ratios for all other age groups at this preview condition (Fig. 5).

Simple main effects of preview condition were present within all age groups ($F(2, 24) = 24.99, 30.00, 14.08,$ and 17.66 for the 4-, 6-, and 8-year-old, and the adult groups, respectively). In the post hoc analysis, the ratio at the limited condition was significantly less than those at moderate and extended preview for the 8-year-old group. All pairwise comparisons were significant for all other age groups. The timing ratios became smaller as preview was increased. These findings reflect the results of the analyses of ADF and of movement time. Those results indicated a significant change in movement time across preview conditions but no significant change for ADF. As a result, the lengthened movement time produced smaller relative timing ratios for the flight phases as preview was increased.

Summary of the relative timing analyses.

From these results, the relative timing of the flight phase was rejected as an invariant feature in the organization of the jump due to the significant change across preview conditions found within this variable. The relative timing of the action phase varied significantly across preview conditions for the 4- and the 6-year-old groups. Finally, the relative timing of the preparation phase varied significantly across preview conditions for all but the 4-year-old group. These results indicate that the relationship between the durations of the jump phases and the movement time of the jump was not constant across preview conditions. None of the age groups investigated within this study demonstrated nonvarying relative timings across preview conditions for all jump phases.

Analyses of the Relative Phasing of the Jump

Relative phasing of the action and the preparation phases.

Only the interaction of age with preview condition was significant in the analysis of the relative phasing between the action and the preparation phases ($F(6, 24) = 3.91, p < .01$). Significant simple main effects of preview condition were present within the 4-year-old group ($F(2, 24) = 5.54$) only (Fig. 6). Post hoc analysis indicated a significantly larger ratio for extended preview when compared to limited preview for this age group. Apparently, the significantly longer ADA produced by the 4-year-old group at the extended preview influenced this ratio.

Relative phasing of the flight and the preparation phases.

Only main effects of preview condition ($F(2, 24) = 27.50, p < .01$) were significant for the relative timing of the preparation and flight phases (Fig. 6). Significant simple main effects of preview were present within all but the 4-year-old group ($F(2, 24) = 5.73, 7.38$, and 16.69 for the 6-year-old, 8-year-old, and adult groups, respectively). All age groups had significantly smaller mean ratios at extended preview when compared to the ratios at the limited condition. All but the 4-year-old group demonstrated a significantly larger ratio at the moderate condition when compared to the ratio at extended preview.

Relative phasing of the action and the flight phases.

The main effects of age ($F(3, 12) = 11.39, p < .01$) and preview condition ($F(2, 24) = 25.57, p < .01$), as well as the interaction of age with preview condition ($F(6, 24) = 4.36, p < .01$), were significant in the analysis of the

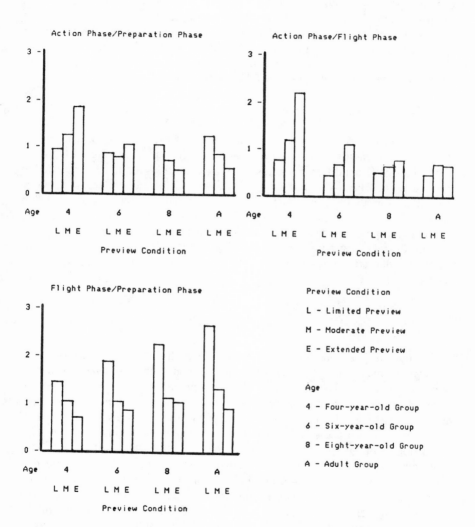

FIG. 6. Relative phasing at limited, moderate, and extended preview conditions for the action phase divided by the preparation phase, the action phase divided by the flight phase, and the flight phase divided by the preparation phase

relative phasing of the action and flight phases. Significant simple main effects of age were present at the extended preview condition only ($F(3, 36) = 19.31$). Post hoc analysis indicated significantly larger ratios for the 4- and 6-year-old groups when compared to the ratios for the 8-year-old and adult groups at extended preview. Simple main effects of preview condition were present within the 4-year-old ($F(2, 24) = 108.33$) and the 6-year-old ($F(2, 24) = 10.63$) groups. The mean ratio at extended preview was significantly larger than the mean at the limited condition for the 4- and the 6-year-old groups in the post hoc analysis. The mean ratio at the moderate preview condition was significantly smaller than the mean at the extended condition for these two age groups.

Summary of the analyses of relative phasing.

As in the analyses of relative timings, none of the age groups within this investigation demonstrated nonvarying ratios for all relative phasings. All groups showed a significant difference across preview conditions for at least one relative phasing ratio. The 4-year-old group demonstrated differences across preview conditions for all three of the relative phasing ratios. The 6-year-old group demonstrated differences for all but the ratio obtained by dividing the duration of the action phase by the duration of the preparation phase. Finally, the adult and the 8-year-old groups showed significant differences across preview conditions for the ratio representing the relative phasing of the flight and the preparation phases.

DISCUSSION

Two conclusions were drawn from the results of this investigation. First, none of the movement characteristics studied were consistently nonvariable across preview conditions. Therefore, none of these characteristics could be accepted as an invariant feature of the temporal organization of the jump. Second, the temporal characteristics of the jump were found to vary across age groups. It was concluded that these differences reflected age-related strategies in the organization of the jump.

Within this study, any movement characteristic which varied significantly across preview conditions was eliminated from consideration as an invariant feature of the jump.[4] According to this criterion, the movement time and both relative timing and relative phasing were rejected as invariant features of the jump. As in the studies by Gentile et al. (1975) and Spaeth (1973), these movement characteristics were found to vary across changes in the performance environment.

Obviously, these results are in conflict with those investigations which support the use of relative timing as an invariant feature of movement organization. However, closer examination of the nature of the skills studied and of the performance environments in which these skills were executed may aid in the resolution of this conflict.

Summers (1975) suggested that invariant relative timing may be an integral part of skills involving rhythmic timing structures. He further suggests that "when the time structure is more arbitrary, the relationship between the sequencing and timing components of a skill becomes less permanent and temporal restructuring can occur" (p. 240). The arm movements studied by Armstrong (1970), as well as the skills of handwheel cranking (Glencross, 1973), lever rotations (Shapiro, 1976), serial key pressing (Summers, 1975), and typing and writing (Viviani & Terzuolo, 1980) are classified as serial movements. Walking or running on a treadmill are continuous movements. It is possible that the various segments or components of these serial movements or skills such as throwing and jumping may possess more arbitrary time structures which allow for less permanent temporal structures within their organizations. These differences in the nature of the skills may account for the conflict between variable and invariant relative timing in the organization of different types of movements.

The second factor which may influence the manner in which a movement is organized is the nature of the performance environment. Handwriting and typing, serial key pressing, handwheel cranking, lever rotations, and the arm movements studied by Armstrong (1970) were performed within a closed environment. Poulton (1957) defines a closed environment as one in which nothing other than the performer is in motion. Movements performed within such an environment are not regulated by the timing of external objects (Gentile, 1972) and may, therefore, be timed by the performer. Both the jump and the dart-throwing movements were performed in what Poulton would define as an open environment (objects other than the performer are in motion).[5] The timing of these movements is regulated by the movement characteristics of objects within the performance environment. Therefore, their timing characteristics may be determined by external events.

Lee (1980), who has investigated the regulation of the timing of movements by external parameters, has supported this hypothesis for the skills of diving (Lee & Reddish, 1981), long jumping (Lee, Lishman, & Thomson, 1982), and a ball interception skill (Lee, Young, Reddish, Lough, & Clayton, 1983). It should be noted that all skills studied by this investigator were discrete, were performed within an open environment, and had coincidence with an object as their goal.

A preliminary search for external parameters which influence the timing of movement has been undertaken for the jump task used within this study (Barnett, 1984). While further investigation is necessary before any conclusions can be obtained, preliminary results do support the use of external parameters for timing discrete movements which are performed within an open environment.

The second conclusion of this investigation concerned the use of age-related strategies in the organization of the jump. Younger children initiated their jumps earlier and covered longer distances. They also appeared to make adaptations to changes in preview condition later in their jumps. Older children and adults covered less distance with their jumps. These subjects were also less variable in the durations of the later phases of their jumps. While it is possible that these differences can be attributed to the tendency of younger children to respond early under conditions of slow moving stimulus or long stimulus travel times, (Williams, 1985), this explanation does not account for all preview conditions within this study. Preliminary investigation of the external cues used by children in the timing of their movements (Barnett, 1984) suggest possible age-related differences, but again, further investigation is necessary.

In summary, the results of this investigation reject the use of relative timing or relative phasing as invariant parameters in the organization of the jump. It was demonstrated that the temporal organization of movements which are performed within an open environment are influenced by the motion characteristics of objects within that environment. Finally, observation of age-related strategies for the organization of the jump were made.

REFERENCES

Armstrong, T. R. (1970). *Training for the production of memorized movement patterns* (Tech. Rep. No. 26). Ann Arbor, MI.: University of Michigan, Human Performance Center.

Ball, C. T., & Glencross, D. (1985). Developmental differences in a coincident timing task under speed and time constraints. *Journal of Human Movement Science, 4*, 1–15.

Barnett, B. E. (1984). *The use of potential visual cues in the organization of the jump by children and adults.* Unpublished doctoral dissertation, Teachers College, Columbia University.

Bernstein, N. (1967). *The Co-ordination and Regulation of Movement.* New York: Pergamon Press.

Gallagher, J. D., & Thomas, J. R. (1980). Effects of varying post-KR intervals upon children's motor performance. *Journal of Motor Behavior, 12*, 41–56.

Gentile, A. M. (1972). A working model of skill acquisition. *Quest, 17*, 3–23.

Gentile, A. M., Higgins, J. R., Miller, E., & Rosen, B. (1975). The structure of motor tasks. *Mouvement*, Actes due 7 symposium en apprentissage psycho-moteur et psychologie du sport, October, pp. 11–28.

Glencross, D. J. (1973). Temporal organization in a repetitive speed skill. *Ergonomics, 16*, 765–776.

Higgins, J. R. (1972). Movements to match environmental demands. *Research Quarterly, 43*, 312–336.

Higgins, J. R., & Spaeth, R. K. (1972). Relationship between consistency of movement and environmental conditions. *Quest, 17*, 61–69.

Hoffman, S. J., Imwold, C. H., & Koller, J. A. (1983). Accuracy of prediction in throwing: A taxonomic analysis of children's performance. *Research Quarterly for Exercise and Sport, 54*, 33–40.

Lee, D. N. (1980). Visuomotor coordination in space-time. In G. E. Stelmach & J. Requin (Eds.), *Tutorials in Motor Behavior* (pp. 181–196). Amsterdam: North Holland.

Lee, D. N., Lishman, J. R., & Thomson, J. A. (1982). The regulation of gait in long-jumpers. *Journal of Experimental Psychology: Human Perception and Performance, 8*, 448–459.

Lee, D. N., & Reddish, P. E. (1981). Plummeting gannets: A paradigm of ecological optics. *Nature, 293*, 293–294.

Lee, D. N., Young, D. S., Reddish, P. E., Lough, S., & Clayton, T. M. (1983). Visual timing in hitting an accelerating ball. *Quarterly Journal of Experimental Psychology, 35*, 333–346.

Moxley, S. E., & Moxley, B. D. (1976). Development of spatial and temporal consistency with extended practice. In D. M. Landers & R. W. Christina (Eds.), *Psychology of Sport and Motor Behavior I* (pp. 70–77). Champaign, IL.: Human Kinetics.

Pew, R. W. (1974). Human perceptual-motor performance. In B. H. Kantowitz (Ed.), *Human Information Processing: Tutorials in Performance and Cognition* (pp. 1–23). New York: Lawrence Erlbaum.

Poulton, E. C. (1957). On prediction in skilled movements. *Psychological Bulletin, 54*, 467–478.

Rothstein, A. L. (1970). *Timing behavior in children*. Unpublished doctoral dissertation, Teachers College, Columbia University.

Schmidt, R. A. (1976). Control processes in motor skills. *Exercise and Sport Science Reviews, 4*, 229–261.

Schmidt, R. A. (1982). The schema concept. In J. A. S. Kelso (Ed.), *Human Motor Behavior: An Introduction* (pp. 219–235). Hillsdale, NJ: Lawrence Erlbaum Associates.

Shapiro, D. C. (1976). A preliminary attempt to determine the duration of a motor program. In D. M. Landers & R. W. Christina (Eds.), *Psychology of Sport and Motor Behavior I* (pp. 17–24). Champaign, IL.: Human Kinetics.

Shapiro, D. C., & Schmidt, R. A. (1982). The schema theory: Recent evidence and developmental implications. In J. A. S. Kelso & J. E. Clark (Eds.), *The Development of Movement Control and Co-ordination* (pp. 113–150). New York: Wiley and Sons.

Shapiro, D. C., Zernicke, R. F., Gregor, R. J., & Diestal, J. D. (1981). Evidence for generalized motor programs using gait analysis. *Journal of Motor Behavior, 13*, 33–47.

Shea, C. H., Krampitz, J. B., Northam, C. C., & Ashby, A. A. (1982). Information processing in coincident timing tasks: A developmental prospective. *Journal of Human Movement Studies, 8*, 73–83.

Spaeth, R. K. (1973). *Skill acquisition under variable temporal constraints: Cinematographic analysis of movement organization*. Doctoral dissertation, Teachers College, Columbia University.

Stadulis, R. E. (1972). Motor skill analysis: Coincident-anticipation. *Quest, 17*, 70–73.

Stadulis, R. E. (1985). Coincidence-anticipation behavior of children. In J. E. Clark & J. H. Humphrey (Eds.), *Motor Development: Current Selected Research* (Vol. 1, pp. 1–17). Princeton, NJ: Princeton Book Company Publishers.

Summers, J. J. (1975). The role of timing in motor program representation. *Journal of Motor Behavior, 7*, 229–241.

Viviani, P., & Terzuolo, C. (1980). Motor engrams in typing and handwriting. In G. E. Stelmach & J. Requin (Eds.), *Tutorials in Motor Behavior* (pp. 525–539). Amsterdam: North Holland.

Williams, H. G. (1973). Perceptual-motor development in children. In C. B. Corbin (Ed.), *A Textbook of Motor Development* (pp. 122–129). Dubuque, IA.: Wm. C. Brown.

Williams, K. (1985). Age differences on a coincident anticipation task: Influences of stereotypic or "preferred" movement speed. *Journal of Motor Behavior, 17*, 389–410.

AUTHOR NOTE

This paper is based on a doctoral dissertation completed under the guidance of Dr. J. R. Higgins at Teachers College, Columbia University.

NOTES

[1] The preview distances did not include the visible five centimeters of the inclined ramp.

[2] Children exhibited some jumps in which their takeoff was late, relative to the arrival of the stick at their starting position behind the white line. In these instances, the stick would contact one or both feet. Trials containing such jumps were classified as unsuccessful and were not included within the analysis.

[3] Investigations of the timing structure of motor skills have not always studied the same movement characteristics. Armstrong (1970), Glencross (1973), and Shapiro (1976) compared phases durations to total movement time. Viviani and Terzuolo (1980) compared pairs of time intervals. Finally, Spaeth (1973) reported a nonstatistical comparison of phase durations. Both relative timing and relative phasing were investigated within this study.

[4] Due to the small number of subjects within each age group, the power of the statistical analyses used within this study was low. Therefore, a bias towards accepting the null hypothesis (and finding no significant difference across preview conditions) existed.

[5] Gentile et al. (1975) divided Poulton's open classification into limited interaction (either spatial or temporal conditions within the performance environment are varied) and open (spatial and temporal characteristics of the environment co-vary) skills. The task of walking or running on a treadmill used by Shapiro et al. (1981) included temporal variation only and would be classified as a limited interaction skill. The skill used within the present study included variation in both the temporal (preview time) and the spatial (preview distance) characteristics of the performance environment and would, therefore, be classified as an open skill.

2

POSTURAL SUPPORT AND FINE MOTOR CONTROL IN CHILDREN WITH NORMAL AND SLOW MOTOR DEVELOPMENT

Donna Adams Johnson and Harriet G. Williams

University of South Carolina

ABSTRACT

*The effects of postural support on fine motor perform-
ance were examined using 60 six-year-old children in
two separate experiments. Children were classified as
normally (NDC) or slowly developing (SDC) on the basis
of scores on a test of gross motor development. In Experiment 1 (n = 30), children performed an object manipulation task and an implement usage task under three
postural support conditions: maximum, moderate, and
no support. The effects of postural support were not
significant. In Experiment 2 (n = 30), only the object
manipulation task was performed. Results showed a significant main effect of postural support conditions on
fine motor control. Although the interaction between
postural support and developmental level was not significant, there were differences between SDC and NDC
when performance was examined across time. These
results suggest that fine motor performance of children,
especially those with gross motor delays, may be affected
by the amount of support provided in sitting.*

Normal motor development is characterized by the emergence and maturation
of a number of postural reactions which provide the foundation for stable body
posture and equilibrium and for performance of skilled movement (Bobath, 1980;
Holt, 1975). The neural mechanisms involved in the development and mainte-

nance of postural control have been studied extensively (Bobath, 1971; Caesar, 1979; Forssberg & Nashner, 1982; Nashner, 1976, 1979) because of the importance of such control (e.g., stability) to efficient motor performance. By quantifying electromyographic activity of the lower extremities and lower trunk muscles during standing and perturbation of standing, Nashner (1979) has described patterns of strategies used by the postural control system to maintain upright stance. Studies have suggested that these postural adjustments become more efficient and consistent with increasing age in normal children (Rosenbloom & Horton, 1971; Shambes, 1976; Williams, Fisher, & Tritschler, 1983). Forssberg and Nashner (1982) assessed the ability of normal children from 18 months to 10 years of age to adapt their patterns of postural control to altered support surface and visual conditions. By studying electromyographic data and measures of reaction forces and body motions, they found that automatic postural adjustments of young children were similar in structure to those of adults, but that the responses of children below 7½ years were significantly slower and more variable than adult responses. In a similar study, Shumway-Cook and Woollacott (1985a) determined that children under 7 years of age demonstrated greater inconsistency in timing and amplitude relationships between lower extremity muscle synergists involved in postural responses than did 7- to 10-year-old children or adults. This suggested to them that the structural organization of postural control is not fully developed in young children (Shumway-Cook & Woollacott, 1985a). Using electromyographic and cinematographic analysis of static balance control, Shambes (1976) demonstrated age-related differences in the number of muscles used and the amplitude of muscle activity exhibited in maintaining balance. Older children generally used fewer muscles and tended to display smaller amplitudes of muscle activity than younger children. Shambes (1976) hypothesized that, as postural control develops with increasing age in the child, the reflexive, automatic components of such control act to suppress extraneous and/or excessive muscle activity and thus produce more skillful movement.

The importance of the automatic movement patterns involved in balance and postural control is most readily observed in children and adults who exhibit pathology of the nervous system. It has been demonstrated that adults with hemiplegia secondary to cerebrovascular accident, for example, tend to display different patterns of muscle activation and sequencing during postural adjustment than normals (Badke & Duncan, 1983). In addition. Nashner, Shumway-Cook and Marin (1983) demonstrated increased variability in the relative strength and sequencing of lower extremity muscle contractions during postural adjustments in children with spastic hemiplegia as compared to age-matched normal children. Individuals with cerebral palsy also have difficulty inhibiting unnecessary muscle activity when performing skilled movements (Harrison & Connolly, 1971; Robertson, Lee, & Jacobs, 1984). Children with Down's syndrome under 6 years of age tend to demonstrate deficits in the postural control system (Shumway-Cook & Woollacott, 1985b). Deficiencies in righting reactions associated with vestibular function have been associated with minor neurological impairment and with those children who are labeled "clumsy" (Ayres, 1973; Steinberg & Rendle-Short, 1977). Children who are delayed or awkward in sensorimotor skill development also frequently exhibit immature postural control (Arnheim & Sinclair, 1979; Cratty, 1975; Williams et al., 1983; Williams, McClenaghan, & Ward, 1985). These children often have difficulty with efficient balance and stability for motor control. Williams et al. (1985) compared electromyographic activity of the lower extremity and trunk muscles of normal and slowly developing children in static standing with superimposed arm movement. Children with delayed motor development displayed more activity in the trunk muscles than in the lower extremity muscles when an arm movement (90° shoulder abduction) was performed. Normal children did not display this pattern. This suggested to the authors that trunk stabilization was more difficult for children who were delayed in motor development.

The increased activity of the trunk muscles observed with superimposed arm movement (Williams et al., 1985) occurs to stabilize or fixate the trunk to allow for movement of the extremities. These postural adjustments occur in all body positions and are particularly important to fine motor skills performed in a sitting position. The development of postural control in sitting appears to be related to the refinement in the use of the upper extremities (Finnie, 1975; Gesell, 1940; Rosenbloom & Horton, 1971). Performance of manipulative activities during sitting has been shown to require additional activity of postural muscles (Anderson et al., 1975). A child with inadequate postural control may therefore have difficulty producing the additional muscular activity needed to maintain a stable sitting posture and also use the hands to perform a task skillfully. For such children, sitting unsupported may require conscious attention or even use of the hands to maintain balance. Thus, minimal energy may be available for controlled activity of the distal musculature. Without the coordinated patterns of muscular activity which normally provide for balance and stability of the head, neck, and proximal musculature of the body, a stable postural framework on which to superimpose distal movement does not exist (Connolly, 1970). Artificial support provided to the trunk in sitting may help to compensate for this deficiency and could improve performance of fine motor tasks.

Adapted supportive seating is used frequently to assist children who lack motor control secondary to spasticity and weakness. This technique is used to enhance use of the hands by providing needed trunk support (Bergen, 1974; Bergen & Colangelo, 1982; Finnie, 1975; Kamath, 1984; Rollefson & Culver, 1972; Trefler, Hanks, Huggins, Chiarizzo, & Hobson, 1978). Cristella (1975) positioned a child with spastic cerebral palsy in a more stable seating position, with abduction of the hips and a higher back support, and reported improvement in functional use of the hands. Using an objective measure, Seeger, Caudry and O'Mara (1984) reported no change in hand function with variation in the angle of hip flexion in sitting. Hulme, Schulein, Hulme, Poor and Pezzino (1983) surveyed caretakers and therapists of multihandicapped clients to determine if behavioral changes were apparent with the use of adaptive equipment for support. They reported significant improvement in activities involving moving a distal extremity on a stabilized trunk. Specifically, eating, drinking, reaching, and grasping behaviors were improved after motorically involved individuals were given postural support in sitting. To date, studies examining the effects of positioning on fine motor skill performance have involved multihandicapped individuals, primarily individuals with spastic cerebral palsy. Improvement in functional hand use has been reported, but has been based largely on subjective observations. The importance of supportive seating for effective use of the distal upper extremities in developmentally delayed or motorically awkward children has not been investigated. Because of abnormal and inefficient patterns of postural muscle activity typically exhibited by this group, performance of manipulative skills might be affected by the amount of trunk support provided in sitting.

The purpose of this study was to investigate the effect of variations in the amount of postural support in sitting on performance of fine motor, manipulative tasks by 6-year-old children, with normal and delayed gross motor development. Two separate experiments were performed. The hypotheses were: 1) there would be no differences in the fine motor performance of normally developing children under different seating or postural support conditions and 2) the performance of fine motor tasks would vary as a function of different seating or postural support conditions in children with gross motor development delays.

METHODS

Subjects

Sixty male and female children, all 6 years of age, participated in the study. The mean chronological age of the children was 6.6 years (SD = .29). Thirty children participated in Experiment 1 and the other 30 in Experiment 2. Normally developing children and children with delays in gross motor skill development were included in both studies. Children in the study were obtained from regular first grade classes in Richland County and Lexington County School Districts in South Carolina, a general call for subjects in a university newsletter, and children enrolled in enrichment programs in the Perceptual Motor Development Laboratory at the University of South Carolina. The majority of the children were from white, middle income backgrounds.

Preliminary Screening

All children were screened initially by a physical therapist with experience in evaluation and treatment of children with developmental disabilities. Screening procedures included assessment of a) joint range of motion; b) selected postural reflexes including three primitive reflexes and several equilibrium reactions; c) muscle tone; d) visual acuity; e) selected visual perception skills. Children who exhibited any of the following characteristics were excluded from the study: 1) abnormally increased muscle tone or spasticity in the upper or lower extremities or trunk; 2) persistence of one or more of the three primitive reflexes tested; 3) significant limitation in joint range of motion, including spinal movement; 4) inability to sit unsupported without losing balance; 5) visual acuity of less than 20/40 that could not or had not been corrected; and 6) inadequate shape discrimination and/or poor figure-ground perception. Children with overt physical handicaps or sensory impairment such as cerebral palsy, blindness, or deafness were automatically excluded from the study.

Screening Instruments

The following procedures were used to screen children for participation in the study.

1. Range of motion.

Active and passive range of motion of all extremity joints, neck, and trunk was evaluated grossly. If deviations from the normal existed, a manual goniometer was used to determine the degree of restriction of movement. Standard procedures of joint measurement were followed (Moore, 1984).

2. Muscle tone.

The level of muscle tone in the extremities and trunk was subjectively assessed based on clinical tests of resistance to passive stretch, joint extensibility, and the ability to hold a posture against gravity. Tone was determined to be "normal" or increased or decreased from the normal on the basis of these observations. Normal muscle tone is difficult to define, but may be assumed to be "tone that is 'high' enough to keep the body from collapsing into gravity, but 'low' enough to allow the body to move against gravity" (Ryerson, 1985, p. 487). Specific areas of increased and/or decreased tone were noted.

3. Postural reflex activity.

Primitive reflexes are "static" in nature and affect changes in distribution of muscle tone throughout the body, either in response to stimulation of the labyrinths or muscle proprioceptors (Fiorentino, 1976). Three primitive reflexes which can act as indicators of central nervous system maturation or dysfunction were evaluated. Standard procedures (Fiorentino, 1976) were used to evaluate the following primitive reflexes: assymetrical tonic neck reflex, symmetrical tonic neck reflex, and the positive support reaction. Persistance of these three reflexes in a 6-year-old child often indicates central nervous system dysfunction and interferes with the development of more advanced righting and equilibrium reactions (Bobath, 1971).

Equilibrium reactions, which are automatic, compensatory movements elicited by stimulation of the labyrinths, were also evaluated. These included a) protective extension of the arms to the sides and rear in sitting and, b) response to tilt in supine, prone, all-fours, kneeling, and standing positions. These reactions serve to maintain equilibrium of the body (Bobath, 1971). The method used for testing equilibrium reactions was that of Fiorentino (1976).

4. Visual acuity.

The Snellen Eye chart was used to assess visual acuity. Standard procedures were followed (Vaughn & Asbury, 1980).

5. Visual perception.

A rough estimate of the level of visual perception development was determined via the use of subjective measures of shape discrimination, shape identification, and a standardized test of figure-ground perception (Ayres, 1980). The child was asked to match like shapes of similar size and to verbally identify six different shapes. Standard protocol described by Ayres (1980) was used for administering the Figure Ground Test.

Assessment of Motor Development

Evaluation of gross motor development was carried out on all 60 children using the Peabody Developmental Motor Scales (PDMS) (Folio & Fewell, 1983). The PDMS includes Gross Motor and Fine Motor Scales; the items in each scale are divided into age-level groupings.

The Gross Motor Scale is divided into five skill categories: 1) Reflexes; 2) Balance; 3) Nonlocomotor; 4) Locomotor; 5) Receipt and Propulsion. All responses are scored on a three point scale (0 = unsuccessful; 1 = clear resemblance to item criterion, but criterion not fully met; 2 = successful performance, criterion met). Standardization of the PDMS is based on a population of 617 children from 0-83 months of age, including 49 six-year-olds. Reported test-retest reliability is .95; interrater reliability correlations .97.

The PDMS was administered according to test protocol (Folio & Fewell, 1983). Children were classified as normally developing (NDC) or slowly developing (SDC) on the basis of performance of the Gross Motor Scale. Children with a Z-score of less than 0 were classified as slowly developing.

EXPERIMENT 1

Method

The first 30 of the 60 six-year-old children screened and evaluated participated in Experiment One (n = 18 NDC; n = 12 SDC). The children performed two fine motor tasks, an object manipulation, and a design copying task, under three postural support conditions. Each child was tested individually in the presence of one or two examiners; testing lasted 1 to 1½ hours. Children were seated at a desk with top dimensions of 43.82 cm × 50.8 cm (17.25" × 20"). Children were asked to sit erect with the arms at the sides and elbows flexed at 90° angles. Desk height was adjusted for each child so that the forearms rested lightly on the desk top. The front edge of the desk was approximately 8 cm from the anterior surface of the child's body.

Postural Support Conditions

Each child was tested in three different postural support conditions. A wooden ladder-back chair with a 35.6 cm (14") seat height and 69.4 (27.33") back height was used. The back of the chair was at a 90° angle to the seat. A stool of appropriate height was placed under the child's feet when necessary to insure that the angle at the hips and knees was 90° for all children in all conditions. Variations in the same style of chair were used to provide different degrees of postural support.

In Condition 1, minimal postural support, the back of the chair was removed. The child sat on the modified chair/stool and performed the fine motor tasks. In Condition 2, moderate postural support, a chair identical to that used in Condition 1 with the back in place was used. In Condition 3, maximal postural support, two seat belts were used to give additional postural support to the child. One belt was fastened snugly across the pelvis to maintain he child's hips against the back of the chair; the second belt was secured around the lower rib cage.

Performance Measures (Tasks)

Purdue Pegboard (PP)

Preferred Hand Test (Tiffin, 1979). The Purdue Pegboard was used to measure manipulative control of the eyes, hands, and fingers. The specific task selected for use involved placing as many metal pins in two parallel rows of holes as possible in 30 sec, using the preferred hand. Test administration was carried out as described in the test manual (Tiffin, 1979). Normative data on 1334 normal children are available, but no reliability data are reported (Gardner & Broman, 1979).

Design Copying Task (DC)

(Ayres, 1980). The Design Copying task is one of 17 tests of the Southern California Sensory Integration Test (SCSIT) battery (Ayres, 1980). The task involves duplication of geometric designs on a dot grid. It is designed to measure a combination of visual perception of geometric designs and the ability to duplicate such designs. The test-retest reliability of the test is reported as .86 for 40 six-year-olds (Ayres, 1980). A modified scoring method was used in this study to increase the maximal possible range of scores instead of assigning a score of 2, 1, or 0 to the entire figure. Each line in each figure was scored as 2, 1, or 0 and these scores were added together to obtain a greater score for the entire figure. If the child's line was less than 1/16″ from a straight line drawn between the two dots, the score for that line was 2; if the line deviated more than 1/16″ from the reference line, it was scored as a 1; if the lines was drawn incorrectly or not at all, the score was 0.

General Experimental Design and Analysis

The two fine motor tasks were administered under each of the postural support conditions. Two trials of the PP were given and one of the DC. A 2 × 3 factorial analysis of variance (level of motor development × postural support conditions) was used for statistical analysis. Separate univariate analysis of variances were run on the two fine motor task performances. There were six randomly selected orders of presentation of the postural support conditions within each of the fine motor tasks. The order of performance of the two fine motor tasks was alternated across subjects.

Results

Purdue Pegboard.

Although there was a trend in mean performance in the expected direction, the main effect of postural support conditions was not significant ($p = .58$). Performance on the PP task was not significantly affected by the kind of postural support provided. The main effect of developmental level was significant ($p = .04$). Children classified as normal in gross motor development performed

Table 1 (Experiment 1)
Purdue Pegboard Performance: Mean Scores as a Function of Developmental Level and Postural Support Condition (sec)

	Group (n = 30)			NDC (n = 18)			SDC (n = 12)		
	Mean	**SD**	**SEM**	**Mean**	**SD**	**SEM**	**Mean**	**SD**	**SEM**
No support (Condition 1)	53.82	8.26	1.51	50.73	7.54	1.78	58.44	7.30	2.11
Moderate support (2)	53.40	8.21	1.50	51.54	6.88	1.62	56.20	9.49	2.74
Maximum support (3)	52.94	6.39	1.17	51.38	5.86	1.38	55.28	6.67	1.92

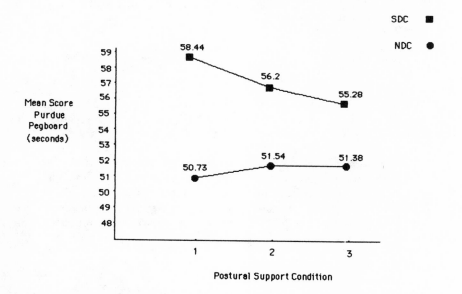

FIG. 1. Fine motor performance as a function of postural support and developmental level (Postural support Condition 1 = no support, 2 = moderate support, 3 = maximum support)

consistently better on the fine motor task than those classified as slowly developing (Table 1).

The interaction between postural support condition and developmental level bordered on significance ($p = .07$). This suggests that performances on the PP task may have been affected both by the kind of postural support provided and by the gross motor development level of the child (Fig. 1). Although performances of NDC were always superior to those of SDC, mean performances of the

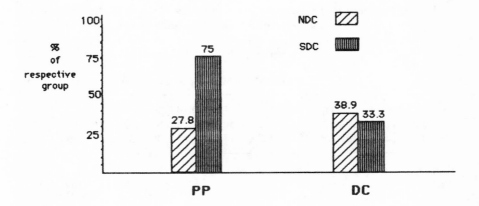

FIG. 2. Percentage of normally and slowly developing children for whom task performance improved with postural support (PP = Purdue Pegboard, DC = Design Copy)

SDC improved consistently as additional postural support in sitting was provided. Children with normal gross motor development, however, did not demonstrate this improvement and performed approximately the same in all postural support conditions.

To provide further support for the apparent differences in performance between the two developmental groups under different postural support conditions, the percentage of children who improved performances when postural support of some kind was provided was calculated (Fig. 2). Seventy-five percent of the slowly developing children displayed some improvement in performance with additional support while only 27.8% of NDC demonstrated improvement.

Design copying.

The main effect of postural support conditions was not significant ($p = .62$). Although the mean scores were in the expected direction, providing additional postural support did not significantly affect performance on the DC task (Table 2). The main effect of developmental level was significant ($p = .0007$). As before, children with normal gross motor development performed significantly better than children who were motorically slow; this was true regardless of the kind of postural support provided (e.g., the interaction between developmental level and postural support was not significant; $p = .82$).

Discussion

The original hypothesis was only partially supported. As predicted, children with normal gross motor development performed both fine motor tasks equally

Table 2 (Experiment 1)
Design Copy Performance: Mean Scores as a Function of Developmental Level
and Postural Support Condition (total points)

	Group (n = 30)			NDC (n = 18)			SDC (n = 12)		
	Mean	SD	SEM	Mean	SD	SEM	Mean	SD	SEM
No support (Condition 1)	56.6	22.96	4.19	67.22	18.65	4.40	40.67	19.76	5.71
Moderate support (2)	57.5	23.54	4.30	67.89	19.79	4.66	42.00	20.41	5.89
Maximum support (3)	58.1	23.18	4.23	69.22	19.02	4.48	41.42	18.76	5.42

well regardless of whether or not postural support was provided. In general, mean performances of children who were motorically slow were in the expected direction; that is, those children with lower levels of gross motor development seemed to profit from some form of postural support when they performed a fine motor, object manipulation task ($p = .07$). They did not show similar improvements in performance (with postural support) on a fine motor task that involved implement usage (e.g., the Design Copy task).

One possible explanation for the difference between the two tasks is that, in addition to fine motor control, the DC task also involved perception of spatial relationships. Since children were not screened for this ability, it is possible that the effect of postural support on fine motor control was confounded or masked by differences in this perceptual characteristic of the children studied. A more likely explanation is that, although the children were asked not to lean on the table in the DC task, they tended to spontaneously support themselves with their arms while writing. To perform the DC task effectively, the child needed to rest both arms (to some degree) on the table. In contrast, because of the nature of the object manipulation task (PP) and the fact that the child was required to place the nonpreferred hand in the lap during performance, the child could not support the arms on the table. Anderson et al. (1975) demonstrated that there is a decreased demand placed on the postural muscles of the posterior trunk when the upper extremities are supported than when they are not. This is in contrast to the greater demand placed on such musculature when the arms are used for unsupported activity. Thus, the motorically slow children may have been able to compensate for "lack" of postural support in the nonsupport condition by leaning on their arms when they performed the DC task.

It should also be considered that the object manipulation task required both dynamic and highly refined control of the fingertips (e.g., finger dexterity) for successful task performance. A greater demand is thus placed on the neuro-muscular system to establish and maintain an appropriate postural framework to support manipulative activity of the arms and hands. Providing additional support to the postural muscles may have allowed the neuromuscular mechanism to activate more selectively the distal musculature where precise motor control was needed. This ability to localize motor control to the necessary areas and to decrease extraneous muscle activity is often deficient in slowly developing children (Williams et al., 1983).

If indeed it is the channeling of activity to properly control movements of the distal musculature that is the basis for the observed postural support effect, one should be able to show a similar and more clear-cut effect by prolonging or extending the amount of time the child is required to spend sitting and performing this fine manipulative activity. When sitting/performing time is increased, the postural muscles of the trunk are more likely to fatigue. Efficient channeling of activity to appropriate muscle groups would then become more critical to successful fine motor performance and thus fine motor performances would be more likely to vary with the presence and absence of appropriate postural support.

EXPERIMENT 2

Method

The remaining 30 children were included in Experiment Two. Preliminary screening, motor development assessment, behavioral characteristics observations, and postural support conditions were identical to those in Experiment One. Children were again classified as NDC (n = 18) and SDC (n = 12). Only the Purdue Pegboard task was administered. Administration procedures for the PP task were as in Experiment One. In this experiment, the child was required to sit in the nonsupport condition for 15 min prior to task performance. During this time, he/she performed unrelated fine motor tasks. Three practice trials of the PP task were then given; this was followed by three trials of the PP task in each of the nonsupport, moderate support, and the maximum support conditions. There were a total of nine trials. Six randomly selected orders of presentation of the postural support conditions were used in assigning order to each child. The performance score was the mean of the three trials.

A 2 × 3 × 3 factorial design (level of motor development × postural support conditions × number of trials) was used for statistical analysis. Univariate analysis of variance was performed to assess the effects of postural support condition on fine motor performance.

Results

The main effects of postural support condition ($p = .014$) and developmental level ($p = .004$) were significant. Overall, task performance in both the moderate

Table 3 (Experiment 2)
Purdue Pegboard Performance: Mean Scores as a Function of Developmental
Level and Postural Support Condition (sec)

	Group (n = 30)			NDC (n = 18)			SDC (n = 12)		
	Mean	**SD**	**SEM**	**Mean**	**SD**	**SEM**	**Mean**	**SD**	**SEM**
No support (Condition 1)	52.68	7.63	1.39	49.58	5.42	1.28	57.32	8.16	2.36
Moderate support (2)	50.52	6.86	1.25	48.10	4.86	1.15	54.15	7.83	2.26
Maximum support (3)	51.62	6.91	1.26	49.30	5.94	1.40	55.10	6.87	1.98

and maximum support conditions was better than in the nonsupport condition (Table 3). Performance was also generally better in the moderate support condition than in the maximum support condition. NDC performed significantly better than SDC under all conditions. Neither the main effect nor any of the second-order effects of trials was significant. Thus, performance in general did not change as a function of practice on the task. The interaction between postural support condition and developmental level was not significant ($p = .39$). This suggests that performance under different postural support conditions was similar for all children regardless of gross motor development level.

The foregoing effects, however, must be interpreted in light of the significant three-way interaction among developmental level, postural support condition, and trials ($p = .04$). The interaction effect is shown in Fig. 3. For NDC, there was little or no difference in performance as a function of treatment or trial. Thus, in general, NDC performed equally well in all seating or postural support conditions. The only exception was in Trial 2 when performance under the moderate support condition (2) was significantly better than performance under either the maximum support (3) or nonsupport conditions (1). Evidence of a practice or trial effect for NDC was seen only in the maximum support condition where performance in Trial 3 was significantly better than in Trial 2. In contrast, for SDC, after the initial trial in which there were no significant differences in performances under the three conditions, performances of motorically slow children were significantly better when they had some form of postural support than when they did not. In Trial 2, performance in both support conditions was significantly better than in the nonsupport condition; in Trial 3 performance in the moderate support condition was significantly better than performance in either of the other two conditions. Interestingly, performance under the maximal support condition was not significantly different than performance in the non-support condition in Trial 3. The only trials effect for SDC was in the moderate support condition where performance improved significantly across trials.

JOHNSON AND WILLIAMS

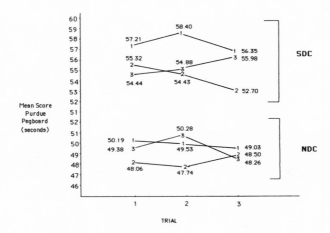

FIG. 3. Fine motor performance as a function of postural support, developmental level and trial

Discussion

In general, the original hypothesis was supported. Overall mean performance scores on the object manipulation task were better when some form of support was provided than when it was not. Peformance under maximum postural support (e.g., with restraints), however, was not superior to performance under moderate support (sitting in a chair with a supportive back).

Although the overall level of gross motor development did not appear to differentially affect the child's performance under different seating positions, there was a difference between the groups when performance across time (e.g., trials) was examined. SDC showed consistent improvement in performance from Trial 1 to Trial 3 in the moderate support condition. They may be indicative of a learning or practice effect; it may also be the result of the effects of providing postural support which allowed more control of the distal musculature needed for object manipulation. Unexpectedly, performance under the maximum support condition did not improve across trials and in fact showed a nonsignificant decrease. During testing, however, many SDC children complained of discomfort from sitting with the restraints. Children in the SDC group tended to be more active than those in the NDC group and were more uncomfortable and less attentive to the task when their movement was constrained. Since children had been confined for two previous trials and were uncomfortable, this could be a major contributing factor to the lack of improvement or change in performance. It is also speculated that the SDC had throughout the years adopted postural habits to compensate for poor stability and that performances were affected when they were prevented from assuming these "compensatory" postures. It should be noted that performance was still significantly better in the maximum support condition than in the nonsupport condition.

For NDC, performance was generally the same under all support conditions. Performance across time under the maximum support condition was the most erratic. Although uncertain, it is possible that NDC also felt confined by the restraints but adapted or accommodated to the new "conditions" and showed an improvement in performance in Trial 3.

An important comparison between NDC and SDC is the difference in the effect of support conditions early (Trial 1) vs later (Trial 3) in performance. For NDC, there was little or no difference in fine motor control under any of the support conditions early or later in task performance. Thus, the child with normal gross motor development did not seem to profit from added postural support. For SDC, however, although fine motor control was at about the same level whether or not some form of support was provided early in task performance, later in task performance their fine motor control was significantly better when some moderate form of postural support was provided. This suggests that, with time, the effects of providing postural support for children with poor gross motor development becomes more evident. Performance scores under the different postural conditions tended to become more similar over time in NDC; in SDC, the differences between performance under nonsupport and moderate support conditions became greater. This could be due to fatigue of postural muscles with time; it might also be reflection of an immature postural mechanism which needs "help" to maintain a stable base of support for control and regulation of fine movement of the distal extremities. Williams et al. (1983) also reported that in contrast to NDC, slowly developing children displayed less efficient and more inconsistent activity of the postural muscles in stabilizing the postural framework necessary for executing simple movements of the arm and shoulder girdle.

Results of this study suggest that there is a relationship between the amount or type of postural support provided to a child with delays in gross motor development and his/her fine motor control. Further investigation is necessary, however, to understand or explain the exact nature of this relationship and the mechanisms involved.

REFERENCES

Anderson, B. J., Ortengren, R., Nachemson, A. L., Elfstrom, G., & Broman, H. (1975). The sitting posture: An EMG and discometric study. *Orthopedic Clinics of North America, 6,* 105–121.

Arnheim, D. D., & Sinclair, W. A. (1979). *The clumsy child* (2nd ed.). St. Louis: C. V. Mosby Co.

Ayres, A. J. (1973). *Sensory integration and learning disorders*. Los Angeles: Western
   Psychological Services.
Ayres, A. J. (1980). *Southern California Sensory Integration Tests Manual*, (Rev. ed.).
   Los Angeles: Western Psychological Services.
Badke, M. B., & Duncan, P. W. (1983). Patterns of rapid motor response during postural
   adjustments when standing in healthy subjects and hemiplegic patients. *Physical Ther-
   apy, 63*, 13–20.
Bergen, A. F. (1971). Table and chair seat for spastic children. *Physical Therapy, 51*,
   1305–1306.
Bergen, A. F., & Colangelo, C. (1982). *Positioning the client with central nervous sysem
   deficits: The wheelchair and other adapted equipment*. Valhalla, NY: Valhalla Re-
   habilitation Publications.
Bobath, B. (1971). *Abnormal postural reflex activity caused by brain lesions*. London:
   Heinemann Medical.
Bobath, K. (1980). A neurophysiological basis for the treatment of cerebral palsy. *Clinics
   in Developmental Medicine, 75*.
Caesar, P. (1979). Postural behavior in newborn infants. *Clinics in Developmental Med-
   icine, 72*.
Connolly, K. (1970). Skill development: Problems and plans. In K. Connolly (Ed.),
   Mechanisms of motor skill development (pp. 3–24). London: Academic Press.
Cratty, B. J. (1975). *Perceptual and motor development in infants and children* (2nd
   ed.). Englewood Cliffs, NJ: Prentice-Hall, Inc.
Cristella, M. C. (1975). Comparison of straddling and sitting apparatus for the spastic
   cerebral palsied child. *American Journal of Occupational Therapy, 29*, 273–276.
Finnie, N. R. (1975). *Handling the young cerebral palsied child at home*. New York:
   E. P. Dutton & Co., Inc.
Fiorentino, M. R. (1976). *Reflex testing methods for evaluating central nervous system
   development* (2nd ed.). Springfield, IL: Charles C Thomas.
Folio, M. R., & Fewell, R. R. (1983). *Peabody Developmental Motor Scales*, Allen,
   TX: DLM Teaching Resources.
Forssberg, H., & Nashner, L. M. (1982). Ontogenetic development of postural control
   in man: Adaptation to altered support and visual conditions during stance. *Journal of
   Neuroscience, 2*, 545–552.
Gardner, R. A., & Broman, M. (1979). The Purdue Pegboard: Normative data on 1334
   school children. *Journal of Clinical Child Psychology, 8*, 156–162.
Gesell, A. (1940). *The first five years of life* (Part 1). New York: Harper & Brothers.
Harrison, A., & Connolly, K. (1971). The conscious control of fine levels of neuro-
   muscular firing in spastic and normal subjects. *Developmental Medicine and Child
   Neurology, 13*, 762–771.
Holt, K. S. (Ed.). (1975). Movement and child development. *Clinics in Developmental
   Medicine, 55*.
Hulme, J. B., Schulein, M., Hulme, R. D., Poor, R., & Pezzino, J. (1983). Perceived
   behavioral changes in multihandicapped individuals using adapted equipment. *Physical
   and Occupational Therapy in Pediatrics, 3*, 63–73.
Kamath, D. G. (1984). The effects of the neck and trunk functional support on spasticity
   in cerebral palsy children. *Proceedings of the 2nd International Conference on Re-

habilitation Engineering. Ottawa, Canada.

Moore, M. L. (1984). Clinical assessment of joint motion. In J. V. Basmajan (Ed.), *Therapeutic Exercise* (4th ed.; pp. 192–224). Baltimore: Williams & Wilkins.

Nashner, L. M. (1976). Adapting reflexes controlling the human posture. *Experimental Brain Research, 26*, 59–72.

Nashner, L. M. (1979). Organization and programming of motor activity during posture control. *Progress in Brain Research, 50*, 177–184.

Nashner, L. M., Shumway-Cook, A., & Marin, O. (1983). Stance posture control in select groups of children with cerebral palsy: Deficits in sensory organization and muscular coordination. *Experimental Brain Research, 49*, 393–409.

Robertson, D. W., Lee, W. A., & Jacobs, M. (1984). Single motor unit control by normal and cerebral-palsied males. *Developmental Medicine and Child Neurology, 26*, 323–327.

Rollefson, V. M., & Culver, B. E. (1972). An adjustable fiberglass chair. *American Journal of Occupational Therapy, 26*, 309.

Rosenbloom, L., & Horton, M. E. (1971). The maturation of fine prehension in young children. *Developmental Medicine and Child Neurology, 13*, 3–8.

Ryerson, S. D. (1985). Hemiplegia resulting from vascular insult or disease. In D. A. Umphred (Ed.), *Neurological Rehabilitation* (pp. 474–514). St. Louis, MO: C. V. Mosby.

Seeger, B. R., Caudrey, D. J., & O'Mara, N. A. (1984). Hand function in cerebral palsy: The effect of hip-flexion angle. *Developmental Medicine and Child Neurology, 26*, 601–606.

Shambes, G. M. (1976). Static postural control in children. *American Journal of Physical Medicine, 55*, 221–252.

Shumway-Cook, A., & Woollacott, M. (1985a). The growth of stability: Postural control from a developmental perspective. *Journal of Motor Behavior, 17*, 131–147.

Shumway-Cook, A., & Woollacott, M. (1985b). Dynamics of postural control in the child with Down Syndrome. *Physical Therapy, 65*, 1315–1322.

Steinberg, M., & Rendle-Short, J. (1977). Vestibular dysfunction in young children with minor neurological impairment. *Developmental Medicine and Child Neurology, 19*, 639–651.

Tiffin, J. (1979). *Purdue Pegboard examiner manual.* Lafayette, IN: Lafayette Instrument Company.

Trefler, E., Hanks, S., Huggins, P., Chiarizzo, S., & Hobson, D. (1978). A modular seating system for cerebral palsied children. *Developmental Medicine and Child Neurology, 20*, 199–204.

Vaughan, D., & Asbury, T. (1980). *General Ophthalmology* (9th ed.). Los Altos, CA: Lange Medical Publications.

Williams, H. G., Fisher, J. M., & Tritschler, K. A. (1983). Descriptive analysis of static postural control in 4, 6 and 8 year old normal and motorically awkward children. *American Journal of Physical Medicine, 62*, 12–26.

Williams, H. G., McClenaghan, B., & Ward, D. S. (1985). Duration of muscle activity during standing in normally and slowly developing children. *American Journal of Physical Medicine, 64*, 171–190.

3.

DEVELOPMENT OF POSTURAL CONTROL IN CHILDREN: EFFECTS OF GYMNASTICS TRAINING

Bettina Debu

Marjorie Woollacott

and

Marilyn Mowatt

University of Oregon

ABSTRACT

We addressed the question of development of postural responses to stance perturbation. Changes occurring in the organization of these responses as a result of both growth and gymnastics practice were examined. Children of two age groups and four levels of training were tested on a movable platform. Electromyographic (EMG) activity was recorded from eight muscles at the leg, trunk, and neck levels. Response latencies were analyzed. The relative importance of visual and proprioceptive information was assessed by including two vision and two stance conditions in the experiment. Comparison of the two age groups of untrained subjects showed that some fine-tuning occurs after the age of 10 in the responses of the upper body muscles. For all groups, latencies of gastrocnemius and trunk muscles were found to be shorter in the one-legged stance conditions, whereas vision had no effect. Advanced gymnasts showed longer latencies of neck muscle responses than untrained subjects.

Although postural control has been studied extensively, there is a surprising lack of research on the development of postural control in children who are

41

highly specialized in motor skills in which balance is fundamental, such as dancers or gymnasts. However, relevant information about the mechanisms underlying postural control might be brought to light by such a study. Indeed, these particular athletes probably need very reliable and perhaps more refined balance strategies than untrained performers, since the execution of their complex gestures depends on their ability to maintain their balance. Moreover, balance control in itself is critical in certain situations (balance beam exercise, for example) and therefore is systematically emphasized and trained during practice sessions.

The available studies on balance control and postural mechanisms underlying stance and movement in both children and adults have emphasized the importance of activating specific neuromuscular response patterns for the successful and efficient execution of a motor act. Two main research themes have been developed on this topic. The first one focuses on the development of anticipatory (or preparatory) postural adjustments preceding voluntary movement. These postural activities serve to compensate in advance (i.e., feed-forward control) for changes in equilibrium caused by the movement itself. A second theme focuses on the development of automatic postural reactions occurring when a person's balance is unexpectedly disturbed. The present research belongs to this second theme.

Compensatory, automatic muscular responses in normal adults can be activated by any of three sensory systems, stimulated by the loss of balance, namely proprioceptive, vestibular, and visual. The relative importance of each type of information is not yet clear in spite of several studies designed to analyze the effects of manipulating sensory inputs on postural reactions. Although early research (Nashner, 1976) emphasized the primary role of ankle joint inputs for the initiation of the leg muscles synergies, more recent work has shown the importance of visual and vestibular cues (Forssberg & Nashner, 1982; Nashner & Berthoz, 1978; Vidal, Gouny, & Berthoz, 1978; Woollacott, Debu, & Mowatt, 1985a, 1985b). These latter findings are in agreement with the results of earlier investigations by Brandt, Wenzel, and Dichgans (1976), Dichgans (1977), and Lee and Aronson (1974). Using a different paradigm, these authors investigated the proprioceptive function of vision in adults and children and assessed its involvement in postural control. In addition, other studies on postural control comparing patients with vestibular lesions to normal adults have demonstrated that vestibular patients show a smaller amplitude of the first component of the postural response when they are suddenly pushed or pulled from behind (Bussel, Katz, Pierrot-Deseilligny, Bergero, & Hayat, 1980). Thus, the vestibular system may also contribute to rapid postural responses.

The above research does not allow us to determine the relative weighting given to each of these subsystems by the postural control system under normal sensory conditions. However, it is possible that, in both adults and children, a general postural control system integrates the information provided by the different sources in order to select the appropriate pattern for the response. It has been hypothesized that the nervous system tests for congruence between at least two of the three sensory subsystems and relies most heavily on those which are congruent (Nashner, Black, & Wall, 1982). The relative dominance of each system also varies during the course of development (Shumway-Cook & Woollacott, 1985; Woollacott *et al.*, 1985a, 1985b). The dominance of the visual system over balance control observed early in childhood, especially when children are learning how to stand, is followed later by somatosensory dominance under normal sensory conditions. According to the hypothesis proposed by Nashner and Berthoz (1978), the suppression of one type of input produces a reorganization of the relative importance of the remaining information for controlling balance.

In order to determine if people who are skilled in an activity which is highly dependent on balance use unique postural response strategies, we conducted an experiment on a group of gymnasts, using a movable platform to perturb their equilibrium. The characteristics of their muscular responses were compared with those of untrained subjects. The main question addressed concerned the similarity of the general organization of automatic postural responses between performers with different levels of motor abilities. If differences were found between trained athletes and "normal" subjects, the well-accepted model of stereotyped patterns of postural adjustments dependent upon a limited set of rigidly wired programs would need to be revised. Conversely, the notion that postural responses are modified in terms of amplitude rather than in terms of muscle sequencing, as a function of sensory conditions (Nashner, 1976), leads to the alternative hypothesis that there will be no differences in postural adjustments between the skilled and the untrained subjects. Specifically, the muscle sequence for both groups should conform to the normal pattern of distoproximal radiating synergies. If this is the case, differences between gymnasts and nontrained subjects are expected to lie in the onset latencies and/or in the amplitudes of the responses or in both features, whereas the sequential activation of the different groups of muscles should be similar in the two groups.

In this experiment, we also attempted to analyze the subjects' postural responses under more difficult balance conditions. We tested them on the platform during one-legged stance, in order to examine whether the sensitivity to proprioceptive or vestibular inputs would be heightened in this situation, or if different balance strategies would appear.

Finally, we were interested in knowing if subjects trained in gymnastics rely more on visual information than do untrained subjects. Indeed, it has been shown that the execution of "simple" acrobatics is regulated through discrete visual information in well-trained trampoline performers (Droulez & Rezette, 1983). Acrobatic skills are unique in that there is an absence of terrestrial support, and, therefore, the role of vestibular and visual inputs is essential. Thus, one can hypothesize that gymnasts, as a result of their training, may become more sensitive to visual information indicating body sway. On the other hand, De Witt (1972) reports that sportsmen and dancers rely more on proprioceptive cues in a static stabilometric task. In order to test these two possibilities, the experiment included trials in which visual information was removed. The difference in amplitude and latencies of muscle responses in eyes-open vs eyes-closed conditions were compared in the two populations (trained and untrained) of subjects. In order to determine if age-related differences in balancing strategies occurred in both untrained and trained populations of children, we analyzed two age groups, 7-10 and 11-16 years of age. Children aged 7 were the youngest included in this study since, in our pool of subjects, involvement in competition started at this age.

METHODS

Subjects

Nineteen children trained and competing in gymnastics and 14 with no gymnastics training participated in the experiment. They were divided into two groups according to their age. The repartition was 7- to 10-year-olds: 5 gymnasts and 7 nongymnasts; 11- to 16-year-olds: 14 gymnasts and 7 nongymnasts. All the

Table 1
Number and Average Age of Subjects by Gymnastics Experience

		7- to 10-year-olds	11- to 16-year-olds
Untrained	N	5	7
	M Age (yrs)	8(1)*	13(1.5)
Trained Beginner	N	5	1
	M Age (yrs)	8(1)	11
Intermediate	N		8
	M Age (yrs)		12.5(1)
Advanced	N		5
	M Age (yrs)		14.2(1.3)

*Standard deviation for age given in parentheses.

gymnasts were provided by the Eugene Academy of Gymnastics, Eugene, Oregon, where they trained at least twice a week for a variable time. In order to study accurately the effects of training on the postural adjustments, the subjects were further divided into four practice groups on the basis of the number of years they had been participating in the gymnastics program. This within-training repartition is described in Table 1, with the average age of the children for each of the groups.

All the gymnasts participating in this study had been competing for at least one year.

Procedures

The children were asked to stand quietly on a platform capable of horizontal movements (Fig. 1). This stance base was hydraulically controlled and consisted of a base plate of 50 × 52 cm suspended at the four corners on strain gauge sensors. The torque (forward and backward shift of the center of pressure) was computed from the difference between the forces applied on the two anterior and the two posterior gauges. Translations consisted of ½ sine waves of 3 cm amplitude and 12 ms duration. Rotations were ½ sine waves, 9° amplitude, and 125 ms duration.

Each subject received a total of 36 trials, distributed randomly, including forward and backward translations. Forward translations were used to provide variety in the stimulus conditions, thus preventing the subjects from anticipating the perturbation direction or adapting to the stimulus. These forward translation trials were not analyzed. The subjects were not informed of the direction of the forthcoming perturbation.

All the subjects were tested in similar sessions, in which two different factors were manipulated. The first factor was the availability of visual information (present, eyes open vs absent, eyes closed), whereas the second one was the difficulty of the balancing task (two-legged stance vs one-legged stance). This procedure enabled us to test the three following designs: for the untrained subjects, age (two levels) × visual information (two levels) × stance condition (two levels); for the 7- to 10-year-old age groups, training (two levels) × visual information (two levels) × stance condition (two levels); for the 11- to 16-year-old age groups, training (three levels) × visual information (two levels) × stance condition (two levels).

Surface electrodes were used to record the electromyographic activity in eight muscles of the left side of the body, four on the anterior aspect and four on the posterior one. Gastrocnemius (G), hamstrings (H), lumbar paraspinal (TE), and cervical paraspinal (NE) were selected for the backside; tibialis anterior (T), quadriceps rectus (Q), rectus abdominus (A), and neck flexor (NF) for the front side. Raw EMGs were preamplified and processed by full-wave rectification and

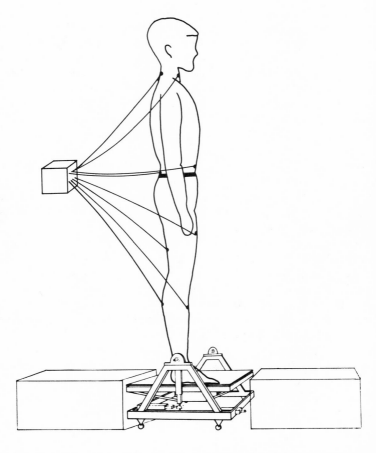

FIG. 1. Diagram of a young subject standing on the platform, showing placement of the surface electrodes.

band-pass filtration (0-40hz). They were stored on magnetic tape after analog to digital conversion. The onset latency was determined by visual inspection of the curves displayed on the computer screen. ANOVA tests were used to compare the results of the different groups.

In order to differentiate the possible mechanisms involved in the regulation of rapid postural adjustments, we chose to separate the muscular responses according to their range of latency. We divided them into 1) very short latency responses (or M1) ranging from 35 to 69 ms in onset latency, believed to be monosynaptic spinal reflexes; 2) medium latency responses (or M2) ranging from 70 to 200 ms, hypothesized to rely on supraspinal mechanisms. In many instances, we also observed long latency responses (or M3), occurring after 200 ms. Since these long latency responses are in the range of transcortical mechanisms, possibly involving voluntary processes, they will not be considered here.

In order to simplify the report of the results, the different conditions used in these experiments will be indicated as follows: 1) the posterior horizontal translations of the platform (HP), inducing a positive (forward) sway; 2) eyes open (O), visual conditions; 3) eyes closed (C), visual condition; 4) one-legged stance condition (differentiated by the addition of a 1 after the other codes). For instance, HPO means horizontal displacement of the platform causing positive sway, eyes open; HPC1 means horizontal platform movement causing positive sway, subject standing on one leg with eyes closed.

RESULTS

Control Groups (untrained subjects, aged 7-10 and 11-16 years)

General pattern.

The pattern of postural responses to the perturbation of normal stance (two legs, eyes open) was very similar in the two control groups. The general organization of M2 responses was the same as described in other studies (Nashner, 1976, 1977; Woollacott & Keshner, 1984; Woollacott et al., 1985a). As illustrated in Fig. 2, a posterior translation of the platform, inducing a forward sway of the body (HPO), provoked a sequential activation of the muscles of the posterior side of the body, beginning in the gastrocnemius and radiating upward to the hamstrings and trunk extensors. On the frontal side of the body, neck flexor, and abdominal muscles were activated at the same short latency as the gastrocnemius (7- to 10-year-olds: G.: 96 ± 10 ms; N.F.: 105 ± 18 ms; A.: 110 ± 15 ms; 11- to 16-year-olds: G.: 103 ± 26 ms; N.F.: 107 ± 8 ms; A.: 100 ± 11 ms). Neck flexors responses occurred in 87% of the trials for the younger group and in 82% of the trials for the older one. It is also noticeable

TAYS/HP0   SAH3S/HPC1

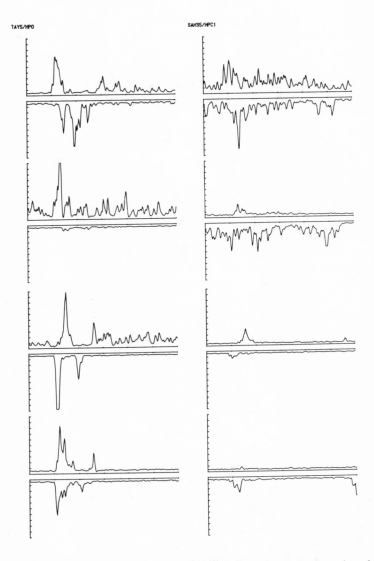

FIG. 2. Surface EMG recordings of muscle responses to a single posterior platform translation causing anterior body sway, untrained subjects. The two muscles recorded from each segment are grouped together with the flexor muscle inverted. The line indicates the onset of platform movement. Time marks are 135 ms. From top to bottom: Gastrocnemius, Tibialis Anterior, Hamstrings, Quadriceps, Trunk Extensors, Abdominals, Neck Extensors and Neck Flexors. Left side of the figure: 11- to 16-year-old subject, HPO condition. Right side, 7- to 10-year-old subjects, HPC1 condition.

that in these two groups of subjects, abdominal muscles were activated very consistently (83% and 96.5% of the trials for the 7- to 10- and 11- to 16-year-olds, respectively) and at the same latency as the neck flexors. This relative timing is similar to the pattern described by Woollacott and Keshner (1984) in adult subjects. These authors described a nearly simultaneous onset for neck flexor and abdominal muscles responses (N.R.: 67 ms; A.: 69 ms, in eyes-open condition).

This general muscle response organization was also observed in the other situations (two-legged stance, eyes closed; one-legged stance, eyes open and eyes closed), (see Table 2).

As can be seen in Table 2, there were some differences in the latencies of the upper body muscles responses across the four conditions (Fig. 3). An analysis of variance (ANOVA) was performed in which age (7-10, 11-16) was treated as a between subjects factor, and visual condition (eyes-open, eyes-closed) and stance condition (two-legged, one-legged) were entered as within subjects factors. This analysis revealed no significant effect of age on the neck muscles or trunk extensors response. However, for the neck extensor muscle, the difference between the younger and older subjects approached significance ($F(1, 15) = 3.4$; $p < .087$).

With regard to stance, the reduction of onset latencies for neck flexors and

Table 2

Mean Response Latencies and Standard Deviations (in parentheses) for Each of the Muscles Recorded in the Two Groups of Untrained Subjects

7- to 10- Year-Olds	N.F.	N.E.	A.	T.E.	Q.	H.	T.	G.
HPO	105(18)	153(18)	110(15)	170(13)	159(24)	137(13)	140(30)	96(10)
HPC	108(18)	155(25)	100(17)	160(15)	161(14)	134(17)	129(38)	93(9)
HPO1	106(15)	151(29)	102(14)	143(12)	126(38)	117(14)	122(18)	89(10)
HPC1	98(7)	150(14)	109(19)	146(11)	133(30)	112(19)	129(32)	93(20)

11 to 16 Year Olds	N.F.	N.E.	A.	T.E.	Q.	H.	T.	G.
HPO	107(8)	144(17)	100(20)	154(14)	143(7)	120(14)	120(30)	103(26)
HPC	106(12)	142(28)	85(24)	153(15)	139(13)	116(1)	122(23)	98(13)
HPO1	97(8)	127(18)	97(17)	142(34)	140(17)	114(12)	135(21)	91(9)
HPC1	101(10)	130(14)	92(12)	142(20)	146(6)	123(17)	140(30)	94(10)

See text for abbreviations used.

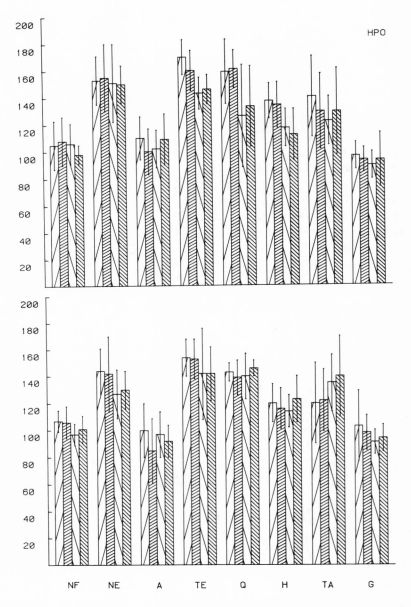

FIG. 3. Histogram of onset latencies of muscle M2 responses for the 2 groups of untrained subjects. For each muscle, from left to right: HPO, HPC, HPO1, HPC1. A (upper panel) 7- to 10-year-olds, B (lower panel) 11- to 16-year-olds.

trunk extensors from the two-legged to the one-legged stance was significant (NF, $F(1, 12) = 5.96, p < .03$); TE, $F(1, 12) = 16.2, p < .002$). The difference observed in the onset latencies of neck exensors did not reach significance ($F(1, 12) = 3.23, p > .094$). Absence or presence of vision had no effect on the onset times for any of the muscles tested, and there were no interactions between the factors.

Cocontraction.

In addition to the reduction in latencies observed between the two-legged and the one-legged stance conditions, both age groups showed a trend toward a decrease in the delay between the agonist and antagonist response onset time of the trunk muscles, thus giving more cocontraction of agonist-antagonist pair in the one-legged stance conditions (Fig. 4).

This effect was more marked for the younger group (delay between trunk extensors and abdominals onset time: 60 $\pm$ 0 ms in the two-legged stance, 39 $\pm$ 3 ms in the one-legged stance conditions) than for the older group (two-legged stance 61 $\pm$ 6 ms, one-legged stance, 47.5 $\pm$ 4 ms). A repeated measures ANOVA of the three factors, muscle (A, TE) $\times$ stance $\times$ vision, confirmed this observation. A significant interaction between muscle and stance was found for the younger group ($F(1, 5) = 16.7, p < .01$), but not for the older one ($F(1, 6) < 1$).

Monosynaptic responses.

In addition to the medium latency responses, short latency (monosynaptic) responses were recorded for both groups in all four conditions. Gastrocnemius showed the highest frequency (7- to 10-year-olds, 35.5%; 11- to 16-year-olds, 20% of the trials, all conditions collapsed). Monosynaptic responses also occurred in the other muscles of the body, although their frequency was much lower (see Table 3). It is interesting to note that the short latency response percentages were higher in the younger group than in the older one, at least for the gastrocnemius and neck flexor muscles in the HPO condition (Fig. 5).

In addition, for the younger group, monosynaptic responses occurred more frequently in the two-legged (38% of the trials) than in the one-legged (27% of the trials) stance condition. There was no pattern of change in the occurrence of monosynaptic responses across the different experimental conditions for any of the groups.

Finally, there were trials in which certain muscles were not activated. This happened especially in the antagonist muscles of the lower and upper leg (tibialis and quadriceps) whose activity does not contribute to bringing the center of gravity back to its initial position. Neck muscles also remained silent on a number

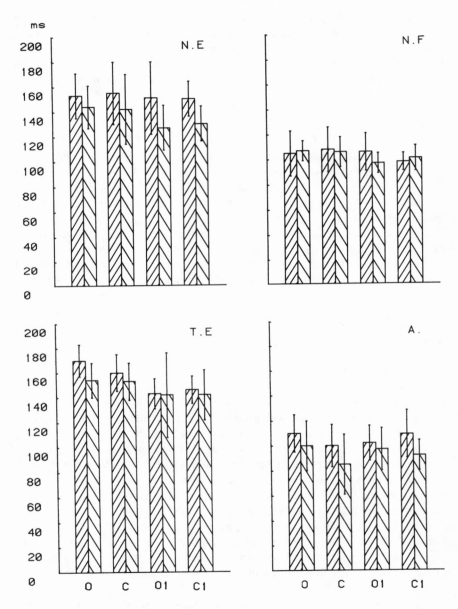

FIG. 4. Differences in onset latencies of responses of the upper body muscles between the 7- to 10- and 11- to 16-year-old untrained subjects. Note that the youngest group (left columns) tends to have longer latencies for the extensor groups, in all situations.

Table 3
**Percentages of Trials in Which Monosynaptic Responses Occurred in Each
Condition for Both Groups of Untrained Subject**

7- to 10-Year-Olds	N.F.	N.E.	A.	T.E.	Q.	H.	T.	G.
HPO	23	7	3	0	7	0	0	43
HPC	7	4	3.5	0	0	0	0	33
HPO1	3	0	6	0	9	6	6	20
HPC1	3	3	3	0	0	3	9	34

11- to 16-Year-Olds	N.F.	N.E.	A.	T.E.	Q.	H.	T.	G.
HPO	0	14	3.5	0	3.5	3.5	0	21
HPC	3.5	0	3.5	0	3.5	0	0	21
HPO1	0	0	0	3.5	0	0	3.5	21
HPC1	11	14	11	3.5	3.5	3.5	11	18

See text for abbreviations used.

of trials. There were no differences in the frequency of occurrence of these "no response" trials across conditions, except for an increase in neck flexors and extensors in the one-legged stance, eyes-closed condition for both groups.

Thus, it appears that the maturational processes are not completed before the age of 11. The adultlike characteristics of M2 responses are reached earlier for the distal leg muscles than for the upper body muscles. In addition, the youngest group seemed to be slightly more sensitive to the manipulation of the task, although there were no major differences in the organization of the responses between the two groups in any of the conditions.

ORGANIZATION OF POSTURAL RESPONSES IN TRAINED GYMNASTS

General Pattern

As expected, the same sequential pattern of muscle activation was observed for the three groups of gymnasts (Beginner, Intermediate, Advanced). There were no differences in the response onset times for the muscles of the ascending ankle synergy in any of the levels of practice. Gastrocnemius latencies range was similar to the one described for the untrained subjects (Beginner, 90 ± 10

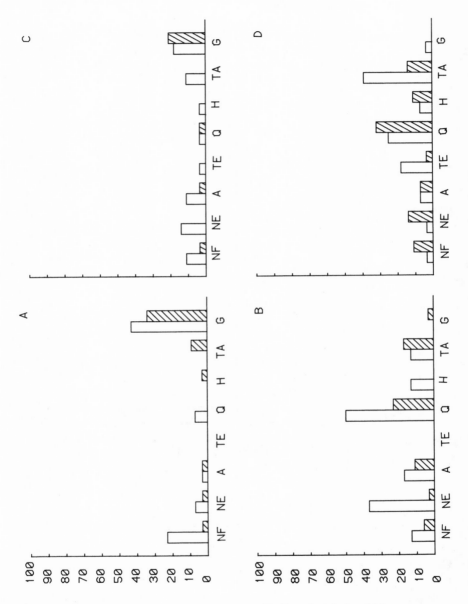

FIG. 5. Percentages of monosynaptic responses (A-C) and trials in which no response occurred in individual muscles (B-D). Comparison between HPO (left, open bars) and HPC1 (right, hatched bars), for the 7- to 10- (A-B) and 11- to 16- (C-D) year-old untrained subjects

TRU4HPO BAN2QHPC1

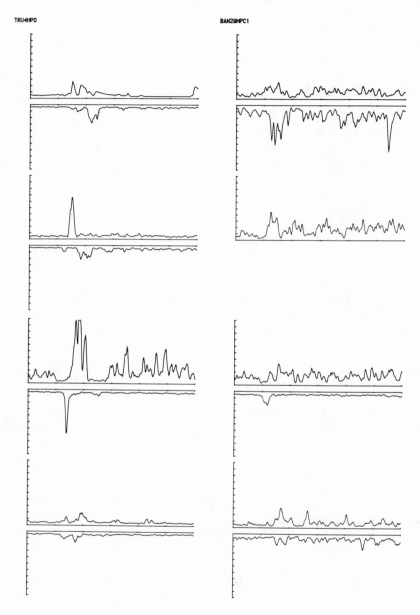

FIG. 6. EMG recordings of the responses of 2 trained subjects to a single posterior platform translation causing anterior sway. Organization of the figure as in Fig. 2

ms; Intermediate, 97 ± 14 ms; Advanced, 91 ± 12 ms). The activity in the gastrocnemius was followed by activation of hamstrings and trunk extensors (Fig. 6). On the front side of the body, a response was recorded in the abdominal muscles at very short latency and was followed by activation of the neck flexor muscles, after a longer delay.

The effect of training was treated separately in the two age groups. In the 7- to 10-year-olds, untrained subjects were compared to beginner gymnasts. In the 11- to 16-year-olds, data from three levels of training were compared (Untrained, Intermediate, Advanced). In all the ANOVA tests performed to analyze the effects of training, visual and stance conditions were entered as two within subjects factors.

7 to 10 year olds

Concerning the gastrocnemius muscle, the ANOVA tests showed no effect of training ($F(1, 10) < 1$). As can be seen from Tables 2 and 4, there was a trend for both trained and untrained subjects to reduce gastrocnemius latencies from the two-legged to the one-legged stance condition (untrained, 94.6 vs 90.6 ms; beginner 88.8 vs 85.6 ms). However, in this age group, this stance factor effect was not significant ($F(1, 10) = 3.54, p < .086$).

Upper body muscles.

No training effect was observed in any of the upper body muscles recorded, although the difference between the two groups was close to significance ($F(1, 9) = 4.58, p < .059$, for the trunk extensor muscles). Response latencies for this muscle group were consistently shorter in the trained group than in the untrained one (Fig. 7A) and it is possible that the small size of the groups is responsible for the absence of statistical difference. Interestingly enough (cf. section on 11- to 16-year-olds), in the trained group, there was a trend toward an increase in neck flexor response latency as the balancing task became harder (Table 4). As already mentioned, this was not the case for the untrained group for which no consistent pattern of change was observed as the conditions of balance changed. The results of the ANOVA test showed that the interaction between training and stance factors was close to significance for this neck muscle ($F(1, 9) = 4.45, p < .062$).

The test also revealed that trunk extensor response onset time was affected by the stance and vision factors (stance factor, $F(1, 9) = 8.19, p < .018$); vision factor, $F(1, 9) = 9.17, p < .013$). The stance effect reflects a decrease in trunk extensor response latencies from the two-legged to the one-legged stance, more marked in the trained group than in the untrained one. The vision effect reflects a decrease in latency in the eyes-closed condition as compared to the eyes-open

Table 4
Mean Latencies and Standard Deviations (in Parentheses) of the Muscle Responses Latencies for the Trained Subjects of Both Age Groups

HPO	N.F.	N.E.	A.	T.E.	Q.	H.	T.	G.
YB	97(10)	155(19)	91(15)	140(9)	*	116(19)	135(28)	90(10)
I	109(16)	146(22)	95(8)	152(16)	136(18)	126(15)	122(9)	97(14)
A	136(30)	172(25)	93(9)	164(9)	145(12)	135(22)	118(30)	91(12)
HPC								
YB	102(2)	169(26)	102(14)	144(13)	*	116(12)	128(12)	93(10)
I	103(7)	155(32)	92(14)	147(16)	141(14)	134(21)	111(13)	95(6)
A	124(34)	173(15)	90(6)	168(15)	124(16)	127(16)	114(20)	107(20)
HPO1								
YB	111(19)	140(30)	86(12)	147(27)	*	109(9)	113(24)	82(4)
I	105(22)	141(19)	85(11)	147(12)	121(26)	118(20)	133(25)	91(9)
A	133(20)	164(21)	86(10)	153(30)	142(15)	125(26)	119(17)	96(11)
HPC1								
YB	115(18)	154(31)	85(7)	131(11)	*	103(20)	111(27)	89(8)
I	108(23)	146(14)	80(7)	153(16)	114(15)	108(18)	118(15)	90(11)
A	128(20)	161(14)	85(5)	152(22)	127(19)	129(19)	122(18)	93(10)

YB: group of beginners belonging to the 7- to 10-year-olds age range
I: 11- to 16-year-old gymnasts of intermediate level
A: 11- to 16-year-old advanced gymnasts
*: data not available

one. On the same aspect of the body, neck extensors also were affected in the same direction by these two factors, but not to a significant extent (stance factor $F(1, 9) = 3.96$, $p > .075$; vision factor, $F(1, 9) = 3.78$, $p < .081$). On the front side of the body, abdominal and neck flexor muscles onset time were not influenced by any of the three factors.

Cocontraction.

In addition, the lengthening of neck flexor response latency across the experimental conditions resulted in an increase in the amount of cocontraction in the agonist-antagonist pair at the neck level in the one-legged conditions as compared to the two-legged ones. The difference between neck extensors and neck flexors onset times was 62 ms in the two-legged stance and was reduced to 34 ms when the trained subjects stood on one leg. Thus, comparing the amount

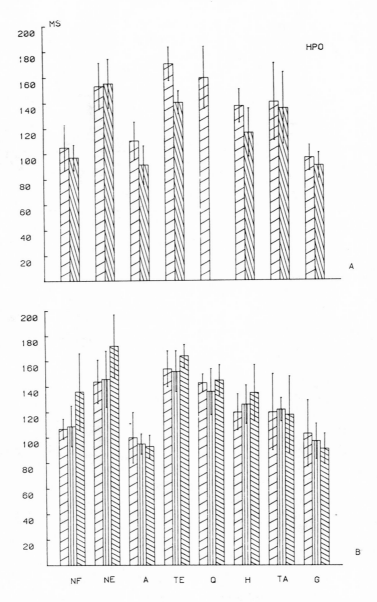

FIG. 7. Histograms showing the differences in onset latencies of muscle responses between untrained and trained subjects. U: untrained; T: trained (7- to 10-year-olds); I: intermediate gymnasts; A: advanced gymnasts. Upper panel 7-10 year olds; lower panel 11- to 16-year-olds

of cocontraction occurring at the neck and trunk levels reveals a shortening of agonist-antagonist onset time delay at the trunk level for the untrained subjects and at the neck level for the trained ones.

Monosynaptic responses.

In the group of trained subjects, monosynaptic responses were exclusively recorded in gastrocnemius, with the exception of HPC1 situation in which M1 responses also occurred in abdominals. This pattern is quite different from the one observed in the untrained group in which short latency responses were seen in all muscles recorded. However, in the latter group as well, gastrocnemius showed the highest frequency.

11 to 16 year olds

As for the younger groups, the response of the lower body muscles did not show any training-related changes. However, the diminution in gastrocnemius response latency from two-legged to one-legged stance was significant in this age group ($F(2, 17) = 7.73$, $p < .012$). No other effect was found for the leg muscles responses (Fig. 7B).

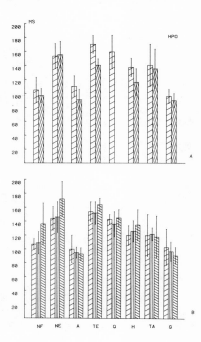

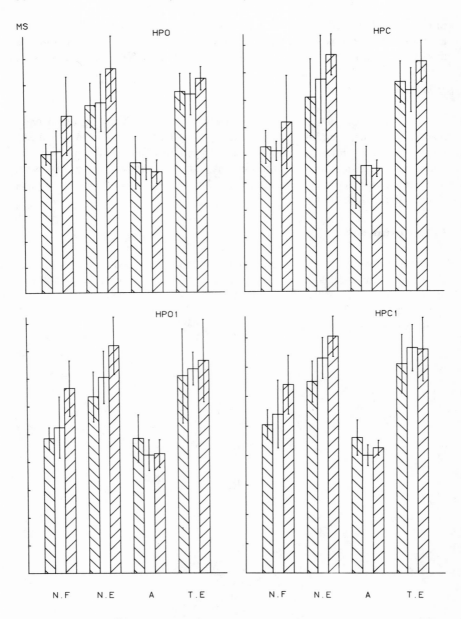

FIG. 8. Bar graph showing the differences in onset latencies of upper body muscle responses in the four experimental situations. For each muscle, from left to right, untrained, intermediate, and advanced subjects. Time scale 20 ms

Upper body muscles.

Surprisingly, we observed longer latencies of upper body muscle responses for the trained subjects than for the untrained ones (Fig. 7B and Table 4). An ANOVA test showed a significant effect of training on the neck flexor ($F(2, 17)$ = 9.34, $p < .002$) and neck extensor ($F(2, 16)$ = 7.82, $p < .004$) muscles responses. There were no significant differences for either the trunk extensors or abdominals. Since there were three groups of training, a t-test was run to determine where the effect occurred. The results showed no difference between untrained and intermediate levels or between intermediate and advanced subjects. The effect was found to exist only between the two extreme groups (untrained vs advanced, $t = 4.25$, $p < .01$).

When the conditions of balance changed, the geneal pattern of the postural response remained similar (Table 4 and Fig. 8). As with the untrained subjects, there was a stance effect on most muscles of the upper body. Response latencies were shorter in the one-legged stance condition than in the two-legged one for abdominals ($F(1, 17)$ = 8.33, $p < .01$), trunk extensors ($F(1, 15)$ = 11.66, $p < .004$), and neck extensors ($F(1, 16)$ = 4.64, $p < .044$). Neck flexor muscles response latencies were identical in the two stance conditions for the trained subjects as opposed to what was observed for the untrained subjects.

Cocontraction.

The amount of cocontraction of agonist-antagonist pairs at the trunk or neck level was more important in the untrained group than in the trained ones. Trained subjects showed longer delays, at both levels, between onset times of the muscles located on the opposite aspects of the body. The increased delay between abdominal and trunk extensor onset latencies also was observed when the trained subjects stood on one leg.

Monosynaptic responses.

In terms of the frequency of occurrence of monosynaptic responses and trials with "no response" (NR) in individual muscles, we did not find any dramatic difference between the untrained and trained subjects, although the percentage of "no response" trials was higher in the advanced group than in the others. As in the younger group, monosynaptic responses occurred in all muscles recorded for the untrained group, whereas they were observed almost exclusively in gastrocnemius, abdominal, and neck flexor muscles for the trained subjects (Fig. 9 and Table 5). Interestingly, the most advanced group showed high percent occurrence of M1 responses in neck flexors in the two eyes-open conditions only (HPO, 20%; HPO1, 16%). The frequency of monosynaptic responses in abdom-

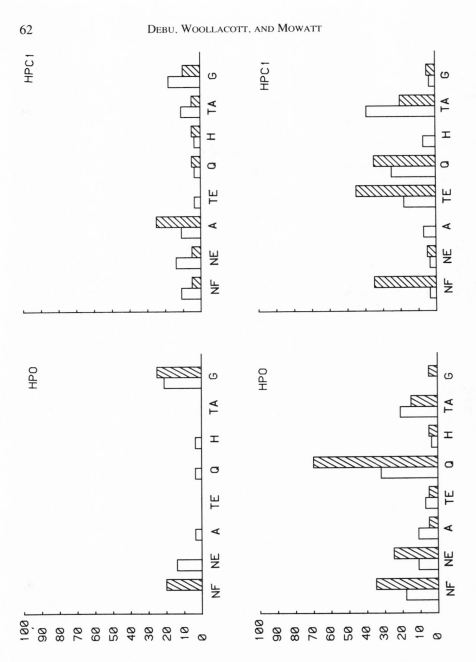

FIG. 9. Histograms showing the percentages of monosynaptic responses (upper graphs) and trials in which no responses occurred (lower graphs); comparison of untrained (open columns) and advanced (hatched columns) 11- to 16-year-old subjects

Table 5
Pecentages of Trials in Which Monosynaptic Responses Occurred, in Each of the Conditions for Trained Gymnasts

7- to 10-year-old Beginners

	N.F.	N.E.	A.	T.E.	Q.	H.	T.	G.
HPO	0	0	0	0	*	5	0	32
HPC	0	0	0	0	*	0	0	50
HPO1	5	0	0	0	*	5	0	37
HPC1	0	0	13	0	*	0	0	27

11- to 16-year-old Intermediates

	N.F.	N.E.	A.	T.E.	Q.	H.	T.	G.
HPO	3	0	0	0	4	0	0	38
HPC	3	0	6	3	0	3.5	0	30
HPO1	0	3	13	0	0	3.5	3	10
HPC1	6	0	18	0	0	7	3	33

11- to 16-year-old Advanced Gymnasts

	N.F.	N.E.	A.	T.E.	Q.	H.	T.	G.
HPO	20	0	0	0	0	0	0	25
HPC	5	9	5	0	0	5	0	35
HPO1	16	10	10	0	0	10	0	37
HPC1	5	5	25	0	5	5	5	10

*Data Not Available

inal muscles was increased for the three groups in the one-legged stance condition. This increase was more important for the trained subjects than for the untrained ones. The gymnasts also showed higher frequency of "no response" trials, especially in the trunk extensor and quadriceps muscles, and, to a lesser extent, in the neck muscles.

Thus, it appears that with training, the advanced gymnasts had acquired the ability to decouple their neck muscle responses from the postural synergies and used an independent mechanism for stabilizing their heads. This ability was not completely mastered by the less trained athletes, although our results show a trend in this direction with increased duration of training. In addition, trained subjects seemed to use more economical postural responses, in which the muscles which are not involved in bringing the center of mass back to its initial position were not activated systematically.

DISCUSSION

The results of our experiments shed new light on two aspects of the automatic postural responses triggered by balance disturbance. First, we have looked at the developmental process, that is, the changes occurring in the organization of the muscular responses during childhood. Second, related developmental questions can be asked by investigating the effects of training, that is, the adaptive specialization acquired with gymnastics practice.

Concerning the developmental issue, previous studies analyzing leg muscles responses to stance perturbation had failed to show any differences in the rapid postural responses between 7- and 10-year-olds and adults (Shumway-Cook & Woollacott, 1985). Our results confirm these findings for leg muscles, but show that the 7- to 10-year-olds' postural responses are characterized by specific features. Some differences exist between this age group and older groups in the responses of the upper body musculature. By recording from the upper body muscles, we have found two interesting observations. First, trunk and neck M2 responses occurred very consistently on nearly every trial in our two groups of untrained children. This indicates a progression in the maturational processes as compared to younger age groups (2-3 and 4-6 years of age) previously studied. In a recent developmental study, Woollacott et al. (1985a) report a low frequency of occurrence of neck flexor responses following platform posterior translations in young children of 2-3 and 4-6 years of age (responses occurred in 42% and 22% of the trials for these two groups, respectively). Second, another point brought by Woollacott et al. in the same paper, was that neck and trunk extensor M2 latencies were longer in the young children groups than in the adult one. Here we have found that the latencies of neck extensor muscles responses are still slightly longer for the 7- to 10-year-old group than for the 11- to 16-year-old one, but not to a significant extent. This means that although the M2 postural responses organization is rather mature by the age of 10, additional fine-tuning takes place after this age before adultlike characteristics are reached. In addition to the shift in onset time for the M2 responses, the 7- to 10-year-old untrained subjects of the present study displayed more monosynaptic responses in gastrocnemius than did the 11- to 16-year-olds. This finding recalls a feature of the reactions of young children to perturbation of stance described by Shumway-Cook and Woollacott (1985). However, these authors reported an increased number of short latency responses in all leg muscles of the younger children, rather than limited to the gastrocnemius alone.

The analysis of the postural responses of the two groups of untrained subjects also showed that some changes occur when the subjects were asked to balance on one leg. Although the same general pattern of sequential activation of muscles was observed in all conditions, when the balancing task difficulty increased we observed 1) a reduction in M2 onset latencies in the gastrocnemius and in the upper body muscles; and, 2) an increase in the amount of cocontraction of agonist-antagonist pairs at the trunk level. These changes were more important in the younger group than in the older one. They may reflect the fact that a more rigid posture was adopted by the subjects in the one-legged stance conditions.

It seems reasonable to assume that the strategy used by the subjects in order to keep balanced on one leg consisted in trying to immobilize their trunk relative to the supporting segment. This stabilization could be achieved by stiffening the hip joint, which implies an increase in the tonic activity of the muscles controlling the pelvic mobility. This could result in an increase of excitability at the level of the motoneuron pool, thus lowering the threshold of postural responses to perturbation of stance. The shortening of the gastrocnemius response latencies from the two-legged to the one-legged stance can be attributed to a similar strategy applied at the ankle level.

Although we did not observe quantifiable changes in the latencies of M2 responses between the vision-present vs vision-absent conditions, this does not rule out the possibility that differences exist in some other response characteristics. Indeed, developmental studies (Woollacott et al., 1985b) as well as studies on adults (Nashner & Berthoz, 1978) have shown that muscle response amplitudes, rather than latencies, are likely to be affected by alterations of visual inputs. Likewise, additional differences between the responses following one- and two-legged stance perturbations may be found in amplitude changes.

Concerning the number of monosynaptic responses, in the developmental study already cited, Woollacott et al. (1985a) report an increased percentage of M1 responses in all groups of children between 18 months and 6 years of age when vision was removed. In the present experiment, we did not observe any similar change in the occurrence of short latency responses in vision-absent vs vision-present conditions. The stability in the number of monosynaptic responses across conditions in the two age groups probably reflects the improvement in stance stability reached by the age of 7.

With regard to the second issue, that is, the effect of training on the organization of postural responses to perturbations of balance, additional points deserve some attention.

First, the absence of training effect in the 7- to 10-year-old group was expected, since the gymnasts of this age group had only had 2 to 3 years of training at the date of the experiment. However, the precise timing of the postural responses of the trained subjects appeared to be more similar to the adult one than to the one of untrained children of the same age. Latencies of trunk extensors M2 responses were shorter in the trained group than in the untrained one and were even shorter than the latencies recorded in the 11- to 16-year-old untrained group. In addition, monosynaptic responses occurred only in a limited number of muscles, which was also a characteristic of M1 responses of the older trained gymnast. These features of M1 and M2 responses of the 7- to 10-year-old trained subjects may be interpreted in two different, but not exclusive, ways. The first hypothesis is that physical training speeds up the final maturational process occurring around the age of 10. The young gymnasts would then reach adultlike characteristics of their postural responses earlier than untrained children. A better timing between the muscles controlling the different levels of the body may contribute to a better stability. This is an important goal to achieve for young gymnasts, given that acrobatic performance depends heavily on a good postural presetting.

Another explanation is that with gymnastics training, children learn to adopt a different alignment of the body during quiet stance. The resulting modifications of the body segment relations could be responsible for the improvement in balancing tasks. Modification of the body alignment would also account for the important number of monosynaptic responses observed in abdominal muscles in the well-trained gymnasts groups. In any case, it is clear that the ease in performing the task during the experimental session was greater for the trained subjects than for the untrained ones in the younger age group especially. In particular, in the one-legged stance conditions only the gymnasts were able to meet the precise requirements of keeping their arms extended behind their back. The untrained children could not help using their upper limbs for balancing.

It is interesting to note that for all groups included in this experiment, the same effect was observed when the subjects were asked to stand on one leg. The constraints of this task seem to be such that even for the very well trained gymnasts, some adaptation of the postural responses were needed to avoid a fall. However, the general organization of the response remained the same in all experimental conditions. The main ankle synergy was observed in all situations. This differs from the results obtained by Horak and Nashner (1986). In their experiment, they reduced the base of support available to the subjects by having them stand on a beam. The beam was placed transversally so that the support surface was short in relation to the foot length. The authors observed a shift in the strategy used by the subjects. Instead of the ascending ankle synergy starting with an activation of the gastrocnemius muscle and radiating upward on the posterior aspect of the body, they describe a descending synergy, beginning with an activation of the abdominal muscles and radiating in the opposite, proximal to distal sequence, on the front side of the body (i.e., in the ankle synergy antagonist muscles). The difference between the results obtained by these authors and ours is explained by the setting of the two experiments. In the Horak and Nashner experiment, the orientation of the beam prevented the subjects from exerting a compensatory torque about the ankle joint in order to move the body center of mass forward. Instead, equilibrium was restored by exerting a compensatory horizontal sheer force against the support surface. In our setting, the whole sole of the foot was able to press on the support plate, and the subjects could exert a torque about the ankle joint.

Another point concerns the absence of training effect on the gastrocnemius M2 response. According to the conclusions of De Witt (1972), sportsmen and dancers tested in a stabilometric task rely more on proprioceptive (viz., pressure, muscular, and/or joint) inputs than do "normal", untrained, subjects for control of equilibrium. His hypothesis is that they do so by lowering the threshold or increasing the gain of proprioceptive reflex loops. The fact that trained subjects tended to show more monosynaptic responses in gastrocnemius than untrained subjects in all situations seems to support this hypothesis. The absence of differences in M2 responses between trained and untrained groups may be explained by the fact that, in the platform situation, ankle inputs are so critical that all the subjects "function" with an optimum sensitivity of their long-loop reflexes, whether it means high gain or low threshold.

Perhaps the most important point is the unexpected finding that latencies of M2 responses of neck muscles appear to be longer in trained subjects than in untrained ones. This results in an uncoupling of the neck muscles from the response radiating in the lower half of the body. Thus, it seems that two relatively independent mechanisms are used to stabilize the center of mass and to stabilize the head. This ability was not completely mastered by the less trained athletes, although our results show a trend in this direction with increased duration of training. What are the implications of this finding? First, it seems to confirm that the responses recorded in the leg muscles actually belong to a synergy which is rather rigid. However, the fact that by varying the quality of the inputs one can change some of the characteristics of this response triggered at the ankle level implies that this synergy is flexible enough to adapt to changing conditions of the environment. In the same way, different inputs are capable of influencing the response triggered at the neck level, thus providing a mechanism of stabilization of the head with the necessary flexibility. The development, or refinement of an independent mechanism of control of the head position relative to the other segments of the body would seem to be very meaningful in the scope of gymnastics skills. Functionally speaking, it would enable the gymnast to collect information about his or her spatial position, while performing acrobatics, without interfering with the evolution of the movement. Indeed, the cephalic segment is carrying two very important informational sources (visual and vestibular systems) for balance control and spatial localization, and its stabilization would improve the reliability of the inputs sampled. Droulez and Rezette (1983), described a comparable strategy used by trampoline performers during the performance of unidirectional figures. In a full backward somersault for example, videoanalysis of head position relative to body position showed that visual information was taken in a discrete manner, at certain points in time, during the execution of the revolution in space. This strategy was no longer used for acrobatics in which the spatial evolution was highly complex, as in a combination of rotations around the longitudinal and transversal axes (full backward twisting). For this latter sault, the authors found that the degradation of the performance was not as dramatic as for the simple backward somersault when the visual information was removed (darkness). However, our experimental situation was much simpler, and the availability of visual inputs was not critical for triggering the postural responses, including the hypothesized independent head position control mechanism. Indeed, there was no difference in the muscles responses whether the eyes were open or closed, except for a slightly larger amount of cocontraction between the agonist-antagonist pairs of the upper body.

In conclusion, we have found that significant differences exist in the postural responses between both our older and younger children, and between gymnasts and nongymnasts. These differences are in the response characteristics of muscles of the upper body. We note that young children (7–10 years) show longer onset delays in upper body extensors responses and more monosynaptic responses in general. Trained gymnasts appeared to be able to decouple the neck muscles from the rest of the postural synergies, and show a larger number of trials in which no response occurred in these muscles. We conclude that 1) the maturational processes are completed later for the upper body muscle responses than for the lower body one; and 2) the organization of these muscle responses is more flexible in the upper body half than in the lower one, and appears to be affected by gymnastics training, as opposed to the leg muscle responses, in which no changes were observed.

REFERENCES

Brandt, T., Wenzel, D., & Dichgans, J. (1976). Die Entwicklung der Visuellen Stabilisation des Aufrechten Standes beim Kind: Ein Reifezeichen in der Kinderneurologie. (Visual stabilization of free stance in infants: a sign of maturity). *Archiv Für Psychiatric and Nervenkrankheiten, 223,* 1–13.

Bussel, B., Katz, R., Pierrot-Deseilligny, E., Bergero, C., & Hayat, A. (1980). Vestibular and proprioceptive influences on the postural reactions to a sudden body displacement in man. In J. E. Desmedt, (Ed.) *Progress in clinical neurophysiology* (Vol. 8., pp. 310–322). Basel: S. Karger.

De Witt, R. (1972). Optic versus vestibular and proprioceptive impulses measured by posturometry. *Agressologie, 13B,* 7–79.

Dichgans, J. (1977). The influence of peripheral vision on ambient ego-orientation. *Neuroscience Research Program Bulletin, 15,* 376–385.

Droulez, J., & Rezette, P. (1983). *Visual control and head trajectories during acrobatic trampoline saults.* Paper presented at NATO Advanced Study Institute, Brain Mechanisms and Spatial Vision, Lyon, France.

Forssberg, H., & Nashner, L. (1982). Ontogenetic development of posture control in man: Adaptation to altered support and visual conditions during stance. *Journal of Neuroscience, 2,* 545–552.

Horak, F. B., & Nashner, L. M. (1986). Central programming of postural movements: Adaptation to altered support surface configuration. *Journal of Neurophysiology, 55,* 1369–1381.

Lee, D. N., & Aronson, E. (1974). Visual and proprioceptive control of standing in human infants. *Perception and Psychophysics, 15*, 529–532.

Nashner, L. (1976). Adapting reflexes controlling human posture. *Experimental Brain Research, 26*, 59–72.

Nashner, L. (1977). Fixed patterns of rapid postural responses among leg muscles during stance. *Experimental Brain Research, 30*, 13–24.

Nashner, L., & Berthoz, A. (1978). Visual contribution to rapid motor responses during posture control. *Brain Research, 150*, 403–407.

Nashner, L., Black, F., & Wall, C. (1982). Adaptation to altered support and visual conditions during stance: Patients with vestibular deficits. *Journal of Neuroscience, 2*, 536–544.

Shumway-Cook, A., & Woollacott, M. (1985). The growth of stability: Postural control from a developmental perspective. *Journal of Motor Behavior, 17*, 131–147.

Vidal, P. P., Gouny, M., & Berthoz, A. (1978). Rôle de la vision dans le déclenchement de reactions posturales rapides. *Archives Italiennes de Biologie, 116*, 273–280.

Woollacott, M., & Keshner, E. (1984). Upper body responses to postural perturbations in man. *Neuroscience Abstracts, 10*, 635.

Woollacott, M., Debu, B., & Mowatt, M. (1985a). Neuromuscular control of posture in the infant and child. (Manuscript submitted for publication).

Woollacott, M., Debu, B., & Mowatt, M. (1985b). The development of balance control in children: Sensorimotor integration. *Proceedings of the North American Society for the Psychology of Sport and Physical Activity.*

AUTHOR NOTE

This research was supported by the Medical Research Foundation of Paris for Bettina Debu.

4

THE EFFECTS OF AGE ON UNRESISTED AND RESISTED FRACTIONATED REACTION TIME

Nancy C. Rich

Miami University

ABSTRACT

*This investigation examined the effects of age upon frac-
tionated reaction time under unresisted and resisted conditions. A total of 48 male subjects in three age groups
(30-40 yrs, 50-60 yrs, 61-70 yrs) were measured on each
of four testing days. The criterion measures were: 20
unresisted reaction time trials of the flexors of one arm
and the extensors of the other arm; 20 resisted reaction
time trials of the flexors of one arm and the extensors
of the other arm. No between-group differences were
found to exist for the fractionated reaction time components. However, the load by group interaction term
for motor times showed that, although groups 2 and 3
were faster than group 1 in the unresisted condition,
they had 6.15% and a 13.91% longer motor times, respectively, than group 1 for the resisted condition. The
load by group interaction term for total reaction time
revealed similar results. Thus it appears that the age-
related decline in the ability to generate the tension
required to move a limb against a resistance is due
primarily to peripheral mechanisms.*

Until recently the area of motor development was defined as a "process of
skill acquisition in children" (Haywood, 1986, p. 4). However, the scientific
community now recognizes that the development of motor skills continues
throughout the entire life span. Performance data, in combination with research
regarding cellular age changes, provides valuable information about the aging

process. For example, research has shown that the number of functional motor units is decreased in older individuals (Brown, 1972; Campbell, McComas, & Petito, 1973; McComas, Sica, Upton, Longmire, & Caccia, 1973), as is the number of fast twitch muscle fibers (Clarkson, Kroll, & Melchionda, 1981; Gollnick, Armstrong, Sanbert, Piehl, & Saltin, 1972; Larsson, Grimby, & Karlsson, 1979; Larsson, Sjodin, & Karlsson, 1978). These data offer physiological explanations for the decreased strength which has been well documented to be a concomitant of the aging process (Kroll & Clarkson, 1978; Montoye & Lamphier, 1977; Shock & Norris, 1970).

It has been well documented that physical performance deteriorates as age progresses (Birren, 1959; Clarkson & Kroll, 1978; Hart, 1980; Hodgkins, 1963; Pierson & Montoye, 1958; Spirduso, 1975). However, little is actually known regarding the control mechanisms which induce the physiological dysfunction associated with age. In an attempt to elucidate the source of the decline in reaction speed, Weiss (1965) employed a research strategy which involved the use of electromyography to fractionate total reaction time into a central nervous system component (premotor time) and a peripheral nervous system component (motor time). Employing a simple finger-lift reaction time task, Weiss reported a significant difference between the reaction times of the young (18-20 yrs) versus the old (65-80 yrs) group, whereas movement times did not show a change of notable magnitude. He commented that the slower reaction times seen with the elderly were caused primarily by differences in the premotor times, thus allowing the deduction that slowing is a result of changes in central processing mechanisms.

Although unresisted reaction time includes measurements which reflect the condition of both the central and peripheral nervous systems, it is not a true measure of all movements as they are performed in daily activities; that is, it measures movements which involve the initiation of a response to a stimulus with only the limb as the primary resistance. Activities involved in daily living are often more complex and may involve movement against a resistance. Resisted reaction time measurement is an attempt to replicate environmental situations which might also be encountered in normal situations. Morris (1975) used an electromagnet to provide resistances equal to 5, 15, and 25% of an individual's maximum isometric knee extension strength. He found that, with resisted reaction times, the premotor time remained consistent with that of the unresisted condition, but the motor times lengthened. Kamen (1980) also observed longer motor times when he measured resisted reaction times employing a resistance equal to 15% of maximum voluntary isometric strength. Kroll and Clarkson (1978) assessed the resisted reaction times of knee extension at 10% of maximum voluntary isometric strength and likewise found that the longer times could be accounted for by an increase of the motor time component. They explained that, with resisted reaction time trials, more time was required to develop the required force to move the limb.

In the present investigation, unresisted and resisted forearm flexion and extension reaction times were measured in young and old male subjects in order to determine the site for the decline in total reaction time that occurs concomitantly with the process of senescence. Developmental differences were examined by comparing three groups of individuals in different decades of life (30-40, 50-60, and 61-70).

METHOD

Subjects

The subject population consisted of a total of 48 males (16 in each group) that were placed into 3 age groups based on chronological age: group 1 = 30-40 yrs ($M = 34.3$ yrs, $SD = 2.9$ yrs), group 2 = 50-60 yrs ($M = 54.0$ yrs, $SD = 3.6$ yrs), group 3 = 61-70 yrs ($M = 66.3$ yrs, $SD = 3.7$ yrs). Calculation of sample size was performed according to the methods outlined by Cohen (1969). It should be noted that a sample size greater than the one calculated was used for the study. This number of subjects allowed more than adequate precision for comparison between age groups.

All subjects volunteered to participate in the study. They consisted of male students and faculty from a university and its community. Each subject was cleared for participation by either the University Health Service or by the subject's personal physician. The methodology employed in this investigation was reviewed by the Human Subjects Review Committee. Each subject was given a verbal description of the testing procedure and was asked to read and sign an informed consent document prior to the first testing session.

Procedures

Each subject reported to the laboratory on four separate days. On each day five silver-silver chloride electrodes were applied to the subject; two on the biceps brachii (forearm flexor) of one arm, two on the triceps brachii (forearm extensor) of the other arm, and one ground electrode on the collar bone. The first measurement procured each day was the maximum voluntary isometric strength of the forearm flexors of one arm and, second, the forearm extensors of the other arm. Strength was measured with a strain gauge. The subjects were required to perform two fast and two slow maximum voluntary isometric contractions. From these four measurements each individual's 15% of maximum strength was calculated for the resisted reaction time trials. Following this each subject performed two blocks of 10 simple unresisted reaction time trials and two blocks of 10 simple resisted reaction time trials. Each subject completed the entire procedure using the forearm flexors of one arm and the forearm extensors of the other arm. The order of presentation for preferred vs nonpreferred arm trials and flexion vs extension trials was balanced over subjects and across days. In addition, the reaction time trials were presented in order from the easiest to the more difficult. That is, unresisted reaction time always preceded the resisted reaction time trials to maximize the effect of practice on the more difficult skill. A second reason for performing the unresisted trials first was to avoid the effects of fatigue that might occur from the resisted trials.

A piece of apparatus was specifically designed for the investigation of both forearm flexion and forearm extension fractionated reaction time. The subject was seated on a stool adjusted for his height in a way that allowed him to place his upper arm on the apparatus parallel to the floor. The subject was positioned so that his chest was placed against a padded rest, and a strap was placed around his back and attached to the apparatus to minimize extraneous movement. The forearm to be tested was attached to a wooden bar 50 cm in length via a leather cuff placed around the wrist. The placement of the cuff on the bar was determined by having the subject place the center of rotation of the elbow joint at the axis of the wooden bar. For the flexion trials the distal end of the wooden bar rested on a microswitch that was mounted on a wooden pedestal which was positioned 15° from horizontal. For the extension trials the wooden bar was positioned so that it pressed against a microswitch which was placed 90 degrees from horizontal.

The visual stimulus for the initiation of the total reaction time trials was a NE-51 neon bulb placed 1.2 m straight ahead at the eye level of the subject. With the wooden bar resting on the microswitch for the trials, the subject was given the verbal command "ready", and simultaneously the investigator activated the Lafayette Interval Timer which controlled the preparatory interval (PI). The light illuminated following preparatory intervals which ranged from 1.5 sec to 3.5 sec in increments of .5 sec. There was an equal number of occurrences of each interval with the addition of two catch trials during which a "ready" command was given but no light flash followed. These catch trials were included in order to discourage anticipatory responses. Upon seeing the light, the subject was instructed to lift the bar as quickly as possible off the microswitch. The onset of the light stimulus initiated an oscilloscope beam and started an electronic timer. Premotor (PMT) time was recorded as the time from light stimulus to the appearance of a muscle action potential on the oscilloscope. The total reaction time (TRT) was recorded from the timer that was started at the onset of the light and stopped when the subject moved off the microswitch. Motor time (MT) was calculated by subtracting premotor time from total reaction time.

The resisted reaction time trials employed identical methodology as for unresisted reaction time, with the addition of an electromagnet to offer resistance to movement. One part of the magnet was attached to the wooden bar at a point that was mechanically equal across subjects. This was accomplished by calculating the radius of gyration of the forearm and hand about the axis of rotation.

The magnetized part of the electromagnet (Edmund Scientific Co., model 60435) was attached to a movable wooden pedestal mounted on the testing apparatus. Magnet force was controlled with the use of a variac (Power Stats, type 116B, Superior Electric Co.). From prior calibration, the voltage applied to the magnet was equal to 15% of the maximum force that each subject exerted each day during his strength trials.

Data Analysis

The data were analyzed in three stages. First, a repeated measures analysis of variance was performed to observe if differences between the four blocks of trials or between the two days existed. If a significant difference was found to exist across all four blocks, a *t*-test was performed to determine if block 3 and block 4 represented stable data. Second, an intraclass correlation analysis was calculated to assess the reliability and variability due to blocks of trials, days, and subjects. Finally, a completely randomized split plot analysis of variance with a between-age group comparison and repeated measures on four factors (flexion vs extension, preferred vs nonpreferred, unresisted vs resisted, and trials) was performed. Results of a post mortem power analysis revealed that the power for all conditions reached a value of 99.

RESULTS

The repeated measures analysis of variance revealed that the means from day 1 and day 2 were significantly different from each other in only five of 72 conditions. Significant differences between the means across all four blocks were found in eight of 72 conditions. There were never any significant differences between the means for block 3 and block 4, which indicates that the parameters were stable for these trials.

Of a total of 24 conditions for each group (flexion and extension, preferred and nonpreferred, unresisted and resisted) only two conditions demonstrated intraclass correlation coefficients below $r = .80$ for group 1, five for group 2, and four for group 3. It was found that the intraindividual variability for trials, bouts, and true score all showed a distinct trend for the largest values to be in the oldest group. Additionally, group 2 also demonstrated a trend to be more variable than group 1 but less variable than group 3. The greater variability associated with the two older groups agrees with previous investigations employing older people as subjects (Birren, 1959; Botwinick & Thompson, 1968; Clarkson, 1977; Kroll & Clarkson, 1978; Hart, 1980).

The means and standard deviations for the day 2 fractionated reaction time components for each group are presented in Table 1 (flexion) and Table 2

Table 1
Age Group Means and Standard Deviations for Reaction Time Components During Simple Unresisted and Resisted Forearm Flexion Reaction Time (ms)

Age Group	Arm		Unresisted			Resisted		
			PMT	MT	TRT	PMT	MT	TRT
	P	M	163.3	68.1	231.4	168.5	86.5	255.0
		SD	17.4	13.9	22.7	21.5	9.7	25.6
1 (30-40 yrs)								
	N	M	167.9	64.3	232.3	172.3	83.7	256.0
		SD	19.1	12.2	24.1	21.6	16.1	25.3
	P	M	168.8	63.9	232.7	173.2	98.4	271.6
		SD	23.8	13.1	26.3	25.6	12.8	28.9
2 (50-60 yrs)	N							
		M	174.0	60.4	234.3	176.7	101.1	277.9
		SD	24.9	15.5	29.2	24.9	22.1	31.5
	P	M	176.9	60.8	237.7	177.7	108.0	285.7
		SD	28.5	13.0	27.1	30.8	23.3	36.8
3 (61-70 yrs)								
	N	M	180.0	60.3	240.3	185.1	109.8	294.7
		SD	31.6	13.9	34.3	40.4	30.6	40.4

P = Preferred Arm
N = Nonpreferred Arm
PMT = Premotor Time
MT = Motor Time
TRT = Total Reaction Time

(extension). Table 3 presents the main effect means on which the analysis of variance was based. It should be noted that the three group means contain pooled data from the flexion, extension, unresisted, resisted, preferred, and nonpreferred trials.

Premotor Time

The results from the premotor time analysis indicate no differences in age category classifications. The analysis of variance revealed that the F-ratio for

Table 2
Age Group Means and Standard Deviations for Reaction Time Components During Simple Unresisted and Resisted Forearm Extension Reaction Time (ms)

Age Group	Arm		Unresisted			Resisted		
			PMT	MT	TRT	PMT	MT	TRT
	P	M	180.1	86.9	267.0	180.8	110.0	290.9
		SD	23.8	16.9	24.3	27.1	16.2	22.4
1 (30-40 yrs)	N	M	179.4	87.3	267.7	177.3	116.6	293.8
		SD	27.9	16.2	27.1	28.6	26.4	21.7
	P	M	179.6	81.2	261.1	182.6	108.9	291.5
		SD	24.8	13.1	27.8	32.2	19.9	37.1
2 (50-60 yrs)	N	M	178.6	82.8	261.4	176.0	112.9	293.8
		SD	28.3	21.9	31.4	28.7	19.6	35.5
	P	M	184.7	83.6	268.3	186.1	118.4	298.9
		SD	31.7	14.4	35.4	29.3	17.8	39.5
3 (61-70 yrs)	N	M	180.7	79.6	260.2	179.4	115.7	295.0
		SD	35.7	15.2	30.0	26.2	22.4	34.2

P = Preferred Arm
N = Nonpreferred Arm
PMT = Premotor Time
MT = Motor Time
TRT = Total Reaction Time

the flexion versus extension main effect was significant ($F(1, 45) = 25.2$, $p < .01$). Extension premotor time was approximately 4% longer than flexion premotor time. A significant groups by flexion-extension interaction was found ($F(2, 45) = 3.42$, $p < .05$). Flexion premotor times for groups 1, 2, and 3 were 168.0, 173.2 and 179.9 ms, respectively, whereas extension premotor times were 179.4, 179.2, and 182.7 ms, for the respective age groups. There was no statistically significant difference between preferred and nonpreferred limb premotor times. There was a significant difference between the unresisted and resisted premotor times ($F(1, 45) = 3.21$, $p < .05$) with means of 176.2 ms and 178.0 ms, respectively.

Table 3

Main Effect Means for Group, Flexion vs. Extension, Side, and Load Main Effects for Premotor Time, Motor Time, and Total Reaction Time

Main Effect		Premotor Time	Means Motor Time	Total Reaction Time
G (Group)	1	173.7	87.9	261.8
	2	176.2	89.3	265.6
	3	181.0	91.3	272.6
F (Flex vs Ext)	Flexion	173.7	80.4	254.1
	Extension	180.4	98.6	279.1
S (Side)	Preferred	176.9	89.1	266.2
	Nonpreferred	177.3	90.9	267.3
L (Load)	Unresisted	176.2	73.3	249.6
	Resisted	178.0	105.8	283.7

Motor Time

The variance analysis for motor time revealed nonsignificant differences between the three age groups. The extension motor time was significantly different (22.6% longer) from the flexion motor time ($F(1, 45) = 135.30, p < .01$) which indicates that extension was a more difficult skill. A significant flexion-extension by groups interaction term demonstrated that there was a progressive lengthening of motor time associated with age for the flexion but not the extension condition. No significant differences were found between preferred vs nonpreferred limbs. The load by group interaction was also significant ($F(2, 45) = 14.60, p < .01$) with unloaded motor times values of 76.7, 72.1, and 71.0 ms for groups 1, 2, and 3, respectively. The loaded motor times for the three respective age groups were 99.2, 105.3, and 113.0 ms. These data show that the two oldest groups required progressively greater amounts of time to develop tension in order to initiate movement under the resisted conditions, as compared to group 1. A significant flexion-extension by load interaction term was found ($F(1, 45) = 4.63, p < .05$). Flexion motor times for the unloaded and loaded conditions were 62.9 and 97.9 ms, respectively. Extension motor times were 83.6 ms for the unloaded condition and 113.8 ms for the loaded condition. Clearly, the extension condition required more time to develop tension to move the limb, compared to the flexion condition.

Total Reaction Time

The results showed that there were no significant differences between age group means for total reaction time. However, the extension total reaction times were 9.8% longer than the flexion total reaction times, and the resisted total reaction times were 13.7% longer than the unresisted total reaction times. The load by group interaction showed that there was a progressive age-related decline in the total reaction times under resisted conditions with means of 273.9, 283.7, and 293.6 ms for groups 1, 2, and 3, respectively.

DISCUSSION

The most revealing statistical results come from analysis of main effect interactions. With respect to premotor time, the flexion-extension by groups interaction term was shown to be significant. Inspection of the means showed that group 2 had a 3.09% slower premotor time than group 1, and group 3 had a 7.08% slower premotor time than group 1 for the flexion movement. For the extension movement, group 2 had a .11% faster premotor time than group 1, and group 3 had a 1.84% slower premotor time than group 1. The larger differences for the flexion movement compared to the extension movement is difficult to explain. Perhaps the extension movement is so uncommon in everyday experience that there is less use of the neuromuscular pathways resulting in slower transmission of messages. With a more uncommon or unpracticed skill, the younger subjects are likely to be closer in performance to the older subjects. Indeed, the standard deviations for the extension movement are all larger than those for the flexion movement across all three age groups. The greater variability in performance observed for extension trials supports the notion that individuals are less familiar with the skill.

The results of this investigation contrast with those reported by Clarkson (1977) and Hart (1980) and indicate that the older subjects could process information as quickly or, in some cases, slightly slower than the younger subjects. A possible explanation is that both Clarkson and Hart measured knee extension whereas the present investigation recorded forearm flexion and extension reaction times. Perhaps the ability to move the forearm quickly is a more common skill and therefore better maintained with advancing age. Indeed, Asmussen and Heeboll-Nielson (1962) found that, as an individual ages, arm strength does not decrease at the same rate as leg strength. They speculated that the reason for the different rates of decline was the ". . . decreasing use of the legs in running and jumping with increasing age as opposed to the more continued use of hands and arms in daily life" (p. 168).

Regarding the motor times, the analysis of variance showed that the load by group interaction was significant. The pooled main effect showed that for the unresisted condition, group 2 had a 6.00% shorter motor time than group 1 and that group 3 had a 7.30% shorter motor time than group 1. However, under the resisted condition, group 2 had a 7.45% longer motor time than group 1, and group 3 had a 12.50% longer motor time than group 1. These data clearly suggest that there is an age-related progressive decline in the ability to generate the tension required to initiate movement of a limb and that the slowing that occurs with aging is due primarily to peripheral mechanisms. The extension movement also requires a longer motor time to initiate movement of the limb than the flexion condition under both the unloaded and loaded condition.

As was the case for the motor time component, the load by group interaction was significant for total reaction time. For the unresisted condition, group 2 was .88% faster than group 1, and group 3 was .80% slower than group 1. However for the resisted condition, group 2 was 3.57% slower than group 1, and group 3 was 7.19% slower than group 1. Thus, there was a definite age-related trend reflecting a progressive decrease in the ability to react to a stimulus when the task was resisted. Also, the extension condition displayed total reaction times that were 9.8% longer than the flexion condition indicating that the extension was more difficult.

The fact that the extension movement produced results so dramatically different from the flexion movement is curious. The exact cause for the flexion vs extension differences cannot be resolved without pathway mapping to determine the number of synapses involved for execution of flexion vs extension movements. However, it is interesting to note that it has been demonstrated that when regions of the brain controlling limb muscles were electrically stimulated, flexor rather than extensor muscles predominated (Penfield & Rasmussen, 1950).

It is intuitively obvious that a resisted movement would produce a longer total reaction time than an unresisted movement. The data from this investigation further demonstrated that, as age progresses, the ability to generate the required tension to move a limb against a resistance declines. Examination of muscle changes at the cellular level offers an explanation for these results. As stated earlier, there is both a reduction of functioning motor units and decrease in the percentage of type II fibers in the older individuals. Larsson, Sjodin, and Karlsson (1978) attributed the type II fiber atrophy to ". . . decreasing trophic influence from the motorneurons caused by a denervation-like process" (p. 37). Since these fibers are required for rapid movements, any reduction in number or size could account for a loss of contractile units in the muscle and, therefore, for a slower contraction time. Additionally, Tomonaga (1977) employed histochemical and electron microscopic methods to examine the muscle fibers in 79 elderly subjects of which the majority was in the range of 60 to 90 years of age. He observed several neuropathic and myopathic changes which included smaller and darker angulated fibers, nuclear clumping, proliferation of the t-system and sarcoplasmic reticulum system, deformed motor end plates, and increased lipid pigment storage. Matsuku, Takeda, and Tonomura (1966) found that the splitting of ATP for muscle contraction increased with age and suggested that the excitation-contraction coupling process becomes less efficient as age progresses. These data suggest that muscle dysfunction and performance decrement are programmed phenomena of the aging process. However, it has been suggested by Larsson (1982) that the type II fiber atrophy may not be a genetically determined developmental characteristic of aging. He demonstrated that the fiber atrophy decreased after four months of strength training in males ranging from 22 to 65 years of age. Thus, it may be that the fiber atrophy is partly due to the hypokinetic lifestyles adopted by older individuals. Many questions regarding universal developmental characteristics of the aging process cannot be answered unless individuals are measured several times throughout their lifespan. Although longitudinal research is administratively difficult, it will identify the predictable physiological concomitants of the aging process so that the practitioners of geriatric care can aim their efforts at increasing the quality of life throughout the lifespan.

REFERENCES

Asmussen, E., & Heeboll-Nielsen, K. (1962). Isometric muscle strength in relation to age in men and women. *Ergonomics, 5*, 167–169.

Birren, J. (Ed.). (1959). *Handbook of Aging and the Individual*. Chicago: The University of Chicago Press.

Botwinick, J., & Thompson, L. W. (1968). A research note on individual differences in reaction time in relation to age. *The Journal of Genetic Psychology, 112*, 73–75.

Brown, W. F. (1972). A method for estimating the number of motor units in thenar muscles and the change in motor unit count with aging. *Journal of Neurology, Neurosurgery, and Psychiatry, 35*, 845–852.

Campbell, M. J., McComas, A. J., & Petito, F. (1973). Physiological changes in aging muscle. *Journal of Neurology, Neurosurgery, and Psychiatry, 36*, 174–182.

Clarkson, P. M. (1977). *The effect of age and activity level on fractionated response and reflex time*. Unpublished doctoral dissertation, University of Massachusetts, Amherst.

Clarkson, P. M., & Kroll, W. (1978). Practice effects on fractionated response time related to age and activity level. *Journal of Motor Behavior, 10*, 275–286.

Clarkson, P. M., Kroll, W., & Melchionda, A. M. (1981). Age, isometric strength, rate of tension development and fiber type composition. *Journal of Gerontology, 36*, 648–653.

Cohen, J. (1969). *Power Analysis for the Behavioral Sciences*. New York: Academic Press.

Gollnick, P. D., Armstrong, R. B., Sanbert, C. W., Piehl, K., & Saltin, B. (1972). Enzyme activity and fiber composition in skeletal muscle of untrained and trained men. *Journal of Applied Physiology, 33*, 312–319.

Hart, B. A. (1980). *Fractionated reflex and response times in women by activity level and age.* Unpublished doctoral dissertation, University of Massachusetts, Amherst.

Haywood, K. M. (1986). *Life span motor development.* Champaign, IL: Human Kinetics Publishers, Inc.

Hodgkins, J. (1963). Reaction time and speed of movement in males and females of various ages. *Research Quarterly, 34*, 335–343.

Kamen, G. P. (1980). *Fractionated reaction and reflex time after fatiguing isometric and isotonic exercise.* Unpublished doctoral dissertation, University of Massachusetts, Amherst.

Kroll, W., & Clarkson, P. M. (1978). Age, isometric knee extension strength, and fractionated resisted response time. *Experimental Aging Research, 4*, 389–409.

Larsson, L. (1982). Physical training effects on muscle morphology in sedentary males at different ages. *Medicine and Science in Sports and Exercise, 14*, 203–206.

Larsson, L., Grimby, G., & Karlsson, J. (1979). Muscle strength and speed of movement in relation to age and muscle morphology. *Journal of Applied Physiology, 46*, 451–456.

Larsson, L., Sjodin, B., & Karlsson, J. (1978). Histochemical and biochemical changes in human skeletal muscle with age in sedentary males, age 22–65 years. *Acta Physiologica Scandinavica, 103*, 31–39.

Matsuki, H., Takeda, Y., & Tonomura, Y. (1966). Changes in biochemical properties of isolated human skeletal myofibrils with age and in myasthenia gravis. *Journal of Biochemistry, 59*, 122–125.

McComas, A. J., Sica, R. E. P., Upton, A. R. M., Longmire, D., & Caccia, M. R. (1973). Physiological estimation of the numbers and sizes of motor units in man. In R. B. Stein, K. G. Pearson, R. S. Smith, & J. B. Redford (Eds.), *Control of Posture and Locomotion* (pp. 55–72). New York: Plenum.

Montoye, H. J., & Lamphier, D. E. (1977). Grip and arm strength in males and females, age 10 to 69. *The Research Quarterly, 48*, 109–120.

Morris, A. F. (1975). *Effects of isometric and isotonic exercise on fractionated reflex and resisted reaction time components.* Unpublished doctoral dissertation, University of Massachusetts, Amherst.

Penfield, W., & Rasmussen, T. (1950). *The cerebral cortex of man.* New York: Macmillan.

Pierson, W. R., & Montoye, H. J. (1958). Movement time, reaction time, and age. *Journal of Gerontology, 13*, 418–421.

Shock, N. W., & Norris, A. H. (1970). Neuromuscular coordination as a factor in age changes in muscular exercise. *Medicine and Sport, 4*, 92–94.

Spirduso, W. W. (1975). Reaction and movement time as a function of age and physical activity level. *Journal of Gerontology, 30*, 435–440.

Tomonaga, M. (1977). Histochemical and ultrastructural changes in senile human skeletal muscle. *Journal of American Geriatric Society, 3*, 125–131.

Weiss, A. D. (1965). The locus of reaction time change with set, motivation, and age. *Journal of Gerontology, 20*, 60–64.

5.

PERCEPTUAL DEVELOPMENT AND ITS DIFFERENTIAL INFLUENCE ON LIMB POSITIONING UNDER TWO MOVEMENT CONDITIONS IN CHILDREN

Katherine T. Thomas
Southeastern Louisiana University
Jerry R. Thomas
Louisiana State University

ABSTRACT

Three experiments using 5-, 7-, 11- and 20-year-old subjects were designed to establish age differences in perceptual sensitivity for a 28-cm movement and then evaluate the influence of this sensitivity under two-movement condition. The experiments used a two-dimensional lever positioning task which was constrained in Experiments 1 and 2, but was not constrained in Experiment 3. Experiment 1 used a well-learned movement (the standard) and seven foils (movements which ended at 0, 3, 6, or 9 cm to each side of the standard) to determine the perception of movement end location (JND). The JNDs were for: 5-year-olds > 9 cm, 7-year-olds $= 9$ cm, 11-year-olds $= 6$ cm, and 20-year-olds < 3 cm. Experiment 2 used the same apparatus in a recognition paradigm where each pair of movements were presented only once, and subjects were asked to determine whether the two movements were the same or different. An age main effect was found with the youngest subjects least able to judge accurately the pairs of movements as same or different. When the judgments for Experiment 2 were corrected for the JNDs estimated from Experiment 1, age differences were eliminated indicating that perceptual sensitivity probably accounted for the age effect.

83

Experiment 3 used the same movement presentations as Experiment 2, but subjects were asked to generate a reproduction estimate of each movement. Again, an age main effect was found; however, when correcting for the JND, the age differences remained. Taken together, these three experiments suggest that while perceptual sensitivity to end location of a movement is greater for older than younger children, younger children still make more errors than older children in movement reproduction.

Perceptual and psychophysical factors affect performance on many movement tasks which are used in motor behavior research (Magill & Parks, 1983; Weeks & Shea, 1984), yet researchers tend to ignore effects when interpreting significant results. Of course one could argue that the influence of the perceptual factor was spread equally across treatment groups, unless the perceptual factor changed between those groups. In the case of adult subjects, Magill and Parks (1983) found that perceptual sensitivity for movement end location and for movement extent varied—that is, perception differentially influenced the dependent variable. Magill and Parks suggested that understanding and being able to quantify perceptual and psychophysical factors in movement are important issues, independent of the potential impact on other research. Weeks and Shea (1984) used a timing task with varying time periods and found that very fast or very slow trials were more susceptible to perceptual error than the trials of moderate speed.

Various studies in the developmental literature indicate substantial age-related differences for performance of perceptual tasks (Vurpillot, 1974; Vurpillot & Ball, 1979). Perceptual tasks, which are not confounded by other factors (e.g., memory, experience) use well-learned or familiar objects, and are usually restricted to dichotomous responses (e.g., same or different, yes or no). There has been no research on perceptual sensitivity for movement using children, yet one would assume that since age differences do exist in perception for other types of information, differences would also exist in kinesthetic sensitivity.

The first of three experiments were designed to determine the kinesthetic sensitivity of children and adults for movement end location. The second and third experiments looked at the impact of the age-related differences in perceptual sensitivity on two conditions of the same movement task.

EXPERIMENT 1

Many experiments have tested perceptual sensitivity using techniques which require the subject to detect the difference between two stimuli; these are called difference thresholds, difference limens (DL), and just noticeable differences (JND) (Magill & Parks, 1983; Shea & Northam, 1981; Woodworth & Schlosberg, 1954). The crucial point is the amount of difference necessary between two stimuli for the subject to detect the difference at a rate better than guessing, i.e., beyond 50%. A JND has been sought for various types of information, e.g., visual—brightness, color, acuity—as an indicator of the precision of the perceptual mechanism (Marteniuk, 1976). One of the classic techniques for determining JND, the frequency method, was used in this experiment. The subject makes a movement (in this instance, moving a lever handle down a trackway); the movement is called the standard. Immediately following that movement, the subject makes a second movement (again moving a handle down a trackway) called the foil. The foil can be any one of six trackways which are equally distributed around the standard, or the standard can be the foil (Fig. 1). The JND is the foil which is judged as different from the standard 50% or more of the time. To equalize possible memory or experience differences between the age groups, the standard was well learned. The age groups were selected to represent those age groups often used in developmental research.

Method

Subjects.

Nine males were randomly selected within age from four age groups of 40 subjects each; 5-year-olds ($M = 67$ mo), 7-year-olds ($M = 85$ mo), 11-year-olds ($M = 131$ mo), and adults ($M = 266$ mo). At the lower ages several subjects had to be replaced during testing (7 of the 5-year-olds, and 2 of the 7-year-olds) for various reasons, which are described later.

Apparatus.

A Numonic Electronic Digitizer (Model #1224) was attached to a template with trackways which guided the reading head. All trackways radiated from a center starting position to points on a circle 28 cm away. The trackways which served as standards were at 40°, 170°, 225°, and 330° when 0° was placed directly in front of the subject at the midline of his body on the farthest edge of the circle (Fig. 1). The seven foils were the standard and three trackways running on each side of the standard at 3-cm intervals. Since all movements begin at the center point, the 3-cm intervals are at the end point of the 28-cm movements, thus the movements radiated outward like the spokes on a wheel.

Procedure.

Each of the subjects was given a pretest to determine his ability to distinguish the terms "same" and "different". This consisted of comparing toy cars placed

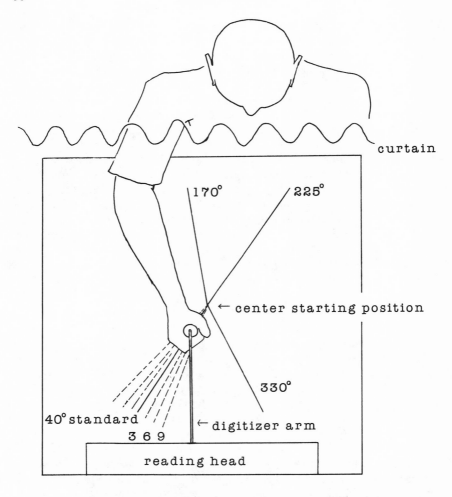

FIG. 1. Apparatus for Experiments 1, 2, & 3

on a road map in pairs of same and different positions. The criterion for correct responses to the pretest was five consecutive or eight of 10 attempts. All 11-year-olds and adults passed the pretest; however, three 5-year-olds and one 7-year-old failed and were replaced by subjects who passed.

Subjects were seated in a chair adjusted for their height, with the apparatus directly in front of them with the center point (180°) at their midline. Vision of the apparatus was prevented by a shield. Within-age, subjects were randomly assigned to two of the four standard movements, with movement order counterbalanced across subjects. Subjects practiced the standard movement before testing began, a minimum of 20 trials, or until the subject reported (and the experimenter observed) he had learned the movement. There is evidence (Kerr, 1978) that movements may be recognized after only one practice trial, so repeated practice on a simple movement indicates familiarity with the standard.

The subject was informed that all movements would be the same length, but some would have different end locations. In addition, some of the movements would have the same end location. Testing began with the subject moving the handle on a trackway representing the standard. Immediately after the standard movement, the experimenter returned the handle to the center start position, then the subject moved the handle along one of the seven foils (3, 6, or 9 cm on either side of the standard or the standard). The subject was then asked if the two movements (first movement as standard, second movement as foil) were the same or different. Each subject made a total of 140 comparisons at each of two sessions, one session for each of the two standards. Each of the seven foils was compared to the standard an equal number of times but in random order. The two sessions were completed within a week.

Results and Discussion

One 5-year-old was replaced because he refused to be tested on the second day. Three other 5-year-olds and one 7-year-old were replaced because they responded to all comparisons in the same way, either same or different. Upon questioning, these children indicated they recognized some differences (or sames), but decided to answer all comparisons with one response. Vurpillot and Ball (1979) found similar results with 4-year-olds who judged houses to be the same regardless of the contents of the windows. These children regarded the houses as alike since each fit into the general class of houses with windows. The children in this experiment may have regarded the standard and foils all as movements, therefore the same. In any case, what was measured for these children was not perceptual sensitivity, so they were replaced.

Three separate ANOVAs were done using age (5, 7, 11, and 20 yrs) with either angle of the standard (40°, 170°, 225°, and 330°) from the starting position, day of testing (first or second), and side of standard (right or left) as classification variables, and the JND for each subject as the dependent variable. The results were that angle and side were not significant, $F(9, 23) = 1.5$, $p > .05$, and $F(2, 34) = 0.1$, $p > .05$. The lack of an angle effect indicated that the position of the standard relative to the subjects made no difference in the sensitivity between age groups. Since the side effect (left or right of the standard) was not significant, the data were collapsed into three foil distances of 3, 6, and 9 cm. Day was significant as a main effect, $F(1, 32) = 12.0$, $p < .05$. While performances on day 2 were better than on day 1, day did not influence the age groups differentially, $F(2, 23) = 1.0$, $p > .05$, suggesting that the day effect was equal for the age groups.

After the data were collapsed across all nonsignificant factors, age was significant, $F(3, 32) = 13.5$, $p < .05$, with JNDs being significantly different among all age groups—5-year-olds > 9 cm, 7-year-olds $= 9$ cm, 11-year-olds $= 6$ cm, and adults < 3 cm (Fig. 2). The exact JND for the oldest and youngest groups was not determined because the actual values were greater or less than the range of the foils.

The judgments on all foils must be corrected for guessing at all age levels by removing the number of different responses to the standard (when the standard was presented as the foil). The amount of guessing increased as age decreased; the 5-year-olds guessed more than once in four trials (27%), whereas the 7-year-olds guessed 22% of the time, 11-year-olds guessed on only 10% of the trials, and the adults guessed on 7% of the trials.

Clearly, the ability of adults to make precise perceptual judgments is greater than that ability in children. The younger the child, the greater the error when making perceptual judgments; guessing, applying inappropriate strategies, and the lack of experience all seem to contribute to errors in perceptual judgment. These perceptual differences are likely to influence both laboratory and real world performance. Experiments 2 and 3 were designed to evaluate that impact on two laboratory tasks.

EXPERIMENT 2

Experiment 1 provides evidence that perceptual judgments for kinesthetic information become more accurate throughout childhood and adolescence. This experiment was designed to examine the impact of JND on the recognition of the end location of a simple lever positioning task. Both the standard movement and the comparison movement are constrained (made with the use of a trackway selected by the experimenter). The apparatus remains the same as in Experiment 1, however 20 additional standards (for a total of 24) are added, and each standard movement is made only once. There are still seven foils (3, 6, and 9 cm and the standard) for comparison to each standard movement. In Experiment 1, after 20 practice trials, the subjects completed 280 pairs of movements using the standard and one of the seven foils. This was a well-learned movement, so the detection of differences was a measure of perceptual sensitivity of the subject. In this experiment the standard movements are all novel. Recognition is greatest when the frequency of the presentation of the target is low (Lockhardt, Craik, & Jacoby, 1976). Each standard is presented once, followed by one foil; the subject then declares them the same or different. Since there were 24 different standards, each subject received 24 trials. Obviously, perceptual judgment is still a factor, but perception has not been isolated as in Experiment 1. The question is how much of the age difference in performance will be accounted for by JND under the conditions in Experiment 2?

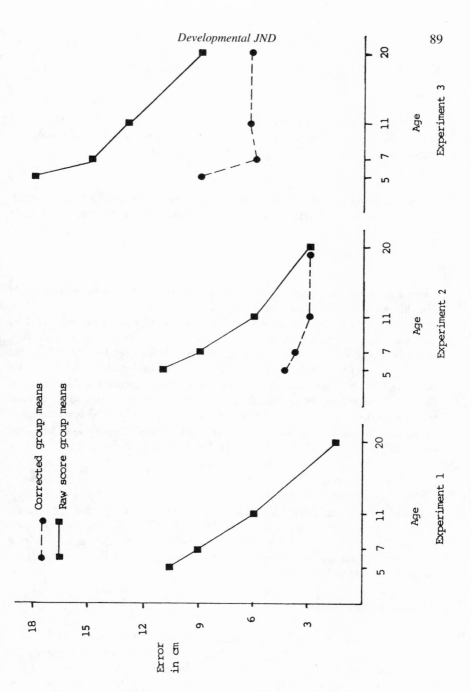

FIG. 2. Results for Experiments 1, 2, & 3

Method

Subjects.

Ten male subjects were randomly selected within age from those remaining in the subject pool—5-year-olds ($M = 67$ mo), 7-year-olds ($M = 85$ mo), 11-year-olds ($M = 130$ mo), and adults ($M = 241$ mo).

Apparatus.

The equipment was the same as in Experiment 1, but used a template with 24 trackways spaced equidistant and radiating outward from the center of a circle (Fig. 1).

Procedure.

Procedures for the pretest to establish the knowledge of same and different were the same as in Experiment 1. Standard movements were 28 cm from the center point radiating outward like spokes of a wheel with grooves every 15°, producing 24 possible pathways. There were 24 trials, one on each trackway, assigned in random order with one of seven possible foils (ending the movement at 3, 6, or 9 cm from the standard or the standard) assigned to each trial with the restriction that each foil occur at least three times during the 24 trials. For a trial the subject moved the handle down a trackway (the standard) to a stop. The experimenter returned the handle to the starting position. The subject moved the handle in one of the foils to a stop (again down a trackway), and then responded either "same" or "different" for the pair of movements.

Dependent Measures.

Two dependent variables were used in this experiment: the percentage of trials in which the subjects made the correct decision (PC = percent correct), i.e., if the foil was the same as the standard the subject said "the same", or said "different" if the foil was different; and the percentage of trials in which the subject said "different" (PD = percent different).

Results and Discussion

A 4 (age level) × 4 (variable locations—standard, 3, 6, or 9 cm) ANOVA with repeated measures on the second factor was applied to each subject's PC and PD response. The age effect was significant, $p < .05$ for PC and PD, $Fs(3, 36) = 26.97, 5.20$. For PC Newman-Keuls follow-ups showed all age groups significantly different: 5-year-olds PC = 38%, 7-year-olds PC = 50%, 11-year-olds PC = 70%, and adults PC = 84%. For PD, the 5- (33%) and 7- (38%) year-olds were not different from each other, but were different from the 11-year-olds (63%) and adults (80%) who were also different from each other.

The distance between the standard and the foils (standard, 3, 6, and 9 cm) was significant for PC and PD, $Fs(3, 101) = 15.37, 41.50$. As would be anticipated, most of the responses were correct for the standard as foil (80%). However, the 9-cm (65%), 6-cm (55%), and 3-cm (40%) foils were of increasing difficulty. The PD responses were a linear function of the distance of the foil from the standard: standard as foil = 25%, 3 cm = 38%, 6 cm = 63%, and 9 cm = 80%. All foils for both PC and PD were significantly different using a Newman-Keuls test.

The two main effects can be summarized as follows: as age increased the judgments became more accurate, regardless of the similarity or difference in the comparison; and considerable guessing occurred (approximaely 25%) with the 0- and 9-cm distances between end locations the positions where accurate decisions consistently exceeded guessing. The age × variable location (difference between the standard and the foils) interaction was the major concern of this experiment and was significant for PD, $F(9, 101) = 2.03$. Age differentially influenced performance on this task depending on the variable location. In Fig. 2 (Experiment 2) the data are graphically presented. These will be described since the F ratios are relatively small, rather than using follow-up tests. Recall that PD represents the percent of trials in which a subject identifies a variable as different at each of the variable locations and is able to respond "different" more than 50% of the time if he actually recognizes that point as "different" more than 50% of the time if he actually recognizes that point as different. The precentages can be translated to estimates of the distance (in cm) necessary for accurate identification. The 5-year-olds were unable to detect the difference half the time, even at 9 cm. Based on this experiment, a difference of nearly 12 cm would be necessary for 5-year-olds to consistently decide the two points were different. The 7-year-olds, 11-year-olds, and adults detected differences half of the time at 3, 6, and 9 cm respectively.

If these data are corrected for guessing (by subtracting the number of false responses for the standard foil from the correct responses for each of the three variable locations) the 7-year-olds only approached the 50% criterion at 9 cm (they knew 46% of the time that a location 9 cm from the standard was different). The 11-year-olds and adults remained unchanged. Apparently guessing occurs less frequently as age increases. When the data were corrected for JND (as determined in Experiment 1) the age differences nearly disappear (Fig. 2., Experiment 2, broken line).

A researcher who looked only at the results of this experiment would see age differences and attribute those differences to the variable of interest (e.g., memory, motivation, etc.) although the differences were, for the most part, due to age differences in perceptual sensitivity.

EXPERIMENT 3

Experiment 3 uses the same task and movement but under a different set of conditions, again trying to assess the influence of perception on performance for the four age groups. In this case the standard movement is constrained (down a trackway), but the comparison movement must be produced by the subject (no trackway—a free moving arm on the positioning task).

Method

Subjects.

At each age level, 9 previously untested male subjects from the subject pool were randomly selected within age: 5-year-olds, (M = 65 mo), 7-year-olds (M = 83 mo), 11-year-olds (M = 133 mo), and adults (M = 247 mo).

Apparatus.

The same equipment described in Experiment 2 was used, the Numonics Digitizer on the template with 24 trackways radiating from a center starting position. A smooth template with no grooves but the same center start was used for the movement reproduction (allowing the movements to vary in two dimensions). The smooth template was moved on top of the experimental task.

Procedure.

Subjects practiced the 28-cm movement until they could reproduce it on five of seven attempts to a criterion of ± 2 cm. The purpose of this practice was to standardize the length of the movement for all subjects (Winther & Thomas, 1981). A trial consisted of the standard location (moving within one of the 24 trackways for 28 cm to a stop) followed by the reproduction movement (digitizer arm was free-swinging from a center start). The 24 positions were presented in one of three random orders and the orders were randomly assigned to subjects within age level (with 24 trials per subject).

Dependent Measures.

Since the digitizer arm was free-swinging for movement reproduction, errors could vary anywhere about the standard's end location. The digitizer provided the x and y coordinates for the reproduction movement's end location. The differences between the standard and reproduction movement's end location yields three error estimates (for more details see Winther & Thomas, 1981):

radial error—the radius in cm of a circle with the standard's end location as the center of the circle, and the edge of the circle as the reproduction movement's end location; distance error—the difference between the reproduction movement's end location and the nearest point of a circle with a radius of 28 cm with its center at the start position (a circle defined by the start point and the 24-28 cm movements); and direction error—angle (in degrees) between the standard and reproduction movements with the starting point as center.

Since radial error is a combination of distance and direction error, practicing the 28-cm movement prior to the task removed the effects of distance error, thus simplifying the scoring as radial and direction error would be approximately equal. Further, since end location varied in Experiments 1 and 2 as a result of altering direction (angle) only, the results of all three experiments would be more directly comparable by eliminating the distance error.

Results and Discussion

Of the 24 standard movements, four were on or immediately adjacent to the horizontal axis. An ANOVA using both direction and radial error identified these four positions as significantly ($p < .05$) different, $F(4, 124) = 32.16$, from the other positions. These four positions were from six times to twice as difficult to reproduce as any of the other 20 locations. Based upon this effect, these positions were eliminated from further analysis. Four separate ANOVAs with age $\times$ quadrant (movements in quadrant 1 = 1 $-90°$), quadrant 2 (91 $-180°$), quadrant 3 (181 $-270°$), quadrant 4 (271 $-360°$) $\times$ locations (five standards within each of the four quadrants) were done with distance absolute error (AE)[1], distance constant error (CE) and direction and radial error as dependent measures.

Age was significant ($p < .05$) for radial and direction error, $F(3, 32) = 10.68$, 7.38, but not for distance AE or CE, Fs(3, 32) < 2.50. The lack of an age effect or any significant interaction (Fs < 2.0) with age for distance error supports the contention that subjects of various ages had learned the 28-cm distance during the practice session. Since distance was not significant, direction error represents the remaining source of movement error (radial becomes equal to direction error). On the average, the 5-year-olds' estimate of the end location of the standard was 30° in error (or 18 cm). This was significantly different (Newman-Keuls test, $p < .05$) from both 7-year-olds (22°, or 12-cm error), and 11-year-olds (24°, or 15-cm error), who were not different from each other. Adults averaged 17° error (9 cm), which was significantly less error than each of the three groups of children.

When locations (five each) were averaged within the four quadrants, the variability (VE)[2] of each type of error could be calculated. Three age $\times$ quadrant ANOVAs (repeated measures on quadrant) were done on the VE estimates for distance, direction, and radial error. The age effect was significant ($p < .05$)

for all three VE estimates, $Fs(3, 32) = 10.10, 11.39, 17.17$. For all three variability estimates using the Newman-Keuls test, adults were the least variable and significantly different from all the younger groups. The 5-year-olds were always the most variable with the 7- and 11-year-olds very similar, but the three younger groups were not significantly different from each other. The children were one and a half to two times as variable in their distance estimates as were the adults. The children were two to three times as variable in their directions estimates as the adults. Quadrant was selected as a factor for two reasons: first, we thought the younger children might have some difficulty crossing the midline (movements in quadrant 3 and 4); and second, quadrant 4 might present length of reach problems for the younger children. The quadrant effect was significant for the four dependent measures (radial error, direction error, and distance AE and CE errors), $Fs(3, 96) = 40.14, 32.14, 5.60, 6.45$. The results of all measures were similar. Quadrants 1 and 3 were easy and not different from each other whereas quadrants 2 and 4 were more difficult and not different from each other; but 2 and 4 were different from 1 and 3. In absolute terms, these differences were relatively small, less than 2 cm for distance and 5° (or 3 cm) for direction. Thus, we choose to make little of these differences except for quadrant 4 where VE estimates (radial, distance, and direction error) were all significantly less than in the other three quadrants. This appears to be a mechanical limitation in reach for all age groups producing less variable performance.

The age × quadrant effect was significant for radial and direction error, $Fs(9, 96) = 3.31, 2.94$, but not for distance AE and CE, $Fs < 1.62$. The interaction was also significant for all variability estimates (distance VE, direction VE, radial VE), $Fs(9, 96) = 34.36, 52.50, 42.02$. The results support the quadrant effect reported earlier. In particular, the 5-year-olds had an extension problem in quadrant 4 producing the age × quadrant interaction. Basically error across quadrant decreased with age while variability increased.

The location effects (20 positions) will not be discussed since they conform with the quadrant effects. Within quadrants, location end points were very consistent, varying 2 to 3 cm.

In this experiment the age group errors were beyond each age group's JNDs from Experiment 1: 5-year-old's error = 18 cm (30°), 7-year-old's error = 15 cm (24°), 11-year-old's error = 12 cm (22°), and adult's error = 9 cm (17°). However, the 5-year-olds were different from all age groups even after adjusting for their JND (Fig. 2). Thus, the differences between the age groups are meaningfully reduced when the perceptual component is considered.

DISCUSSION

These three experiments have established the need to consider the impact of perceptual sensitivity on the performance of movement tasks. This is especially true in developmental research where perceptual sensitivity increases across the age groups.

Experiment 1 established that perceptual sensitivity for movement end location becomes more acute as children age (at least for this laboratory task). This change in perceptual sensitivity appears to account for most of the age differences that are observed in a simple movement recognition task (Experiment 2). However, when movement reproduction is required as in Experiment 3, age differences in movement positioning are greater than just perceptual sensitivity differences. Yet, these movement production differences are not as great as they appear at first glance as correcting for perceptual sensitivity does make age groups more similar, particularly 5- to 7-year-old children. We believe that this suggests that all of the changes noted in movement response as children age are not due to increases in motor skill and control, but may be partly explained by the younger child's inability to distinguish the quality of the motor response.

The results of these three experiments support previous work indicating that some movement characteristics can be remembered after only one trial (Kerr, 1978), and others may be learned after only a few trials (e.g., distance in Experiment 3). The fact that error was low after a few practice trials for distance when movement was not constrained also supports the contention in Experiment 1 that a constrained movement where only end location varies can be well-learned after about 20 trials.

Another robust finding, which is consistent with most developmental research, is that as age increases the amount of variability decreases. This could be observed in the performance on the pretest, by the use of unique strategies by young subjects in Experiment 1, by the high guessing rates in younger children and was statistically noted by the significant VE scores (Experiment 3). Since variability measures are not sensitive to age differences when other measures are not, research using children should measure variability whenever possible. Children's increasing consistency (as estimated by decreases in the variability of movement) as they age may be the most robust and interesting characteristic in movement.

REFERENCES

Kerr, B. (1978). The effects of invalid task parameters on short-term motor memory. *Journal of Motor Behavior, 10*, 261–273.

Lockhardt, R. S., Craik, F. I., & Jacoby, L. (1976). Depth of processing, recognition and recall. In J. Brown (Ed.), *Recall and recognition* (pp. 75–102). Bath, England: John Wiley & Sons.

Magill, R. A., & Parks, P. F. (1983). The psychophysics of kinesthesis for positioning responses: The physical stimulus–psychological response relationship. *Research Quarterly for Exercise and Sport, 54*, 436–451.

Marteniuk, R. G. (1976). *Information processing in motor skills*. New York: Holt, Rinehart & Winston.

Shea, C. H., & Northam, C. (1982). Discrimination of visual linear velocities. *Research Quarterly for Exercise and Sport, 53*, 222–225.

Vurpillot, E. (1974). The developmental emphasis. In E. C. Carterette & M. P. Friedman (Eds.), *Handbook of perception,Vol I*, (pp. 364–376). New York: Academic Press.

Vurpillot, E., & Ball, W. A. (1979). The concept of identity and children's view of selective attention. In G. A. Hale & M. Lewis (Eds.), *Attention and cognitive development* (pp. 23–42). New York: Plenum Press.

Weeks, D. L., & Shea, C. H. (1984). Assimilation effects in coincident timing responses. *Research Quarterly for Exercise and Sport, 55*, 89–92.

Winther, K. T., & Thomas, J. R. (1981). Developmental differences in children's labeling of movement. *Journal of Motor Behavior, 13*, 77–90.

Woodworth, R., & Schlosberg, H. (1954). *Experimental psychology*, New York: Holt, Rinehart and Winston.

NOTES

[1]Absolute error (AE) is the difference between the standard end location and the estimate of the end location regardless of whether the estimate is long or short. Constant error (CE) is assigned a plus (+) value if the estimate is too long and a (−) value if the estimate is too short. Thus, CE takes into account the bias (+ or −) of the estimate while AE does not.

[2]Variable error (VE) is the standard deviation of several trials of a subject's CE score.

6.

THE EFFECTS OF CONTROLLED VIDEOGAME PLAYING ON THE EYE-HAND COORDINATION AND REACTION TIME OF CHILDREN

Patricia J. McSwegin
Emporia State University
Cynthia Pemberton
University of North Dakota
Nancy O'Banion
Emporia State University

ABSTRACT

The purpose of this study was to investigate the effects of 7 weeks of videogame playing on the eye-hand co-ordination and reaction time of children, as measured by the Lafayette Rotary Pursuit and a reaction time test. Thirty 7- and 8-year-old boys and girls were pretested for eye-hand coordination and reaction time. Fifteen students then played selected videogames for 10 min a day, 4 days a week, for 7 weeks. The 15 control subjects did not play any videogames for the same 7-week period. Scores were analyzed by analysis of covariance. The experimental group scored significantly better than the control group on both the eye-hand coordination test and reaction time test. It was concluded that videogame playing experience contributed to improved eye-hand coordination and reaction time of these children.

Since the early 1900s, behavioral scientists have studied how learning of one task can facilitate learning of successive tasks. Theorists advocating transfer of training suggest that the strategies used to learn one task and the experience of

97

manipulating the information required to learn that task can be generalized to the learning of other tasks which are similar in nature. Although not all learning theorists subscribe to a transfer of learning paradigm, it is probable that transfer of learning can occur, especially in the initial stages of learning a new task (Magill, 1985).

As Singer (1982) points out, the greater the similarities between the task-to-be-learned and the previously learned task, the greater is the potential for positive transfer, that is, transfer which will aid in learning of the new task. How closely the stimuli and responses involved in the new task are related to stimuli and responses of the previously learned task is important. Of particular importance is the similarity of responses desired. Even if the stimuli for the two tasks differ, if the responses elicited are similar, learning of the first task can aid in learning of the second task. Transfer processes appear to facilitate initial learning of the new task. Another important element in transfer is the degree to which the first task was learned. Thorough learning of the first task aids transfer. As learning of the new task progresses, it is crucial to practice the unique skill and apply the unique strategies of that task in order to achieve the highest level of skill learning.

Singer (1982) makes an important distinction between learning which occurs in laboratory situations and learning which occurs in a field setting. Laboratory conditions aid the learner in recognizing relationships between tasks. This identification of the similarities between tasks aids positive transfer. In field situations recognition of the relationships between tasks is more difficult due to the presence of distracting variables. Therefore, situations which assist the learner in recognizing similarities or which help the learner realize how to approach a new task (i.e., develop learning strategies) might be useful in initial learning of tasks of similar nature. Two studies (Singer, Gerson, & Ridsdale, 1979; Singer, Ridsdale, & Korienek, 1979) support the concept that use of learning strategies and experience with a previous task can have a positive transfer effect.

However, there remains a need to investigate transfer effects in field situations. The recent increase in videogame playing poses an interesting situation for studying transfer of learning. Although there has been little research investigating the effect of videogame playing on motor development, a study by Favaro (cited in Thornburg, 1982) revealed that videogame experience improved the eye-hand coordination and reaction time of young children. Because eye-hand coordination and reaction time are fine motor skills which involve small muscles and precise movements and because videogame playing requires similar movements and coordination, it is reasonable to expect that playing videogames might aid in development of motor skill. Furthermore, motor skill development, particularly reaction time, shows marked improvement in children 6 to 10 years of age who are given adequate opportunity to participate in proper experiences (Fairweather, 1978; Hodgkins, 1963).

Leonard, Karnes, Oxendine, and Hesson (1970) have suggested three elements to consider in potential transfer between tasks. These elements are: the perceptual elements, the motor elements, and the strategy elements. If care is taken in selecting videogames which fulfill the criteria for transfer of learning, then learning to play videogames should enhance the transfer of learning. It was the purpose of this study to investigate the effects of videogame playing experience on the eye-hand coordination and reaction time of children.

METHODS

Subjects

The subjects for this study were 30 boys and girls aged 7 or 8 years. All subjects were volunteers, and informed consent was obtained from parents and children prior to testing. Fifteen of the volunteer girls and boys served as controls and the remaining fifteen girls and boys were assigned to the experimental group.

Procedures and Apparatus

The preferred hand of each child was determined by observing each child write a sentence on a piece of paper and was used for all testing. Each subject was pretested on an eye-hand coordination test and on a reaction time test.

The eye-hand coordination test was conducted on the Lafayette 30013 Photoelectric Rotary Pursuit. The circular disc moved in a clockwise direction at 25 revolutions per min. Scores were recorded for the amount of time the subject was on target. Subjects were given two 30-sec practice trials, followed by five 30-sec trials, with 30-sec rest intervals between each trial.

The reaction time test was a simple hand reaction test, with a light stimulus, using a Dekan Automatic Timer. A variable foreperiod (1-5 sec) was employed, with a 10 sec intertrial interval. Scores were recorded for the amount of time it took the subject to react to the light stimulus. Subjects had two practice trials, followed by 10 recorded trials, with 10-sec rest intervals between each trial.

The total time for testing each child was approximately 10 min per test session. The reaction time test and the eye-hand coordination test were chosen for their simplicity, appropriateness for the age group, and similarity to videogame responses. The videogames chosen were selected on the basis of their similarity to the movements and strategies needed to successfully keep a stylus on target (pursuit rotor test) and/or to make hand movements in reaction to a light stimulus (reaction time test).

The experimental group played videogames 10 min a day, 4 days a week, for 7 weeks. Each subject played the games 24 to 28 times during the 7-week period.

Two games were selected for the subjects to play. "Sink the Ship" involved dropping a bomb on a ship at the correct time to score the maximum number of points. "Nightmare Gallery" involved shooting a movable gun at a moving target on the screen.

The subjects in the control group were instructed to refrain from playing videogames for the same 7-week period. Because it was essential to the study's validity that the subjects assigned to the control group not play videogames during the experimental period, parental assistance was sought in monitoring the children from playing videogames during the 7-week experimental period.

At the end of 7 weeks, each subject was retested on the eye-hand coordination test and the reaction time test. Confidentiality regarding all data collection was ensured through coding, and all tests were conducted in a quiet room with minimum distractions. Data were analyzed using analysis of covariance to determine if there were significant differences between the control group and the experimental group on the eye-hand coordination test and the reaction time test.

Results

Analysis of covariance on the eye-hand coordination scores revealed that the experimental group had significantly higher scores than the control group $F(1,$

Table 1

Means (seconds) and Standard Deviations for the Experimental and Control Groups on the Rotary Pursuit Test

Group	n	Pretest M	Pretest SD	Posttest M	Posttest SD	Adjusted Means
Control	15	.464	.196	.533	.278	.566
Experimental	15	.513	.265	.957	.529	.924

Table 2

Means (seconds) and Standard Deviations for the Experimental and Control Groups on the Reaction Time Test

Group	n	Pretest M	Pretest SD	Posttest M	Posttest SD	Adjusted Means
Control	15	.319	.040	.312	.052	.308
Experimental	15	.295	.054	.263	.037	.268

27) = 11.767, $p < .01$. Subjects from the experimental group stayed on target (light stimulus) for a significantly greater period of time than did the control group subjects (Table 1).

Analysis of covariance on the reaction time scores revealed that the experimental group had significantly higher scores than the control group $F(1, 27) = 6.344$, $p < .05$. These results indicate that the subjects in the experimental group had significantly faster reaction times than did the subjects in the control group (Table 2).

DISCUSSION

The results of this study suggest that videogame playing produces a transfer effect for improving eye-hand coordination and reaction time for children. The findings associated with the eye-hand coordination test support the results of Favaro's study (cited in Thornburg, 1982). Favaro found that the training subjects received playing videogames enhanced their performance on other videolike games. Singer, Ridsdale, and Korienek (1979) suggest that experience with a visual tracking task has a positive effect on learning of a similar visual tracking task. They also indicate that strategies may be important elements of transfer.

The findings related to reaction time may be partially explained by improvement in appropriate response selection and categorization (Fairweather & Hutt, 1978). Fairweather (1978) and Fairweather and Hutt (1978) have established that children aged 5 to 11 can improve reaction time. However, their research suggests that stimulus input and response execution are not as effective as categorization and appropriate response selection in improving reaction time in children.

Data from the present study suggest that 7- or 8-year-old children can significantly improve eye-hand coordination and reaction time following videogame training. Furthermore, as found in this study, such improvement can be made through only a few minutes of practice (10 min per day for 4 days per week), over a relatively short period of time (7 weeks), practicing games that hold great appeal for children, thereby making the experience enjoyable.

The results of this study should not be interpreted as suggesting that videogame playing would in itself be an appropriate substitute for participation in more conventional physical activities such as are normally provided in elementary physical education classes. However, these data suggest that videogame playing might be considered an adjunct experience useful in developing eye-hand coordination and reaction time in 7- and 8-year-old children. Future studies should identify the magnitude and stability of these transfer effects through retention studies and the quantification of a videogame ability.

REFERENCES

Fairweather, H. (1978). Choice reaction times in children: Error and post-error responses, and the repetition effect. *Journal of Experimental Child Psychology, 26*, 407–418.

Fairweather, H. & Hutt, S. (1978). On the rate of gain of information in children. *Journal of Experimental Child Psychology, 26*, 216–229.

Hodgkins, J. (1963). Reaction time and speed of movement in males and females of various ages. *Research Quarterly, 34*, 335–343.

Leonard, S., Karnes, E., Oxendine, J., & Hesson, J. (1970). Effects of task difficulty on transfer performance on rotary pursuit. *Perceptual and Motor Skills, 30*, 731–736.

Magill, R. (1985). *Motor learning: Concepts and applications*. Dubuque: W. C. Brown Publishers.

Singer, R. (1982). *The learning of motor skills*. New York: Macmillan.

Singer, R., Gerson, R., & Ridsdale, S. (1979). *The effect of various strategies on the acquisition, retention, and transfer of a serial positioning task* (Report No. 399). Alexandria, VA: U.S. Army Research Institute.

Singer, R., Ridsdale, S., & Korienek, G. (1979). *The influence of learning strategies in the acquisition, retention, and transfer of a visual tracking task* (Report No. 402). Alexandria, VA: U.S. Army Research Institute.

Thornburg, D. (1982). Computers and society. *Compute!, 4*, 240.

7

THE INTERACTION OF CONCEPTUAL TEMPO AND MODELING ON THE MOTOR PERFORMANCE OF 10- AND 11-YEAR-OLD CHILDREN

Shirley DeVard Brown

Southern University

Amelia M. Lee

Louisiana State University

ABSTRACT

This study was designed to examine the effects of conceptual tempo and modeling on performance of a serial motor task. There were 48 subjects, 10- and 11-year-old males and females, classified as impulsive or reflective. Subjects were randomly assigned to one of three modeling groups or a control group. The three types of models included a silent model, a verbal model, or a verbal model with self guidance. The task was a motor skill obstacle course in which both speed and errors were scored. Data were analyzed by a 2 × 4 (Cognitive Style × Model Type) MANOVA with the number of trials to criterion, the average number of errors per trial, and the average amount of time on the three trials after criterion as the dependent variables. The results indicated that reflective children performed more accurately than impulsive children. There were no differences in the time scores of reflective and impulsive children. More importantly, a Cognitive Style × Model Type interaction revealed that student characteristics play a role in the modeling process. The impulsives performed equally as well after observing a silent- or verbal-model, or after observing a verbal-model and participating in self-instruction. The reflective children performed equally as

*well after observing a silent- or verbal-model and slightly
better with a verbal-model plus self-instruction.*

Cognitive style refers to how a learner processes information and is concerned with the form rather than the content of cognitive activity (Witkin, Moore, Goodenough, & Cox, 1977). Specifically, the construct refers to the manner in which an individual perceives, thinks, and solves problems. Conceptual tempo is one way in which cognitive style has been classified and identifies an individual as either reflective or impulsive. Impulsive learners respond quickly making many errors whereas reflective learners respond more slowly making few errors (Kagan, 1965). Reflective children have shown more ability to sustain attention (Campbell, 1973; Zelniker, Cochavi, & Yered, 1974), have better auditory and visual memory (Kagan, 1966; Siegel, Kirasic, & Kilburg, 1973) can selectively attend to relevant cues more efficiently (Weiner & Berzousky, 1975) than impulsive students, and make fewer errors of omission in serial recall (Kagan, 1966).

Several researchers have studied the relationship of age to conceptual tempo and found that children typically become more reflective as they get older (Messer, 1976; Kagan & Kogan, 1970; Salkind & Nelson, 1980). In both cross-sectional and longitudinal studies the developmental nature of reflection-impulsivity has been confirmed. Thus, the impulsive child at 10 years of age may solve problems and relate to others much like a member of a younger age group. When Drake (1970) studied the scanning strategies of reflectives and impulsives at two ages, differences of younger and older subjects resembled the differences found between impulsives and reflectives. In this investigation, the subjects' eye movements were studied and recorded during a visual discrimination problem. It was found that reflectives examined the alternatives in an analytic way before choosing an answer. The viewing behavior of the impulsives was more global, resulting in the selection of many incorrect answers.

Because impulsive children tend to be at a disadvantage in most classroom situations (Messer, 1976; Readence & Bean, 1978), many attempts have been made to make impulsive children more reflective. Modeling and self-instructional training have been used successfully to modify impulsivity (Messer, 1976; Thompson, Teare, & Elliot, 1983). Modeling is an important social process in which individuals can acquire new behaviors or change old ones (Bandura, 1969). Using both natural models in a classroom (Yando & Kagan, 1968) and experimental models (Kagan, Pearson, & Welch, 1966), the response time and accuracy of the impulsive have been altered successfully by researchers in the cognitive domain. Self-instructional techniques are based on the notion that internalization of verbal comments is a necessary step for a child to learn voluntary control of motor behavior (Luria, 1961).

For years physical educators have used modeling as an effective means of acquiring knowledge and skills related to movement and sport (Feltz & Landers, 1977; Gould & Weiss, 1981; Landers & Landers, 1973). Because of the demonstrated effectiveness of modeling in motor skill performance, researchers have recently started studying factors which might affect the modeling process. The type of model is one example of a factor which has been found to affect the relationship between modeling and motor performance. Gould and Weiss (1981) concluded that model talk should be an important variable to be considered by researchers. At least two studies (Thomas, Pierce, & Ridsdale, 1977; Weiss, 1983) have demonstrated that developmental factors interact with modeling. The study by Weiss (1983) revealed that verbal models were more effective than silent models in directing young children's attention to relevant task cues. While it was predicted that a verbal self-instructional training procedure would facilitate modeling for the younger child, this finding was not evident.

Taken together, these studies generally show that conceptual tempo influences the manner in which children approach and perform cognitive tasks, and that impulsive behavior can be modified to improve chances of success in learning situations. Whereas reflectives have a definite advantage in achievement of a cognitive task requiring problem solving strategies, little information is available as to what to expect with motor skills. Brown, Singer, Cauraugh, and Lucariello (1985) suggest that skills requiring precision and accuracy may be associated with the reflective style, whereas others may require the characteristics of the impulsive. These researchers found that reflective adults traversed a maze more slowly and with fewer errors than did impulsive adults. Further, performance of reflectives and impulsives was facilitated by an appropriate model. Finally, although several studies have demonstrated that models can provide information that observers can use during motor skill practice, the findings from the cognitive style literature could have important implications for modeling researchers. Because modeling serves as a guide to performance, the observer must be able to symbolically code the modeled behavior which requires visual memory and attentiveness. An impulsive learner might need verbal self-instruction with modeling or at least a verbal model, whereas a silent model may be sufficient for the reflective.

The research findings on gender differences in the conceptual tempo paradigm are not conclusive. Some studies have found females to be more reflective than males (Harrison & Nadelman, 1972; Messer, 1976), but the differences were not significant. Gender has consistently not affected the outcome of conceptual tempo studies. There is, however, evidence that males and females perform differently on a number of motor skills. Several summaries indicate superior performance of males in most movement tasks (Herkowitz, 1978; Thomas & French, 1985). The body of research on conceptual tempo can still be considered relatively new, and gender might, therefore, continue to be a variable that is included in these studies. This is especially true when studying the relationship between conceptual tempo and motor skills. Thus, the specific purpose of this study was to examine the interaction of cognitive style, gender, and modeling on children's performance on a serial movement task.

Upon the basis of the literature reviewed, the following predictive hypotheses were stated: (a) during acquisition, reflective children would perform more accurately (fewer errors) than impulsive children; (b) after a movement sequence is learned, impulsives and reflectives would not differ on a measure of speed; (c) for reflective children, a silent- or verbal-model, or verbal-model with self-instruction would be equally effective and better than no model; (d) for impulsive children a verbal-model or a verbal-model with self-instruction would be more effective than a silent-, or no-model.

METHOD

Subjects

In this study, 93 children ranging in age from 10 to 11 years who were enrolled in private schools were tested. All subjects in this study were black with middle-class backgrounds. Students were tested individually using the Matching Familiar Figures Test (MFFT) (Kagan, 1965) until a sample of 24 reflective (12 males and 12 females) and 24 impulsive (12 males and 12 females) subjects were identified, using error and latency scores based on norms provided by Messer (1976). After reflective and impulsive subjects were identified, the ages ranged from 121 months to 148 months, with a mean age of 133 months.

Matching Familiar Figures Test

In this test the child is presented a picture of a familiar object and six alternatives, only one of which is identical to the criterion. Directions provide two practice items and 12 test items, each using an object and six alternatives. The object appears on a page and the alternatives appear on an adjacent page. The child is asked to find the picture on the second page that is exactly like the picture on the first page. If the choice is correct, the child is praised; if incorrect, additional trials are allowed until the correct alternative is located. The two scores are (a) time to the first response, and (b) the number of errors on each item. Upon completion of the items, a separate score is computed for the mean response time to the first choice and the total number of errors. The subjects in this study were classified on a median split of both time and error scores. Impulsive subjects are those who scored below the median on time and above the median on errors, and reflectives are those who scored above the median on time and below the median on errors, using the normative data reported by

Messer (1976). In a comprehensive review of different samples (N = 423), Messer provides medians and ranges of response time and errors by age groups. For this age group the median number of errors was 7.7 and the median time was 13.6 sec. Messer reports the reliability estimates to be .92 to .98 for errors and time, respectively.

Testing Equipment

Obstacle Course.

The perceptual motor obstacle course by Johnson and Nelson (1979) was revised so as to be appropriate for 10- and 11-year-old children. The course required children to perform specified motor tasks at each of six stations in a sequential order. At the first station, the subject was required to hop right, hop right, jump, jump, hop left, and hop left. At the second station, the subject was directed to jump over, go around, jump over, and go around a rectangle on the floor. Then, at the third station, the subject jumped to geometric patterns using the sequence: square, square, triangle, circle, square. A playground ball had to be (a) dribbled around five cones using the right hand, (b) tossed three times against the wall and caught, (c) dribbled around five cones with the left hand, and (d) tossed against the wall and caught two times at the fourth station. The subject walked forward, backward, and sideward on a 2-in. (5.08-cm) balance beam at the fifth station. The sixth station required the subject to bounce a ball on the ground inside a hoop with a paddle three times and to stand inside a hoop and bounce the ball off of the paddle three times against the wall. Finally, the subject ran to a designated spot.

The time to complete the course and any performance or sequence errors were recorded. Performance errors were such violations as the subject using the wrong locomotor skill, losing control of the ball, or failing to stay on the balance beam. A sequence error occurred when the subject could not perform the correct pattern or missed a part or all of a pattern. The time score was the time in seconds that it took each subject to complete the obstacle course.

Procedures

Subjects were first administered the MFFT to identify their cognitive style. The experimenter continued to test until 24 reflective and 24 impulsive subjects were classified for this study. The mean MFFT response time for the reflective boys was 21.44 sec (*SD* = .84), and the mean number of errors was 2.6 (*SD* = 1.92). The impulsive boys had a mean response latency of 7.46 sec (*SD* = .27) with 8.8 as the average number of errors (*SD* = 2.08). The results for the reflective girls on response latency was 18.47 sec (*SD* = 5.51), and the mean number of errors was 2.5 (*SD* = 1.62). The impulsive girls had a mean time of 7.99 sec (SD = 2.78), and the mean number of errors was 8.0 (SD = 2.04).

Subjects were randomly assigned within gender and cognitive style to one of three modeling groups or a no-model group. The random assignment was completed with one constraint: to ensure that each model and cognitive style group was represented by the two age groups; equal number of males and females were sometimes not possible. The model types used were either a silent-model, a verbal-model, or a verbal-model with self-instruction. A black female (who was one of the experimenters) served as the model. The silent-model demonstrated the movement sequence involved in the obstacle course, moving at a medium speed but making no errors. The verbal-model demonstrated the movements at a medium speed and verbalized aloud the sequence. In addition to the sequence, the verbal-model made statements about performance such as: "I am going to keep the ball low so I will not lose control"; and "I am holding my arms out for balance on the beam". The verbal-model plus self-instruction demonstrated the movements, verbalized aloud the sequence, made statements about technique, and trained the subjects to recite the sequence and make the statements about technique. Children in the no-model group were given verbal instructions only.

Each subject was tested individually beginning with the no-model group. The three remaining groups were tested in random order. The no-model group was tested first to try to diminish as much sharing of information as possible from the other three treatment groups. Further, the no-model group was required to wait the average amount of time needed to observe a model before beginning the run. This was done to eliminate any differences in the cognitive style groups to use a rehearsal strategy. Upon arrival at the test station, the subjects were told that the experimenter wanted them to go through the obstacle course with no errors. All treatment groups were given verbal instructions two times for completing the course. The subjects in the no-model group were then asked to complete the course. Subjects in the silent- and verbal-model groups observed the appropriate model and then completed the course. After observing the model, subjects in the verbal-model self-instruction group practiced the sequence until it could be verbalized without error. These children were also required to include some hints for successful performance.

A maximum of 15 trials was given for each child to reach a criterion of three or less errors. The maximum number of trials as well as the length and difficulty of the sequence was determined by pilot testing. It was confirmed that children 10 and 11 years old would maintain interest for approximately 15 trials and could learn the selected sequence. For each of the acquisition trials, error scores were recorded. The error score included both sequence and performance errors. If a subject forgot the sequence, the child was encouraged to continue to the next station, and a maximum number of errors for the station was recorded.

The subject continued until the criterion of three errors or less was reached.

After criterion, each subject was given three additional trials. For these trials, the children were told: "Now I want you to see if you can complete the course in a faster time but still without errors. You know the sequence, now think about speed." Time scores were recorded for these three trials.

Analysis

The results were analyzed in a 2 × 2 × 4 (Learning Style × Gender × Model Type) MANOVA to compare group differences on the following performance measures: (a) number of trials to criterion, (b) average number of errors per trial, and (c) average time on the three trials after criterion.

RESULTS

The 2 × 2 × 4 (Cognitive Style × Gender × Model Type) MANOVA[1] performed on the data to compare group differences on the number of trials to criteria, the errors per trial, and the average amount of time on the three trials after criteria revealed a significant main effect for cognitive style, $F(3, 30) = 4.13$, $p < .01$ and model type, $F(9, 73) = 3.99$, $p < .01$. There was also a significant Cognitive Style × Model Type interaction, $F(9, 73) = 2.37$, $p < .05$. Because there were no gender differences, the decision was made to complete all subsequent analyses collapsed across gender. Considering the small sample size, this decision increased the power of the test and was, thus, considered appropriate.

The follow-up ANOVA (2 × 4), with the number of trials as the dependent

Table 1
Means for Cognitive Style and Treatment Groups

Variable	Number of Trials		Errors per trial		Time	
Cognitive Style	*M*	*SD*	*M*	*SD*	*M*	*SD*
Impulsive	6.8	3.3	12.0	3.7	98.2	22.8
Reflective	5.0	2.5	8.6	4.2	95.0	20.3
Model Type						
No-model	9.0	3.8	12.3	3.7	164.6	36.9
Silent-model	5.5	1.2	10.4	2.9	146.4	52.3
Verbal-model	5.1	2.3	9.5	4.7	149.2	38.0
Verbal-model with self-instruction	3.9	1.6	9.0	5.0	152.9	49.5

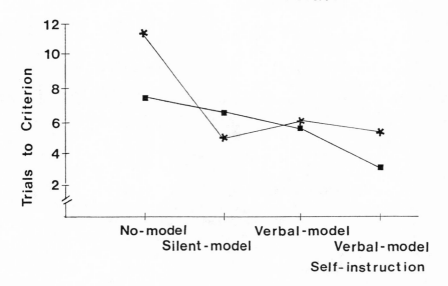

FIG. 1. Trials to criterion for Cognitive Style × Model Type interaction

variable, yielded significant differences for cognitive style, $F(1, 40) = 9.17$, $p < .01$, model type, $F(3, 40) = 13.06$, $p < .01$, and Cognitive Style × Model Type, $F(3, 40) = 3.37$, $p < .05$. Impulsive children had significantly more trials to criterion than did reflective children. The means and standard deviations are shown in Table 1. Results of Newman Keuls follow-up analysis indicated that subjects who did not receive a model took significantly more trials to reach criterion than did subjects with a silent-model, a verbal-model of a verbal-model and self-instruction. The latter three model groups were not significantly different (Table 1). These findings, however, must be discussed in light of the Cognitive Style × Model Type interaction which is shown graphically in Fig. 1. Planned comparisons indicated that the impulsive subjects in the no-model treatment had significantly more trials to criterion ($M = 11.2$; $SD = 3.4$) than the reflective subjects ($M = 6.8$; $SD = 3.1$) in the no-model group. All modeling strategies helped the impulsive subjects to reach criterion with fewer trials than with no-model. Inspection of Fig. 1 shows that, with one minor exception, the participants receiving any of the modeling treatments, regardless of cognitive style, displayed essentially the same behavior. The one exception is that reflective subjects learned the task to criterion with slightly fewer trials with a verbal-model and self-instruction.

The ANOVA with the number of errors per trial as the dependent variable yielded significant differences for cognitive style, $F(1, 40) = 9.76, p < .01$. The impulsives had significantly more errors per trial ($M = 12.0; SD = 3.7$) than the reflectives ($M = 8.6; SD = 4.17$) (Table 1). There were no significant differences for the main effects of model group, nor for any of the interactions.

The same univariate procedure used on the number of trials to criterion and the number of errors per trial was used to examine differences in the time scores after criterion had been reached. Neither the main effects nor any of the interactions approached significance.

DISCUSSION

The findings in this study support the notion that motor skill performance accuracy of children classified as impulsive or reflective will differ. Reflective children performed with fewer errors and used fewer trials to criterion than did the impulsive children. These results support previous research in the cognitive domain which has shown that reflectives make fewer errors of omission in serial recall (Kagan, 1966). The tendency of reflective children to be more accurate extends to performance in motor tasks which involve memory of a sequence. The reflective subjects appeared to cognitively encode the elements of the task more readily than the impulsive, thereby reducing the number of trials required to reach criterion and the mean number of errors per trial.

Children, regardless of conceptual tempo, had similar time scores for the obstacle course after reaching criterion for accuracy. These results support a major hypothesis of this study. It appears that the impulsive child was at a disadvantage only during the acquisition trials when it was important to remember the movement sequence. With the cognitive component removed from the task, there is no reason for the two groups to differ on a speed test.

The significant Cognitive Style × Model Type interaction indicates that a model is extremely important and effective in helping the impulsive learner perform more accurately in a serial motor task. These children performed approximately the same under the three modeling conditions and significantly better than with no model. It was hypothesized that the impulsive students would perform best with a model plus self-instruction since these techniques have been used successfully to modify the behavior of the impulsive. Findings failed to substantiate this prediction. It appears that the accuracy of the impulsive was increased equally by a demonstration, a demonstration with verbal cues, or a demonstration with verbal cues and self-instructional training. The requirements of the children in the verbal-model self-instruction condition may help explain why this condition did not enhance the performance of the impulsive. The children in the silent- and verbal-model conditions had to process visual and visual plus auditory information, respectively. The children in the verbal-model with self-instruction conditions had to process visual and auditory information, plus, make a verbal response. Perhaps the methodology used to train the children in this group did not allow the impulsives the opportunity to benefit from the self-instructional training. Previous researchers (Meichenbaum & Goodman, 1971), using modeling plus self-instruction to make impulsives more reflective, have used a multistep procedure. First, the student observed a model and was then carefully guided through the problem. Later, the student solved the problem with overt self-instructions. Even though the subjects in this study observed the model before learning the verbal sequence of actions, the procedure probably did not provide the time and guidance needed by the impulsive to benefit from the training. The reflective children, on the other hand, learned the task in slightly less time (trials to criteria) when provided a verbal-model and self-instructional training. Apparently these children could obtain more easily helpful information from the visual and verbal cues and at the same time combine this with self-instruction to improve performance. Figure 1 suggests that the reflectives became slightly more accurate with each model condition.

In summary, these findings have implications for school learning. Whereas providing a demonstration to facilitate performance in motor skills has been accepted as a valuable process in physical education for years, this technique appears to be extremely necessary for the impulsive learner. The reflective student might successfully obtain information concerning what is required from verbal instructions alone. The impulsive learner, in contrast, needs something more than a verbal explanation. Following the same line of thinking, reflectives may be more adept at discerning information from a written task sheet. This study was one of the first attempts to relate cognitive style to an instructional process in physical education. The findings suggest that the performance of a student with an impulsive conceptual tempo is different from that of a reflective on a sequential motor task. The impulsive subject's performance can be altered by a modeling strategy and, thus, facilitate performance.

REFERENCES

Bandura, A. (1969). *Principles of behavior modification*. New York: Holt, Rinehard & Winston.

Brown, H., Singer, R., Cauraugh, J., & Lucariello, G. (1985). Cognitive style and learner strategy interaction in performance of primary and related maze tasks. *Research Quarterly for Exercise and Sport, 56,* 10–14.

Campbell, S. B. (1973). Cognitive styles in reflective, impulsive and hyperactive boys and their mothers. *Perceptual and Motor Skills, 36*, 747–752.

Drake, D. M. (1970). Perceptual correlates of impulsive and reflective behavior. *Developmental Psychology, 2*, 202–214.

Feltz, D. L., & Landers, D. M. (1977). Informational-motivational components of models' demonstration. *Research Quarterly for Exercise and Sport, 48*, 525–533.

Gould, D., & Weiss, M. (1981). The effects of model similarity and model talk on self-efficacy and muscular endurance. *Journal of Sport Psychology, 3*, 17–29.

Harrison, A., & Nadelman, L. (1972). Conceptual tempo and inhibition of movement in black pre-school children. *Child Development, 43*, 657–668.

Herkowitz, J. (1978). Sex role expectations and motor behavior of the young child. In M. V. Ridenour (Ed.), *Motor development issues and applications* (pp. 83–98). Princeton: Princeton Book Company.

Johnson, B., & Nelson, J. (1979). *Practical measurement for evaluation in physical education*. Minneapolis: Burgess.

Kagan, J. (1965). Impulsive and reflective children. In J. D. Krumboltz (Ed.), *Learning and the educational process* (pp. 133–161). Chicago: Rand McNally & Company.

Kagan, J. (1966). Developmental studies in reflection and analysis. In A. Kidd & J. Reverre (Eds.), *Perceptual development in children* (pp. 487–522). New York: Inernational Universities Press.

Kagan, J., & Kogan, N. (1970). Individual variation in cognitive processes. In P. H. Mussen (Ed.), *Carmichael's manual of child psychology* (Vol. I, pp. 1273–1365). New York: Wiley.

Kagan, J., Pearson, L., & Welch, L. (1966). Modification of an impulsive tempo. *Journal of Educational Psychology, 57*, 359–365.

Landers, D. M., & Landers, D. M. (1973). Teacher versus peer models: Effect of model's presence and performance level on motor behavior. *Journal of Motor Behavior, 5*, 129–139.

Luria, A. R. (1961). *The role of speech in the regulation of normal and abnormal behavior*. New York: Liveright.

Meichenbaum, D. H., & Goodman, J. (1971). Training impulsive children to talk to themselves: A means of developing self-control. *Journal of Abnormal Psychology, 77*, 115–126.

Messer, S. B. (1976). Reflection-impulsivity: A review. *Psychological Bulletin, 83*, 1026–1051.

Readence, J. E., & Bean, T. W. (1978). Modification of impulsive cognitive style: A survey of the literature. *Psychological Reports, 43*, 327–337.

Salkind, N. J., & Nelson, C. F. (1980). A note on the developmental nature of reflection-impulsivity. *Developmental Psychology, 16*, 237–238.

Siegel, A. N., Kirasic, K. C., & Kilburg, R. L. (1973). Recognition memory in reflective and impulsive preschool children. *Child Development, 44*, 651–656.

Thomas, J. R., & French, K. E. (1985). Gender differences across age in motor performance: A meta-analysis. *Psychological Bulletin, 8*, 260–282.

Thomas, J., Pierce, C., & Ridsdale, S. (1977). Age differences in children's ability to model motor behavior. *Research Quarterly for Exercise and Sport, 48*, 592–597.

Thompson, R. W., Teare, J. F., & Elliot, S. N. (1983). Impulsivity: From theoretical constructs to applied intervention. *Journal of Special Education, 17*, 157–169.

Weiner, A. S., & Berzousky, M. D. (1975). Development of selective attention in reflective and impulsive children. *Child Development, 46*, 545–549.

Weiss, M. R. (1983). Model and motor performance: A developmental perspective. *Research Quarterly for Exercise and Sport, 54*, 190–197.

Witkin, H. A., Moore, C. A., Goodenough, D. R., & Cox, P. W. (1977). Field-dependent and field-independent cognitive styles and their educational implications. *Review of Educational Research, 40*, 1–64.

Yando, R. M., & Kagan, J. (1968). The effect of teacher tempo on the child. *Child Development, 39*, 27–34.

Yando, R., Seitz, V., & Zigler, E. (1978). *Imitation: A developmental perspective*. New York: Wiley.

Zelniker, T., Cochavi, D., & Yered, G. (1974). The relationship between speed of performance and conceptual style: The effect of imposed modification of response latency. *Child Development, 45*, 779–784.

NOTE

[1]Statistics for MANOVA are Wilks' Lambdas converted to approximate Fs.

8

CONTRIBUTIONS OF MOTOR, CONCEPT, AND COMMUNICATION SKILLS TO PRESCHOOL LEARNING

Geoffrey D. Broadhead and Gabie E. Church
Louisiana State University

ABSTRACT

The focus of the study was to examine the conribution of gross motor, fine motor, concept, and communication skills in showing developmental differences among 3-, 4-, and 5-year-old Caucasian children. As assessed by the DIAL test, Developmental Indicators for the Assessment of Learning (Mardell & Goldenberg, 1975), each component of behavior—gross motor, fine motor, concept, and communication skills—is assessed by seven test items, with communication skills as the primary criterion for identifying normal development in preschoolers. Separate stepwise multivariate discriminant analyses of the vector of 28 variables were completed for 275 Caucasian boys and 207 Caucasian girls who took part in a school district preschool screening project. In each case both discriminant functions were statistically significant (p < .01), with the first function accounting for over 88% of the explained variance. For each analysis, 11 of the 18 variables (61%) included in the functions assessed motor performance, whereas no more than 23% assessed communication. Results support the existence of four components of performance but not the emphasis on communication skills.

The importance of the preschool years in influencing the course of a child's total development has long been recognized (Bloom, Davis, & Hess, 1965; Lorton & Walley, 1979; Pringle, 1965). However it is only during the last quarter century that the number of instructional programs for 3- to 5-year-old children has increased significantly (Allen & Goetz, 1982; Lorton & Walley, 1979; Pringle, 1965; Spodek, 1982). But attendance at preschool is voluntary, costs frequently prohibitive, sites not always accessible to parents from all sections of the community, and the benefits not always thought to be superior to experiences gained at home (Barnes, 1982; Chazan, 1973; Travers & Light, 1982; Weikart, Deloria, Lawser, & Wiegerink, 1970). Thus, it seems reasonable to suggest that the opportunities vary greatly for children to acquire and develop cognitive, language, movement, and social skills during these years.

For the most part, preschool programs are cognitively and socially oriented and use the techniques of verbal bombardment, social play, and parental involvement to elicit change in behavior (Bloom, Davis, & Hess, 1965; Chazan, 1973; Payne, Mercer, Payne, & Davison, 1973; Spodek, 1982; Stanley, 1972; Travers & Light, 1982; Westinghouse Learning Corporation & Ohio University, 1979; Weikart, Bond, & McNeil, 1978; Zigler & Valentine, 1979). The literature neither stresses the importance of motor development for preschoolers nor describes movement education programs for such children.

The absence of structured movement programs for these young children is difficult to understand, for several well-known tests, which purport to evaluate the skills acquired by young children, aged from birth through 6 years, include movement tasks. Among these are the Bayley Scales of Infant Development (Bayley, 1969), the Denver Developmental Screening Test (Frankenburg & Dodds, 1967), the Portage Guide to Elementary Education (Bluma, Shearer, Frohman, & Hilliard, 1976a, 1976b), the Learning Accomplishment Profile (LeMay, Griffin, & Sanford, 1977; Sanford, 1970), Assessment in Infancy (Uzgiris & Hunt, 1975), and the DIAL, Developmental Indicators for the Assessment of Learning (Mardell & Goldenberg, 1975).

The inclusion of movement tasks in these test batteries does not automatically mean that movement competence is particularly important in showing whether or not children are developing normally. If, however, it is demonstrated that the level of performance on movement tasks discriminates among preschool children in the same way as language and cognitive tasks in the same battery, then there would be a strong argument for influencing instructional content by including movement education/physical education in preschool programs.

Of the above mentioned tests, only through the use of DIAL can the question of the relative importance of movement tasks be answered. For in DIAL four components of development—gross motor, fine motor, concepts, and communication skills—are assessed by equal numbers of test items and an identical range of possible component scores. However, though no specific rationale is provided by Mardell and Goldenberg (1975), the level of performance on the communication component of DIAL is the predominant criterion for identifying normal development.

The purpose of this study was to examine the contribution of gross motor, fine motor, concept, and communication skills as measured by DIAL, in showing developmental differences among 3-, 4-, and 5-year-old Caucasian children.

METHOD

Sample

The subjects for this study were 275 Caucasian boys and 207 Caucasian girls, aged 3 to 5 years, residing in a geographically large, mostly urban school district in Louisiana (Table 1). It should be noted that subjects 2 years 6 months to 3 years 5 months were considered as 3-year-olds, etc.

Subjects were volunteer participants in a preschool screening program mandated by state and federal laws and regulations designed to determine whether children were developing normally (Louisiana Legislature, 1977; Louisiana State Department of Education, 1978; United States Congress, 1975; United States Department of Health, Education, & Welfare, 1977). Because fewer than 3% were later judged to need special education, the sample is believed to be representative of 3- to 5-year-old Caucasian children.

Test Instrumentation

DIAL (Mardell & Goldenberg, 1975) consists of four components, each with seven items. *Gross motor* tasks are throwing, catching, jumping, hopping, skipping, standing still, and balancing. *Fine motor* tasks are matching, building, cutting, copying shapes, copying letters, touching fingers, and clapping hands. *Concept skills* are sorting blocks, naming colors, counting, positioning, following

Table 1
Descriptive Statistics for Chronological Age (months) by Yearly Age Group

Age Group		Boys	Girls
3	M	34.81	34.86
	SD	5.45	3.90
	n	67	76
4	M	47.71	47.72
	SD	3.38	3.71
	n	97	55
5	M	59.85	60.38
	SD	4.40	4.74
	n	111	76

directions, identifying concepts, and identifying body parts. *Communication skills* are articulating, remembering, naming nouns and verbs, coping, naming self, age, sex, classifying foods, and telling a story. Mardell and Goldenberg (1975) believe that the test battery includes all the behaviors separately identified in studies such as those of Bayley (1969), Frankenburg and Dodds (1967), and Gesell (1940).

From the standardization process involving 4,356 children, norms were established separately for boys and girls at 3-month age intervals from 2 yrs. 6 mos. to 5 yrs. 5 mos.; at all ages, and for each of the four components of development, girls are expected to outperform boys. Cutoff scores for each age group indicate the level of performance of the lowest 10% of the age by sex group. No separate norms are provided which take into account demographic setting, race, or socioeconomic status.

The above performance characteristics were confirmed by Docherty (1983). However, in a study of movement traits of preschoolers, Broadhead and Church (1985) reported significant differences between sexes (favoring girls) for yearly age groups but not for 3-month age groupings. It was reported also that movement performance differences occurred between races, black and Caucasian, some favoring black subjects, others favoring Caucasian subjects (Broadhead & Church, 1985).

Mardell and Goldenberg (1975) used evaluations of student performance from a team of professionals—a psychologist, guidance counselor, school nurse, and social worker—to compare against DIAL results of youngsters in a Headstart Day Care Program and reported concurrent validity of the test as an 85.3% item agreement. In another study, Hall, Mardell, Wick, and Goldenberg (1974) compared DIAL scores of children in kindergarten and grade one with standardized achievement subtests from instruments such as the Metropolitan Reading Readiness and Achievement Tests and reported multiple correlations with the test criterion and the DIAL scores ranging from $R = .45$ to $.73$ ($p < .05$). Wick (1973) reported high test-retest reliability coefficients after examining data from low versus high functioning children over a 12-month period. No reports on validity and/or reliability of DIAL, by researchers independent of the test authors and their colleagues, were found.

Evaluation Procedures

Subjects were administered the 28 items of DIAL individually. A team of four testers was trained in the practice and execution of the test items using the exact procedures outlined in the Training Manual which is part of the DIAL kit (Mardell & Goldenberg, 1975). Training was under the supervision of the then School District Coordinator of Preschool Screening, who had previously been trained by the test authors. A central location which used four separate rooms, one for each DIAL component, helped to ensure the appropriateness of the testing environment.

Analysis of Data

Separate discriminant analyses were completed for the samples of 275 Caucasian boys and 207 Caucasian girls. The 28 items of DIAL were used as discriminating variables to test for developmental differences across 3-, 4-, and 5-year-olds. The DISCRIMINANT procedure of SPSS[x] (SPSS, Inc., 1983) was employed with a stepwise selection of variables, based on the Mahalanobis distance criterion, in order to produce an optimal subset of the 28 items which maximally discriminated among the yearly age groups. Estimates of the percent of correct classification were obtained for the purpose of assessing how well the functions actually discriminated among the three age groups. Because the sample size was considered sufficiently large the split-sample holdout validation technique was used, rather than the more frequently used resubstitution method (Kerlinger & Pedhazur, 1973; Klecka, 1980; Thorndike, 1978). This technique consists of randomly splitting a sample into two approximately equal subsamples to produce classification functions which are used to classify the other (independent) subsample. These two independently obtained estimates are then averaged to obtain an unbiased estimate of the percent of correct classification from use of the discriminant functions (Toussaint, 1974).

RESULTS

Means and standard deviations for each of the 28 DIAL items for the sample of 275 Caucasian boys and 207 Caucasian girls appear in Tables 2 and 3.

Discriminant analysis for the boys produced two discriminant functions, both statistically significant ($\chi^2(36) = 335.12$, $p < .01$, $\chi^2(17) = 47.80$, $p < .01$), with differences between all pairs of yearly age groups also significant ($p < .01$); the first function accounted for 90.85% of the explained variance. Eighteen variables were selected for inclusion in the functions, including five gross motor items (throwing, hopping, skipping, standing still, balancing), six fine motor items (matching, building, cutting, copying shapes, copying letters, clapping hands), four concept items (naming colors, positioning, identifying concepts, identifying body parts), and three communication items (naming nouns and verbs, coping, classifying foods). Standardized discriminant function coefficients for the two functions appear in Table 4. Average correct classifications from the split-sample holdout validation were 67% for 3-year-olds, 48% for 4-year-olds, 76% for 5-year-olds, yielding an overall 64% correct classification.

Discriminant analysis of the sample of girls yielded similar results. Two

Table 2
Means and Standard Deviations of 28 DIAL Items for 3-, 4-, and 5-year-old Caucasian Boys

	Age Group					
	3		4		5	
Item	**M**	**SD**	**M**	**SD**	**M**	**SD**
Gross Motor						
Throwing	2.75	0.70	2.88	0.48	2.98	0.13
Catching	1.46	1.26	2.21	1.03	2.56	0.77
Jumping	2.12	1.35	2.88	0.60	2.94	0.41
Hopping	0.33	0.61	1.29	0.96	2.18	0.92
Skipping	0.66	0.77	1.52	0.81	2.09	0.87
Standing still	1.15	1.18	2.26	1.09	2.72	0.65
Balancing	1.49	1.02	2.47	0.84	2.74	0.61
Fine Motor						
Matching	2.27	1.07	2.80	0.57	2.95	0.35
Building	1.76	0.72	2.39	0.67	2.80	0.40
Cutting	1.28	0.95	2.49	0.86	2.85	0.45
Copying shapes	1.00	0.55	1.82	0.71	2.46	0.55
Copying letters	0.72	0.55	1.49	0.88	2.34	0.76
Touching fingers	0.84	1.05	1.96	1.20	2.54	0.85
Clapping hands	1.07	1.03	1.95	1.03	2.50	0.74
Concept						
Sorting blocks	1.01	1.25	2.11	1.23	2.69	0.80
Naming colors	1.43	1.08	2.43	0.91	2.82	0.41
Counting	1.19	0.96	2.05	0.78	2.64	0.57
Positioning	1.55	0.91	2.30	0.71	2.51	0.59
Following directions	2.58	0.80	2.90	0.47	2.90	0.49
Identifying concepts	1.72	0.73	2.35	0.54	2.72	0.49
Identify body parts	1.96	0.91	2.67	0.53	2.85	0.36
Communication						
Articulating	2.04	1.15	2.65	0.78	2.87	0.49
Remembering	1.43	0.92	2.31	0.85	2.71	0.59
Naming nouns/verbs	1.70	0.84	2.58	0.66	2.76	0.49
Coping	0.55	0.80	1.32	0.85	1.71	0.55
Naming self/age/sex	1.81	1.20	2.56	0.82	2.86	0.46
Classifying foods	1.03	0.83	2.18	0.88	2.44	0.75
Telling a story	1.87	1.51	3.02	1.01	3.37	1.04

Table 3
**Means and Standard Deviations of 28 DIAL Items for 3-, 4-, and 5-Year-Old
Caucasian Girls**

| | Age Group | | | | | |
| | 3 | | 4 | | 5 | |
Item	M	SD	M	SD	M	SD
Gross Motor						
Throwing	2.62	0.83	2.78	0.69	2.86	0.60
Catching	1.49	1.30	2.31	0.81	2.64	0.56
Jumping	2.30	1.22	2.87	0.58	2.96	0.34
Hopping	0.61	0.71	1.78	0.96	2.54	0.66
Skipping	0.99	0.92	1.76	0.98	2.51	0.64
Standing still	1.52	1.24	2.13	1.20	2.51	0.89
Balancing	1.46	1.12	2.65	0.70	2.82	0.45
Fine Motor						
Matching	2.29	1.11	2.95	0.23	2.96	0.20
Building	1.61	0.78	2.44	0.54	2.80	0.46
Cutting	1.20	1.01	2.62	0.78	2.80	0.65
Copying shapes	0.97	0.66	1.87	0.79	2.54	0.53
Copying letters	0.71	0.58	1.76	0.86	2.62	0.59
Touching fingers	0.96	1.10	2.53	0.92	2.80	0.61
Clapping hands	1.09	1.11	2.22	0.83	2.57	0.77
Concept						
Sorting blocks	1.05	1.26	2.40	1.16	2.84	0.61
Naming colors	1.83	1.12	2.78	0.57	2.91	0.37
Counting	1.38	0.94	2.42	0.57	2.76	0.46
Positioning	1.55	0.89	2.47	0.72	2.62	0.56
Following directions	2.58	0.91	3.00	0.00	2.99	0.11
Identifying concepts	1.74	0.88	2.49	0.60	2.68	0.50
Identify body parts	2.24	0.89	2.89	0.31	2.89	0.31
Communication						
Articulating	1.97	1.14	2.91	0.35	2.86	0.60
Remembering	1.28	1.04	2.65	0.64	2.79	0.52
Naming nouns/verbs	1.84	1.01	2.62	0.59	2.74	0.53
Coping	0.76	0.94	1.75	0.67	1.76	0.59
Naming self/age/sex	1.72	1.21	2.73	0.65	2.87	0.44
Classifying foods	1.07	0.96	2.18	0.86	2.51	0.76
Telling a story	2.08	1.52	2.87	1.07	3.61	0.83

Table 4

Standardized Discriminant Function Coefficients of DIAL Items Selected in
Stepwise Discriminant Analysis among 3-, 4-, and 5-Year-Old Caucasian Boys

Items	Function 1	Function 2
Throwing	−0.11	−0.27
Hopping	0.22	−0.51
Skipping	0.19	−0.03
Standing still	0.15	0.07
Balancing	0.05	0.36
Matching	−0.21	0.23
Building	0.14	−0.28
Cutting	0.27	0.44
Copying shapes	0.22	−0.33
Copying letters	0.07	−0.40
Clapping hands	0.11	0.13
Naming colors	0.18	0.24
Positioning	−0.07	0.29
Identifying concepts	0.04	−0.35
Identifying body parts	−0.04	0.25
Naming nouns, verbs	0.20	0.22
Copying	0.13	−0.12
Classifying foods	0.18	0.36

functions were derived, both statistically significant ($\chi^2(36) = 339.62, p < .01$, $\chi^2(17) = 63.75, p < .01$), with differences between all pairs of yearly age groups also significant ($p < .01$); the first function accounted for 88.94% of the explained variation. Eighteen variables were selected in the stepwise procedure with six gross motor items (catching, jumping, hopping, skipping, standing still, balancing), five fine motor items (matching, building, cutting, copying letters, touching fingers), three concept items (sorting blocks, following directions, identifying body parts), and four communication items (articulating, remembering, coping, telling a story). Standardized discriminant function coefficients for the two functions appear in Table 5. Estimates of percent of correct classification were 74% for 3-year-olds, 53% for 4-year-olds, 80% for 5-year-olds, for an overall 71% correct classification.

DISCUSSION

From the results it was apparent that for boys and for girls fewer than 65% (18) of the 28 test items of DIAL were influential in discriminating among the

Table 5
**Standardized Discriminant Function Coefficients of DIAL Items Selected in
Stepwise Discriminant Analysis among 3-, 4-, and 5-Year-Old Caucasian Girls**

Items	Function 1	Function 2
Catching	0.11	−0.19
Jumping	−0.14	0.12
Hopping	0.33	−0.05
Skipping	0.13	−0.26
Standing still	−0.15	−0.19
Balancing	0.14	0.29
Matching	−0.28	0.14
Building	0.11	−0.28
Cutting	0.19	0.38
Copying letters	0.37	−0.54
Touching fingers	0.24	0.33
Sorting blocks	0.28	−0.02
Following directions	0.20	0.32
Identifying body parts	−0.16	0.10
Articulating	−0.06	0.27
Remembering	0.34	0.28
Coping	−0.03	0.46
Telling a story	−0.03	−0.83

three age groups. Items from each of the four components of DIAL were included in the discriminatory process, ranging from at most 22% for nonmotor components, to at least 27% for motor components. The results were similar for boys and girls, with 61% of the 18 items being for gross and fine motor components of DIAL. From this it seems that two conclusions are justified. First, the inclusion of movement oriented tasks, and, more specifically, the inclusion of separate gross and fine motor components of this screening inventory is supported by this sample of Caucasian preschoolers. Second, there appears to be no support for the emphasis of any one component of behavior over the other three, as suggested by Mardell and Goldenberg (1975).

By inspecting the individual test items which were influential in discriminating among the three age groups (Tables 4 and 5), it is noticed that the discrepancy between the items selected for the functions for boys and for girls is related to the nature of the component, motor or nonmotor. For each nonmotor component only six of the seven items were selected, with one item from each being common to both boys and girls (concept: identifying body parts; communication: coping). On the other hand, all seven items were selected from each motor component, with four items from each common to both sexes (gross motor: hopping, skipping, standing still, balancing; fine motor: matching, building, cutting, copying letters).

In summary, it is apparent that each of the four components of DIAL—gross motor, fine motor, concepts, and communication skills—contributes to a discrimination among the age groups. What is interesting to note is that, of the optimal set of variables (18 of 28), movement tasks contribute more than nonmovement tasks and the inclusion of separate gross and fine motor components is sound.

The notion, in DIAL, that communication skills are of much greater educational significance than other components of development is not supported by the data. Because of the greater disparity of performance between the sexes among items in the nonmotor components, there seems to be some justification for providing somewhat different test batteries for preschool boys and girls.

REFERENCES

Allen, E. K., & Goetz, E. M. (1982). *Early childhood education*. Rockville, MD: Aspen Systems Corp.

Barnes, K. E. (1982). *Preschool screening: The measurement and prediction of children at-risk*. Springfield, IL: Charles C Thomas.

Bayley, N. A. (1969). *Manual for Bayley Scales of Infant Development*. New York: Psychological Corporation.

Bloom, B. S., Davis, A., & Hess, R. (1965). *Compensatory education in cultural deprivation*. New York: Holt, Rinehart, & Winston.

Bluma, S. M., Shearer, M. S., Frohman, A. H., & Hilliard, J. M. (1976a). *Portage Guide to Early Education: Manual*. Portage, WI: Cooperative Educational Service Agency 12.

Bluma, S. M., Shearer, M. S., Frohman, A. H., & Hilliard, J. M. (1976b). *Portage Guide to Early Education: Checklist*. Portage, WI: Cooperative Educational Service Agency 12.

Broadhead, G. D., & Church, G. E. (1985). Movement characteristics of preschoolers. *Reseach Quarterly for Exercise and Sport, 56*, 208–214.

Chazan, M. (Ed.). (1973). *Compensatory education*. London: Butterworths.

Docherty, E. M. (1983). The DIAL: Preschool screening for learning problems. *The Journal of Special Education, 17*, 195–202.

Frankenburg, W. K., & Dodds, J. B. (1967). The Denver Developmental Screening Test. *Journal of Pediatrics, 71*, 181–191.

Gesell, A. (1940). *The first five years of life: A guide to the study of the preschool child*. New York: Harper.

Hall, J., Mardell, C., Wick, J., & Goldenberg, D. (1974). *Further development and refinement of DIAL: Final report.* Springfield, IL: Office of the Superintendent of Public Instruction.

Kerlinger, F. N., & Pedhazur, E. J. (1973). *Multiple regression in behavioral research.* New York: Holt, Rinehart, & Winston.

Klecka, W. R. (1980). *Discriminant analysis.* Sage University Paper series Quantitative Applications in the Social Sciences (series no. 07-019). Beverly Hills, CA: Sage Publications.

LeMay, D. W., Griffin, P. M., & Sanford, A. R. (1977). *Learning Accomplishment Profile: Examiner's manual (Diagnostic ed.).* Winston Salem, NC: Kaplan Press.

Lorton, J. W., & Walley, B. L. (1979). *Introduction to early childhood education.* New York: Van Nostrand.

Louisiana Legislature. (1977). *Education of All Exceptional Children, Act 754.*

Louisiana State Department of Education. (1978). Education of All Exceptional Children, Act 754 Regulations.

Mardell, C. K., & Goldenberg, D. S. (1975). *Manual for the Developmental Indicators for the Assessment of Learning.* Elmer, NJ: Childcraft Education Corporation.

Payne, J. S., Mercer, C. D., Payne, R. A., & Davison, R. G. (1973). *Head Start: A tragicomedy with epilogue.* New York: Behavioral Publications.

Pringle, M. L. K. (1965). *Deprivation and education.* London: Longmans.

Sanford, A. R. (1970). *The Learning Accomplishment Profile.* Winston Salem, NC: Kaplan Press.

Spodek, B. (1982). Early childhood education: A synoptic view. In N. Nir-Janiv, B. Spodek, & D. Steg (Eds.). *Early childhood education: An international perspective* (pp. 1–13). New York: Plenum Press.

SPSS, Inc. (1983). *SPSS^x user's guide.* Chicago: Author.

Stanley, J. E. (Ed.). (1972). *Preschool programs for the disadvantaged: Five experimental aproaches to early childhood education.* Baltimore, MD: The Johns Hopkins University Press.

Thorndike, R. M. (1978). *Correlational procedures in research.* New York: Gardner Press.

Toussaint, G. T. (1974). Bibliography on estimation of misclassification. *IEEE Transactions on Information Theory, IT-20,* 472–479.

Travers, J. R., & Light, R. J. (Eds.) (1982). *Learning from experience: Evaluating early childhood demonstration programs.* Washington, D.C.: National Academy Press.

United States Congress. (1975). *The Education for All Handicapped Children Act (Public Law 94–142).*

United States Department of Health, Education, & Welfare, Office of Education. (1977). Education of Handicapped Children: Implementation of Part B of the Education of the Handicapped Act. *Federal Register, Part II,* August 23.

Uzgiris, I. C., & Hunt, J. M. (1975). *Assessment in infancy: Ordinal scales of psychological development.* Urbana, IL: University of Illinois Press.

Westinghouse Learning Corporation, & Ohio University. (1979). *The impact of Head Start: An evaluation of the effect of the Head Start on children's cognitive and affective development. Executive summary.* Washington, D.C.: Clearinghouse for Federal Scientific & Technical Information. Report to the U.S. Office of Economic Opportunity (EDO 36321)

Weikart, D. P., Bond, J. T., & McNeil, J. (1978). *Ypsilanti Perry Preschool Project: Preschool years and longitudinal results through fourth grade. Monograph No. 3.* Ypsilanti, MI: High/Scope Educational Research Foundation.

Weikart, D. P., Deloria, D. J., Lawser, S. A., & Wiegerink, R. (1970). *Longitudinal results of the Perry Preschool Project. Monograph No. 1.* Ypsilanti, MI: High/Scope Educational Research Foundation.

Wick, J. (1973). *Validation and normative study of the DIAL battery.* Springfield, IL: Office of the Superintendent of Public Instruction.

Zigler, E., & Valentine, J. (Eds.). (1979). *Project Head Start: A legacy of the war on poverty.* New York: The Free Press.

REVIEW SECTION

9

THE WEAVER'S LOOM: A DEVELOPMENTAL METAPHOR

Mary Ann Roberton
University of Wisconsin

ABSTRACT

Persistent in the motor development literature is the metaphor of the weaver's loom. Movement of the loom is used to describe the interweaving between processes of development, between parts of a motor pattern, and even across parts of the body. In like fashion, it may be time for the subdisciplines of motor control/learning, motor development, and sport psychology to attend to the potential for interweaving their ideas and methods. We could more frequently integrate 1) the action systems we study, 2) the methods we use for research, 3) our levels of analysis, and 4) the ideas or paradigms with which we deal. Even with the benefits of this interweaving, the uniqueness of motor development will always be the perspective *from which it views behavior. To developmentalists, present behavior is only "interesting" as a way station or temporary pause in the process of change.*

As a developmentalist, I would like to encourage more frequent integration of the subdisciplines of motor development, motor learning/control, and sport psychology. At the same time, I value the uniqueness of each area; so, I am proposing "integration" but not "obliteration" (see Thomas, in press, for a different view). Each subdiscipline has much to contribute on its own; yet, each could learn from the other two areas.

Motor development may be the oldest of these three areas. It had an official start in the 1800s with the famous "baby biographers," such as Darwin (1877) and Shinn (1900), and unofficial starts as far back as Pestalozzi's observations of his son in 1774 (Irwin & Bushnell, 1980). Despite such early beginnings, motor development is still the least understood and, possibly, the least studied of the three areas. Perhaps for this reason, changes in the thinking of its scholars have come slowly. Equally slow to change have been perceptions of the field on the part of those outside it. Early doomed to be the polar opposite of "learning" in that infamous dichotomy, "maturation vs learning" or "development vs learning," motor development has yet to shake its nativistic connotations and its traditional association with the study of children.

Yet, I bear good news. Motor development is not just about kids anymore! Those who study motor development are discovering what their parent field of developmental psychology has already discovered (Bayley, 1963). The old end point of development, known as "maturity," does not really exist. As long as there is life, there is change. As long as there is change, there is development. Indeed, development *is* lifelong change.

For this reason, then, the study of motor development is now defined as the attempt to describe and explain life span change in motor behavior (Halverson, 1978). The breadth of this definition means that those who study motor development are *no longer constrained to study only those phenomena defined a priori as caused by "maturation."* (Indeed, I had always wondered: if we already knew what caused development, then why did we study it?) Freedom from this constraint has already breathed new vigor into the study of motor development. Studies of adulthood, studies of aging, and—dare I say it?—studies of learning can now all fall under the rubric of "development."

In addition to allowing a broader content for study, the breadth of this definition also demands the use of a greater variety of research methods. Since realizing that their focus is *change* rather than *children*, some motor development specialists have already started to integrate method and content from other perspectives on motor behavior. Hopefully, this paper will promote even more sharing of these perspectives.

In what sense, then, does motor development still differ from motor control, motor learning, and sport psychology? It seems that now we are *all* trying to explain why people behave as they do! The basic difference is simply the *perspective* from which we view the phenomena in question. The developmentalist always studies behavioral content at any point in the life span using three questions: 1) what is the behavior like now, and why? 2) what was it like before, and why? and 3) how is it going to change in the future, and why? Question one is no different, I would imagine, from what the motor control specialist or the sport psychologist asks. The developmental specialist, however, asks question one with questions two and three also in mind. Present behavior is always related to past behavior and to future behavior. Present behavior is *only* "interesting" as a way station or temporary pause in the process of change.

Given these definitions and distinctions, what are examples of the integration of perspectives already occurring today, or what would I urge should occur even more frequently in the future? I have organized these examples into four areas: I believe we should more frequently integrate 1) the action systems we study, 2) the methods we use for research, 3) our levels of analysis, and most importantly, 4) the ideas or paradigms with which we deal.

ACTION SYSTEMS

Scientists have frequently talked about the "whole child" or the whole person; yet, in order to study that person we have always had to divide him/her into artificial and arbitrary sections, like the distinction between perceptual and motor systems, or cognitive and affective systems. Of course, the motor development of individuals depends on or is *intertwined with* their perceptual, cognitive, affective, and whatever-else-selves. Of course, all scholars believe we are "whole persons;" our research simply has not stressed this perspective enough.

Let me cite examples of how the action systems studied by motor development and sport psychology interrelate. I would hypothesize that, ultimately, how or what one feels about one's self—one's self-concept, if you will—may be the key factor in determining one's willingness to try new motor skills or to experience new movement situations. Similarly, one's success or satisfaction in performing those same skills feeds back into one's confidence-in-movement. I cannot help but believe that competent movers are confident movers and confident movers will gain competence.

One motor development specialist who has been exploring this relationship is Jack Keogh. He and Norma Sue Griffin (Crawford & Griffin, 1986; Griffin & Keogh, 1982) have presented a series of pilot studies directed toward ultimately being able to evaluate children's movement confidence or feelings of adequacy in a movement situation. They hypothesized that movement confidence influences whether youngsters choose to participate in motor activities, how they perform given they do choose to participate, and whether they will persist in that participation. Each of these affective variables is theoretically an important factor in determining a child's degree of motor development progress. Feelings of confidence and self-esteem also appear as important variables in the work of Tara Scanlan (1977, 1979; Scanlan & Passer, 1980) on children's perceptions of youth sport competition.

I cannot help but believe that movement confidence is also a critical variable to study across the life span. One of my most daredevil and skillful friends (now 40) announced to me that she had purposely gone down some particularly treacherous, cross-country ski paths last winter—on her seat—having stood at the top of the ravine and thought, "I'm getting too old for this." Or, I think of some of my elderly friends whose bodies simply are no longer trustworthy. How their deteriorating motor development affects their own feelings of self-worth and competence seems a critical and fruitful area of inquiry.

A last example of how questions typically associated with sport psychology can be intertwined with questions of interest in motor development comes from the provocative work of Solomons (1980). After a formal assessment of fifth-graders' throwing and catching abilities, she formed four-person teams which combined high-ability girls with low-ability boys and high-ability boys with low-ability girls. She then placed the teams in a competitive game which stressed individual catching and forceful, accurate throwing. She found that the high-ability girls voluntarily gave away twice as many chances to score as the high-ability boys, while receiving half as many passes as the high-ability boys. In fact, girls who were the second highest ability players on their teams received fewer passes than boys who were the lowest-ability players.

While the implications about gender bias are obvious in this study, what I would like to stress is the implication that children in the same game/practice situation did not receive the same practice on their motor skills, in this case because of the perceptions of their team/playmates. Clearly, this fact has tremendous importance when we try to understand why individuals differ in their motor development even though their environments *appear* similar.

Psychology and motor behavior are intertwined. Motor development specialists need to include psychological variables in their studies more frequently. Likewise, I would like to see sport psychologists include motor development variables more often.

METHODS

In addition to integrating the action systems that we study, we can also speak of integrating the methods we use to study these systems. In a very real sense, despite our differing paradigms (Reese & Overton, 1970), the key difference between motor development and motor learning has been in the methodological approaches we have taken. Let me suggest that many of the historical battles (Bijou & Baer, 1961; Gesell, 1946; McGraw, 1935/1975; Russell, 1957; Spiker, 1966; Stevenson, 1983; Watson, 1919) between developmental psychology (read: motor development) and experimental psychology (read: motor learning) were mainly artifacts of the methods used. The experimentalists manipulated the environment with great care; they studied the organism's responses with less care and, lo and behold, they discovered that the *environment* controlled the organism. The developmentalists studied the organism in its natural environment with great detail; they made little attempt to manipulate that environment and, lo and behold, they discovered that the *environment had no effect* on the organism. We indeed see what our methodologies condition us to see.

Yet, the great strength of motor development research is the care which has gone into providing detailed descriptions of the observable changes that occur in motor behavior over time. The field is often criticized for being overly descriptive. A more valid criticism of motor development research is that it has only described the organism. What we developmentalists have forgotten to do is to provide an equally careful and detailed description of the environment surrounding that moving organism.

Clearly, from this perspective, research in motor learning or control has suffered from the reverse problem. The environmental manipulations have been carefully performed and measured. The moving organism has been only perfunctorily examined or has been constrained so it is hardly moving at all. I will never forget one of our top motor control specialists saying to me, "But, Mary Ann, what difference does it make if the wrist goes this way (showing flexion) or this way (showing extension)?" Somehow, he had never considered that the *movement* of the moving organism was of interest; that it was a window on the nervous system and the result of all forces acting on the body. How could we *not* care whether the wrist went "this way" or "that?" Yet, many in motor behavior have not cared.

Clearly, one of the first methodological integrations that we developmentalists should perform in our study of motor behavior is to combine our descriptions of the moving organism with a careful assessment and, preferably, manipulation of the environment. Let me briefly describe the first of a series of studies in which I am trying to do just that (Roberton, 1987). I filmed 22 children throwing 1) for force with no specific target, 2) at a stationary target which did not change position across trials, 3) at a stationary target which did change position across trials, and 4) at a moving target which, in addition to moving, changed pathway across trials. The children (mean age 5.6 yrs) performed 20 throws each, five in each condition. After the filming I used the films to assess their developmental levels using the developmental sequences for throwing that I had previously validated over the last several years using traditional motor development procedures (Roberton, 1977, 1978; Roberton & Langendorfer, 1980). The category data were subjected to a Friedman two-way ANOVA (subjects $\times$ conditions). This analysis indicated that the mean developmental levels did not differ across the environmental conditions for any of the body components studied (stepping action, action of the humerus, action of the forearm, pelvic-spinal action) ($p > .05$). In other words, the changing environment had no effect on the children's movement as a total group. Further analysis of individual children, however, suggested that the developmental level exhibited by a child when throwing for force alone determined whether that child would change developmental levels as the environment became more complex. Primitive throwers were not responsive to the environment; intermediate throwers were. These findings held true regardless of the child's age. These data suggested, therefore, the validity of that old developmental truism: Change occurs due to the *interaction* of the organism and its environment. Perhaps the organism, in this case a child, must reach a certain level of competence before it can be responsive to a changing environment.

Although this study represents only a preliminary look at environment-organism interactions, it does represent a study which employs rather traditional "motor learning," independent variables with rather traditional "motor development" dependent variables. Indeed, the original source for the independent variables is the motor task taxonomy proposed by Gentile, Higgins, Miller, and Rosen (1975). By combining methodologies from both fields, I am hoping to see phenomena, such as the interaction of organism and environment, that neither field could see alone.

Combining the experimental and descriptive approaches is what gave ethology such powerful tools and such compelling results (see, for example, Hinde, 1983). I strongly feel the ethological approach, which emphasizes describing behavior in its natural setting while systematically manipulating that setting, could be a powerful tool in motor behavior research (Roberton, in press).

LEVELS OF ANALYSIS

A third integration that comes to mind is, again, a methodological one, one to which we usually refer as a level-of-analysis difference. Development has recognized for years that there are many ways to measure motor behavior; yet, it has stayed with its traditional inclination to measure so-called products of the behavior—where balls went or how fast they travelled to get there—or scores on motor proficiency tests, such as the now popular Bruininks-Oseretsky Test of Motor Proficiency (Bruininks, 1978). Also popular with developmental researchers has been the tendency to describe what the movement that produced the product looked like. Usually this description is carefully done, with considerable attention to timing and spatial relationships occurring in the movement.

What the movement looks like can be measured on finer scales, however; it is time we began to employ those scales, instead of or along with our more traditional measures. For instance, kinematics, kinetics, and electromyography are tools that motor development specialists can borrow from biomechanics to study the phenomena of changing motor behavior. It is of more than passing interest to note that motor control specialists are borrowing these same tools (Kelso, Southard, & Goodman, 1979; Shapiro, Zernicke, Gregor, & Diestel, 1981). They are rediscovering the value of describing the movements of their subjects. Motor development is discovering the need for finer-grained analyses of the movements that it has historically described.

A caveat is in order here: The questions which one can ask at each level of measurement or analysis are slightly different. A continuing reduction to a finer level may not necessarily reveal the answers to questions asked at other levels. On more than one occasion I have recently seen kinematic analyses collapsed back into verbal description in order to see and communicate the developmental sequences apparent in the data (see, for instance, Clark, Phillips, & Boyer, 1983). On the other hand, one can argue the old "the whole is greater than the sum of its parts" adage well beyond usefulness. The logical solution, until we know better, would be for motor behavior scholars to take multiple dependent measures at different levels of analysis, whenever they are able to do so.

IDEAS OR PARADIGMS

Finally, I would like to discuss how the ideas of the different subdisciplines might be integrated. Let me begin with what the motor control area sometimes refers to as the "phenomenon of constancy" (Turvey, 1974). Simply put, this is the observation that the same motor product can be produced by dissimilar muscle/limb patterns. This observation, coupled of course with many others, has led to the notion that a motor control system has a set of rules which are held in memory or form a "deep structure" for the production of movements. It is these rules which are drawn upon to produce a given movement rather than specific, held-in-memory orders for specific muscles. Thus, sentences written by hand, foot, or mouth are supposed to be similar in spatial-temporal characteristics even though the same muscles did not produce the product.

On the whole, the notion of "rules" or "deep structures" for generating movements is quite appealing. I do wonder, however, about the empirical observations of movement constancy. First of all, I wish motor control specialists would think of another example of movement constancy—handwriting is a little overused! More importantly, this apparent phenomenon is often used to criticize those motor development researchers who laboriously describe the limb actions characteristic of specific skills. Obviously, this is a nonsense task if "a required result can be attained by an indefinitely large class of movement patterns" (Turvey, 1974, p. 309). What seems to be ignored, however, is the fact that although the body may be able to generalize a set of rules across limbs and to do the same task "another way," *under normal circumstances it does not do so*. The common motor patterns seen across individuals and the predictable, sequential changes in these patterns suggest that the *system has preferred ways of moving*. Motor control theories need to acknowledge these system preferences; motor development theories, on the other hand, need to acknowledge the variability possible in the system.

A second motor behavior problem for which we could pool our knowledge is the so-called "degrees of freedom" problem presented by Bernstein (1967).

This is basically the question of how a multilink system, such as the human skeleton, with many movement possibilities at each joint, can be controlled. Several motor control theorists, in addition to Bernstein, have argued very persuasively that muscle groups must somehow be constrained to act together as collectives or functional units or "coordinative structures" (Kelso, Holt, Kugler, & Turvey, 1980). Easton (1972) has argued that postural reflexes and, perhaps, even the so-called "primitive" reflexes may be the constraining or "coordinative structures." Most of this discussion, however, is theoretical with little empirical data generated thus far.

It strikes me that motor development's descriptive research contains considerable evidence for how the body solves the degrees of freedom problem. Indeed, as Bernstein (1967) implied, the degrees of freedom question is really a developmental question of the first order. For instance, the humerus at the shoulder joint is capable of medial/lateral rotation, flexion/extension, abduction/adduction, horizontal abduction/adduction . . . and all the combinations. Over which of these actions does the child gain first control? Which comes next? Given that information, we would at least know what the system does to answer the problem; knowing that, we might better be able to analyze *how* the system comes up with the answer that it does.

First of all, the answer is probably task-specific. Indeed, Kelso, Tuller, Vatikiotis-Bateson, and Fowler (1984) defined a coordinative structure as a task-specific functional unit. In the overarm throw, for instance, the shoulder degrees of freedom problem is solved by the advanced performer in this way: he/she omits almost all the movement possibilities at the shoulder joint when throwing, thus greatly reducing the degrees of freedom. The only movement that occurs at the shoulder is lateral, then medial rotation. The performer stabilizes the humerus at 90° of abduction so it becomes an extension of the rotating shoulders. Neither horizontal adduction nor flexion occur (Roberton, 1977, 1978).

By examining the developmental sequence that precedes this advanced action (Roberton & Langendorfer, 1980), we could begin to understand how beginners cope with the same degrees of freedom problem. For instance, primitive throwers cannot stabilize against the forward/backward nor the up/down possibilities for movement at this joint. They cope by omitting lateral/medial rotation, the very movements the advanced performer uses and move through paths created by the other two planes. Intermediate performers are able to stabilize against the up/down possibilities by assuming the fixed 90° of abduction. They cannot yet resist against forward movement (i.e., horizontal adduction). Some lateral rotation may also begin to occur, but they are unable to time the rotation in relation to their position in space. Finally, they are able to resist forward movement of the humerus as well as abduction so that the limb is locked in place. Even then they still may not be able to time the lateral rotation, which is the last thing to occur in the development of humerus action within the throw for force.

Though sketchy, this analysis indicates grossly how the degrees of freedom problem is handled over time at this one joint in this one skill. The sequence is robust: most people pass through it (Roberton, 1977; 1978; Roberton & Langendorfer, 1980), so it clearly could have important implications. What rules could we generate from this description for how the body has developmentally handled the problem? Would these rules generalize to other skills or body joints? Do these rules suggest cognitive processes, such as schemas (Schmidt, 1976), or do they reflect dynamic relationships characteristic of systems, such as mass-springs (Tuller, Turvey, & Fitch, 1982)?

Many sequences for other joint actions and skills are available in the motor development literature. They could be a goldmine for motor control specialists interested in the degrees of freedom problem. Similarly, I am suggesting that the motor development specialists who are generating these sequences ought to pay attention to the degrees of freedom issue and to other issues like it, which are addressing fundamental questions about motor control.

Lastly, and most briefly, I would like to suggest that both motor control and motor development could profit from the perspectives of ecological psychology, as espoused by Gibson (1979). Here, I believe, is an instance where both of our perspectives could use the freshness of his approach to the organism-environment relationship. The approach is fresh because it presents a new metaphor for our consideration. Rather than modeling development after the embryo (which is the pervasive model in motor development) or modeling control after the machine (the computer is the pervasive model in motor control), Gibson suggests we look to ecology and the ever evolving mutuality between species and their environment or ecological niche. The "environment" of an animal is only that specific aspect which provides information which the animal has evolved to find meaningful. Certain configurations of shapes, apertures, and edges signal them "dangerous or safe," "jump-on-able" or not, "step-over-able" or not. Since the animal evolved with its environment, the synergy may require little in the way of intervening variables, such as programs or schemas (Kugler, Kelso, & Turvey, 1982).

So much motor control research, especially in the information processing paradigm, seems to be describing what the organism can do under unusual circumstances. There is no question that we seem to act like information processors in these experiments. The real question is do we always act this way or is there a more "natural" connection between our motor systems and the environment? Ecological psychology suggests there is.

So much motor development research focuses on the organism with no regard for the environment, or gives lip service to the notion of organism-environment interactions, but never investigates them. Ecological psychology would suggest that the *only* topic for study is the organism-in-its-natural-environment, since the two are really one thing. Gibsonian psychology, in a very real sense, is finally breaking down that other false dichotomy: the organism vs the environment.

While the ecological approach is legitimately criticized for being difficult to test empirically, it has produced some simple but elegant experiments in both animals and humans. Our tendency to duck or draw back when an object in the visual field expands rapidly is shared with fiddler crabs and chicks (Schiff, 1965). Even the postural sway of our bodies is finely tuned to our visual field (Lee & Thomson, 1982).

Although models and metaphors come and go in the history of science, they can be very powerful heuristic devices or they can be blinders about our eyes. Gibson's metaphor of ecology may be just the heuristic device to push motor behavior into a most rewarding direction.

THE WEAVER'S LOOM

So what has all this to do with the title of this paper, "The weaver's loom: a developmental metaphor"? As I mentioned earlier, the pervasive model in development is the developing embryo, passing through stages, showing differentiation of cells and hierarchical ordering of systems. Less noticed, but almost as ubiquitous, is the metaphor of the weaver's loom:

> It is natural that the metaphor of the loom should constantly reappear in the description and interpretation of the developmental process. The products of growth are envisioned as a fabric in which threads and designs are visible. . . . this process [of reciprocal interweaving] implies an intricate cross-stitching or involuted interlacing which organizes opposing muscle systems into reciprocal and increasingly mature relationships. (Gesell, 1946, p. 302)

We find the same analogy in the writings of Myrtle McGraw (1935/1975):

> Development works back and forth, yet steadily forward; here and there it strikes rapids, in other spots it pauses or regresses. . . . It is a gradual twining and interweaving of movements and phases of developing patterns which make it difficult to allocate the rhythms and spurts of growth. (pp. 305–306)

On a more contemporary note, even Roberton and Langendorfer (1980) unconsciously described the developmental relationship of body components as an "interweaving" of developmental steps across the body. The loom is a comfortable metaphor in the face of the exquisite regularity and interpatterning of motor development.

What I have tried to suggest in this paper is that the ideas, the methods, and action systems we study could be more greatly interwoven across our subdisciplines. The weaver's loom is an appropriate analogy for the back and forth sharing of ideas that could enrich our mutual study. Hopefully, the resulting fabric formed of our joint knowledge will be a stronger, more vibrant, and heuristic approach to the study of motor behavior.

REFERENCES

Bayley, N. (1963). The lifespan as a frame of reference in psychological research. *Vita Humana, 6*, 125–139.

Bernstein, N. (1967). *The co-ordination and regulation of movements.* Oxford, England: Pergamon.

Bijou, S., & Baer, D. (1961). *Child development. Vol. 1. A systematic and empirical theory.* New York: Appleton-Century-Crofts.

Bruininks, R. (1978). *The Bruininks-Oseretsky test of motor proficiency.* Circle Pines, MN: American Guidance Service.

Clark, J., Phillips, S., & Boyer, J. (1983). Temporal characteristics of infant gait across speeds. *Psychology of motor behavior and sport—1983.* Abstracts of the Annual Conference of the North American Society for the Psychology of Motor Behavior and Sport and the Canadian Society for Psychomotor Learning and Sport Psychology. Michigan State University.

Crawford, M., & Griffin, N. S. (1986). Testing the validity of the Griffin/Keogh model for movement confidence by analyzing self-report playground involvement decisions of elementary school children. *Research Quarterly for Exercise and Sport, 57*, 8–15.

Darwin, C. (1877). A biographical sketch of an infant. *Mind, 2*, 285–294.

Easton, T. A. (1972). On the normal use of reflexes. *American Scientist, 60*, 591–599.

Gentile, A., Higgins, J., Miller, E., & Rosen, B. (1975). The structure of motor tasks. In C. Bard (Ed.), *Mouvement* (pp. 11–28). Actes du 7 symposium en apprentissage psycho-moteur et psychologie du sport.

Gesell, A. (1946). The ontogenesis of infant behavior. In L. Carmichael (Ed.), *Manual of child psychology* (pp. 295–331). New York: Wiley.

Gibson, J. J. (1979). *The ecological approach to visual perception.* Boston: Houghton Mifflin.

Griffin, N. S., & Keogh, J. (1982). A model of movement confidence. In J. A. S. Kelso & J. E. Clark (Eds.), *The development of movement control and co-ordination* (pp. 213–236). New York: Wiley.

Halverson, L. E. (1978). *Motor development.* Unpublished application for academy status in the National Association for Sport and Physical Education, American Association for Health, Physical Education, Recreation, and Dance, Reston, VA.

Hinde, R. (1983). Ethology and child development. In P. Mussen (Ed.), *Handbook of child psychology* (Vol. II, 4th ed., pp. 27–93). New Yok: Wiley.

Irwin, D. M., & Bushnell, M. M. (1980). *Observational strategies for child study.* New York: Holt, Rinehart, & Winston.

Kelso, J. A. S., Holt, K. G., Kugler, P., & Turvey, M. (1980). On the concept of coordinative structures as dissipative structures: II. Empirical lines of convergence. In G. Stelmach & J. Requin (Eds.), *Tutorials in motor behavior* (pp. 49–70). New York: North Holland.

Kelso, J. A. S., Southard, D. L., & Goodman, D. (1979). On the nature of human interlimb coordination. *Science, 203*, 1029–1031.

Kelso, J. A. S., Tuller, B., Vatikiotis-Bateson, E., & Fowler, C. (1984). Functionally specific articulatory cooperation following jaw perturbations during speech: Evidence for coordinative structures. *Journal of Experimental Psychology: Human Perception and Performance, 10*, 812–832.

Kugler, P., Kelso, J. A. S., & Turvey, M. (1982). On the control and co-ordination of naturally developing systems. In J. A. S. Kelso & J. E. Clark (Eds.), *The development of movement control and co-ordination* (pp. 5–78). New York: Wiley.

Lee, D., & Thomson, J. (1982). Vision in action: The control of locomotion. In D. Ingle (Ed.), *Analysis of visual behavior* (pp. 411–433). Cambridge, MA: MIT Press.

McGraw, M. (1975). *Growth, A study of Johnny and Jimmy.* New York: Arno. (Original work published 1935.)

Reese, H., & Overton, W. (1970). Models of development and theories of development. In L. R. Goulet & P. Baltes (Eds.), *Life-span developmental psychology: Research and theory* (pp. 115–145). New York: Academic Press.

Roberton, M. A. (1977). Stability of stage categorizations across trials: Implications for the "stage theory" of overarm throw development. *Journal of Human Movement Studies, 3*, 49–59.

Roberton, M. A. (1978). Longitudinal evidence for developmental stages in the forceful overarm throw. *Journal of Human Movement Studies, 4*, 167–175.

Roberton, M. A. (1987). Developmental level as a function of the immediate environment. In J. E. Clark & J. H. Humphrey (Eds.), *Advances in Motor Development Research* (Vol. 1) (pp. 1–15). New York: AMS Press.

Roberton, M. A. (in press). Future directions in motor development research: Applied aspects. In J. Skinner (Ed.), *Future directions in sport and exercise research.* Champaign, IL: Human Kinetics.

Roberton, M. A., & Langendorfer, S. (1980). Testing motor development sequences across 9–14 years. In C. Nadeau, W. Halliwell, K. Newell, & G. Roberts (Eds.), *Psychology of motor behavior and sport—1979* (pp. 269–279). Champaign, IL: Human Kinetics.

Russell, W. (1957). An experimental psychology of development: Pipe dream or possibility? In D. Harris (Ed.), *The concept of development* (pp. 162–174). Minneapolis: The University of Minnesota Press.

Scanlan, T. (1977). The effects of success-failure on the perception of threat in a competitive situation. *Research Quarterly, 48*, 144–153.

Scanlan, T. (1979). Sources of competitive stress in young female athletes. *Journal of Sport Psychology, 1*, 151–159.

Scanlan, T., & Passer, M. (1980). Anxiety-inducing factors in competitive youth sports. In F. Smoll & R. Smith (Eds.), *Psychological perspectives in youth sports* (pp. 105–122). New York: Halsted.

Schiff, W. (1965). Perception of impending collision: A study of visually directed avoidant behavior. *Psychological Monographs, 79*, 1–26.

Schmidt, R. (1976). The schema as a solution to some persistent problems in motor learning theory. In G. E. Stelmach (Ed.), *Motor control: Issues and trends* (pp. 41–65). New York: Academic Press.

Shapiro, D., Zernicke, R., Gregor, R., & Diestel, J. (1981). Evidence for generalized motor programs using gait pattern analysis. *Journal of Motor Behavior, 13*, 33–47.

Shinn, M. (1900). *The biography of a baby.* New York: Houghton Mifflin.

Solomons, H. (1980). Sex role mediation of achievement behaviors and interpersonal interactions in sex-integrated team games. In E. Pepitone (Ed.), *Children in cooperation and competition* (pp. 321–364). Lexington, MA: Heath.

Spiker, C. (1966). The concept of development: Relevant and irrelevant issues. *Monographs of the Society for Research in Child Development, 31*, 40–54.

Stevenson, H. (1983). How children learn–The quest for theory. In P. Mussen (Ed.), *Handbook of child psychology: Vol. I. History, theory, and methods* (4th ed., pp. 213–236). New York: Wiley.

Thomas, J. (in press). As children get older, motor performance gets better: The question is why? In J. Skinner (Ed.), *Future directions in sport and exercise research*. Champaign, IL: Human Kinetics.

Tuller, B., Turvey, M., & Fitch, H. (1982). The Bernstein perspective: II. The concept of muscle linkage or coordinative structure. In J. A. S. Kelso (Ed.), *Human motor behavior: An introduction* (pp. 253–270). Hillsdale, NJ: Erlbaum.

Turvey, M. T. (1974). A note on the relation between action and perception. In M. Wade & R. Martens (Eds.), *Psychology of motor behavior and sport—1973* (pp. 307–313). Champaign, IL: Human Kinetics.

Watson, J. B. (1919). *Psychology from the standpoint of a behaviorist*. Philadelphia: Lippincott.

AUTHOR NOTE

A previous version of this paper was presented at the R. Tait McKenzie Sympoisum, University of Tennessee, Knoxville, May, 1984.

10.

THE DEVELOPMENT OF VISUALLY DIRECTED REACHING: FROM DESCRIPTION TO EXPLANATION

Jill Whitall
University of Maryland

ABSTRACT

The development of visually directed reaching has been studied extensively for over half a century. Early work described the changes in overt behavior while more recent research has focused on the underlying mechanisms of reaching development. In the first half of this paper, the trend from description to explanation is laid out chronologically with reference to seminal papers. The second half of the paper begins with an examination of the three phases of reaching: prereaching behaviors, early successful reaching, and skillful reaching. This three-phase framework is subsequently discussed in relation to current theoretical perspectives on motor behavior and future directions for research are offered.

Visually directed reaching is one of the most prominent developments during the infant's first half-year of life. The neonate is born exhibiting what appear to be random spontaneous movements and rather more stereotypic reflexive movements. Gradually these neonatal movements give way to voluntarily controlled movement manifested in reaching for objects within the field of vision. Such a significant change in behavior has interested many researchers for well over half a century. Apart from technological advances which generally have refined the observations, the last 50 years have seen a shift from studies which attempt to describe to studies designed to elucidate the mechanisms underlying the development of visually directed reaching. This change in purpose is a natural trend in scientific research (Wohlwill, 1973). In the present paper, this trend will be described and explored in an attempt to understand where we have been and where we might be going in our understanding of visually directed reaching.

The paper is divided into four sections. The first reviews a few early descriptive studies (1931–1964), which were typically longitudinal in nature and involved measuring the overt changes in behavior of infants in a qualitative way. Investigators during this era moved from a maturationist to an interactionist position concerning the origin of the observed behaviors, but there was little attempt to determine what mechanisms were underlying the interactive process or the exact nature of the interaction.

The second section begins with experimental cross-sectional studies conducted within a short time span (1970–1974). These are seen as the watershed between the earlier descriptive studies and the newer, more explanatory approach which evolved to infer the processes or mechanisms underlying the development of visually directed reaching. These early 1970s studies essentially challenged the prevailing belief that the sensory and motor systems are separate at birth, and consequently, subsequent research attempted to replicate and/or refute the first experimental studies. An examination of these replicated studies (1976–1982) concludes the second section.

Section three attempts to reconcile the extant work in the area and reviews some of the most recent studies (1975–1985). This section starts with the neonate and proceeds chronologically through the first year of life. All of the studies here may be characterized by a concern not only with underlying processes but in accurately quantifying behavior. The methodology used ranges from an experimental/manipulative to a descriptive/ecologically valid approach.

Finally, in section four, a heuristic framework for the study of visually directed reaching is assembled. In the light of current conceptualizations of development, the framework is discussed as a potential tool for directing future research.

The Early Descriptive Period

The first period of research on visually directed reaching lasted from about 1931 to the late 1960s and was characterized by descriptions of reaching and grasping. Early studies in this period were conducted by Halverson (1931, 1933, 1937a, 1937b, 1937c). As an example of his work, Halverson (1933) filmed 8 infants, every month from 3 to 15 months of age as they were reaching for a pellet on a table top. Infants were supported when necessary. Halverson's purpose was to look at the infants' accuracy and error reductions over the time period. Briefly, Halverson formed three major conclusions. First, reaching movements were always characterized by lateral, zigzag movements which increased in frequency until the 6th month, after which they decreased in both frequency and amplitude to almost zero. Second, the accuracy of reaching increased slowly at first, then dramatically between the 5th and 7th month when all reaches were successful, before declining briefly at 12 months and finally increasing again. Third, Halverson found, as he predicted, that large muscle groups, such as those controlling the shoulder, tended to be more effective and thus under better control than smaller muscles, such as those controlling the digits and wrist. However, all body parts were equally effective by 10 months of age. In comparison with 5-year-olds and adults, Halverson concluded that a 15-month infant showed a mature form of reaching. The important point for our purposes here is to realize that Halverson implicitly assumed a "maturational" view of motor development, which implied an "unfolding" of abilities without regard to sensory inputs or environmental constraints. His concern was in describing the behavioral outcomes of the maturing neuromuscular system, descriptions which, for the most part, have not been refuted by more recent researchers.[1]

Two further examples of early descriptive research on visually directed reaching are Gesell and Ames (1947) and Piaget (1952). In both cases, their attention to the development of reaching appears to have been peripheral (White, Castle, & Held, 1964). Gesell and Ames looked at the development of visually directed reaching primarily for the purpose of identifying normative levels for various stages of reaching. In this regard, like Halverson, they assumed a maturational viewpoint for the development of motor abilities. Piaget, on the other hand, was interested in cognitive development. His descriptions of his 3 children's reaching was primarily to understand their cognition. Piaget, more than Gesell, however, stressed the importance of an interaction between child and environment as the key to the developmental process. Thus to Piaget an object as part of the environment was necessary to stimulate the construction of mental schemas from which responses were made. Piaget offered the underlying mechanisms of assimilation and accommodation to explain cognitive development. But these mental processes seem not to be intended for explaining the motor control of reaching. Thus, his work may be regarded as essentially providing yet another description of reaching. The Gesell and Ames, and Piaget observations are included here as examples of early work in the field; their actual contributions to the knowledge of visually directed reaching were the basis for the culminating descriptive study of this period, White, Castle, and Held (1964).

White et al. studied 34 normal, but institutionalized, infants during the first 6 months of their life. Infants were tested, every week, in a supine position using a 10 min. observation pretest and a 10 min. standardized test session. The latter consisted of using a "fringed, multicolored paper party toy" as a stimulus object to elicit visual pursuit, prehension, and grasping responses. From their analysis, the authors described a detailed normative developmental sequence categorized into eight stages of 2 weeks each. Significantly they found that subjects first exhibited object-oriented arm movements, i.e., swiping with fisted movements, at about 2 months of age. Unilateral arm responses decreased at 3 months in favor of bilateral patterns with hands clasped at the midline. At 4 months uni-lateral responses reappeared with the hand open and raised to the vicinity of the object. The infant then shifted his glance repeatedly from hand to object until the object was crudely grasped. Just prior to 5 months, the infants began to reach for and successfully grasp the test object in a fairly rapid motion.

It is interesting that the White et al. description of successful visually directed reaching revealed that it occurred 2 months earlier than Halverson had reported. This difference may be explained by the methodological differences between the two studies. Although one might suspect that supporting an infant as Halverson had done might assist the infant's reaching, the motivational effect of a bright and larger object, and/or the practice effects of weekly testing, as in the White et al. study, may have counteracted this advantage. Differing testing environments may well have affected the reaching response patterns. Indeed, White et al. are at pains to point out that as interactionists they believe that neurological growth is in large part critically dependent upon experience or some kind of informative contact with the environment.[2]

Like Piaget, White et al. recognized the importance of primitive sensory and motor schemas present at birth. The grasp reflex and a primitive form of visual pursuit were observed and postulated to be both innate and particularly relevant to the development of visually directed reaching.

In summary, by the mid 1960s, a complete description of the relevant pre-ceeding and the accompanying behaviors of visually directed reaching had been meticulously described. All of the studies were based on the same philosophical assumptions that sensory (mind) and motor (body) schemas are distinct at birth and that their development and ultimate coordination are a result of either ma-turation or an interaction between the environment and innate schemas. From either developmental perspective, the underlying processes of visually directed reaching had not been investigated.

EXPERIMENTAL STUDIES ON INTERSENSORY COORDINATION

The second period of research sharply differs from the earlier descriptive work in its emphasis on cross-sectional studies designed to infer the underlying mech-anisms of development. The early 1970s saw a wave of experimental studies challenge the prevailing belief in separate sensory and motor systems at birth. First, a claim was made that "reaches" were observable practically at birth. Bower, Broughton and Moore (1970a) presented five 1- to 2-week-old infants with a small sphere in five different positions. They reported that 70% of all extensions were within 1.5 cm of the ball regardless of the ball's position. Bower (1974) later reported that 40% of all extensions led to direct contact with the ball. The conclusion from this work would appear to be that infants have a primitive form of hand-eye coordination at a very early age.

Bower (1974) argued that such competencies displayed at birth can only be the consequence of pure growth since there is no psychological environment and no experience per se. A neonate enters a 3-dimensional world and yet the pattern of stimulation of the retina is only 2-dimensional. Does the infant learn through experience or can it already perceive the third dimension and consequently link vision with the sensing of touch?

Bower, Broughton, and Moore (1970b) tested this question in infants from 3 to 20 days old.[3] With the infants lying supine, they moved an object towards the face and found that the infants did not blink. Supposing the infants to be virtually asleep in this position, Bower held them upright and found they performed a coordinated defensive movement consisting of eyes opening wide, head moving back, and both hands coming up between the object and face. Air movement by itself produced a different response while 2-dimensional stimulation (i.e., film) still elicited the defense response. This sensory-motor reaction to a visual stimulus was assumed, by Bower, to have adaptive significance.

In a third experiment Bower, Broughton, and Moore (1970c) demonstrated visual-manual coordination in infants of 1 to 3 weeks. Using point source lamps, polaroid goggles and a screen, they projected a virtual image of an object within reaching distance of their infants. In time the infant brought his/her hand to the locus of such an object but, of course, the hand contacted nothing. All of the infants expressed surprise and distress at this event, which Bower inferred to mean that they had expected to feel a tangible object. These reactions were consistent up to 5 months of age.

These experiments are interesting because a neonate does not have good binocular vision, necessary for depth perception, until 3 to 4 months of age (Fox, Aslin, Shea, & Dumais, 1980). Von Hofsten (1977) confirms the importance of binocular convergence at later ages when he made a 4.5-month-old infants look through prisms which changed convergence only. The majority of reaches were clearly aimed at the position of the virtual object as specified by the new convergence. For younger infants, Bower (1974) argues that spatial position is specified largely by the expanding optical array consequent upon the approach of an object. This variable can be picked up by one eye as well as two and is independent of growth processes. The latter would demand a continuous adjustment of any representational structures involved in translating the visual information. Thus, the infant appears to be born with a primitive unity of the senses such that visual variables specifying tactile consequences is already built into the structure of the nervous system.

Further evidence for this primitive unity of the senses comes from Bruner and Koslowski (1972) who were looking for visually preadapted constituents of manipulatory action. Every 2 weeks, 10 infants from 2 to 5.5 months, were shown two balls, one at a time. Although both balls were within reach, one was of a graspable size, and the other was too large to grasp. Categories of behavior were coded while the infant was looking at the balls and the analysis included only those weeks before an infant was able to reach and grasp the smaller ball. As predicted, the infants were more likely to bring their hands to the midline and engage in manipulative-like action in the presence of the graspable rather than the nongraspable ball. Conversely, more swiping actions were recorded in the presence of the nongraspable ball. The authors concluded that grasping activity is coordinated with visual information about the graspability of an object, even before the infant has had experience in reaching. Thus, the frustration of the infants in the study by Bower et al. (1970c), when encountering a virtual object is accounted for by a violation of the preadapted coordination of visual and manipulatory space.

Finally, the work of Trevarthen (1974) is exemplary in trying to disprove the assumption of innate separate sensory and motor control mechanisms which have to be built up and then coordinated. Trevarthen argues that if space is "learned" by exploring it with locomotion, or reaching and touching, then infants should show signs of groping with limbs before they see space and they should, at first, have no eye movements or only random movements. However, by recording spontaneous displacements of the newborn's eyes, Trevarthen found conjugate saccades of varying length and direction produced in a regular scanning rhythm. Furthermore, the pattern of these saccades was almost indistinguishable from that of an adult scanning a field of visual information.

Trevarthen speculates that a prenatally established neural pacemaker determines oculomotor scan. Scanning itself does not necessarily imply perception, much less understanding, and Trevarthen admits that infants do not use the scanning well because the visual perception processes are still undifferentiated. However, he is an ardent advocator of a fundamental hand-eye coordination from the moment of birth. Using frame-by-frame analysis, he found a regular pattern of space-controlled form and definite temporal regularity in the arm movements of 1- to 2-week neonates *if* they were suitably supported. For example, directed finger extension and flexion, anticipating capture of the object, were coupled to arm extension and withdrawal, respectively. These "embryonic expressions of intention" (Trevarthen, 1974, p. 575) towards the object were rarely successful and this fact, one might speculate, is the reason why earlier researchers did not focus on their coordination. At 2 to 3 months, Trevarthen noticed a loss of fluency in the extension movements of the fingers, coupled with an increase in jerky arm extensions. He explained the loss of fluency by correlating it with the increase in growth and strength of the proximal segments. Finally, at 5 months a more controlled form of reaching was exhibited in which the timing of the arm movements was of a regular pattern and often precisely synchronized with head movements.

While the kind of evidence cited above was enough to convince many researchers that a rudimentary hand-eye coordination exists at birth, this fact implied such a radical change in the previous conceptions of neonatal abilities that it was hardly surprising when many investigators were prompted to replicate this work. Ruff and Halton (1978) attempted to replicate the Bower et al. (1970a) study. Bower had reported a preponderance of directed arm extensions to a ball for 1- to 2-week-old neonates. Hampered somewhat by lack of detail in the original study, the replication did not support the earlier results. The percentage of contacts or near contacts to the total number of extensions was 36% or half that reported by Bower, suggesting that early extensions may not be directed. Also the hit rate was far less at 7% compared to the 40% quoted by Bower (1974). Worse, the authors found that there were as many extensions in the absence as in the presence of the stimulus, a control condition which Bower did not report.

The single most likely explanation for the differences is not that Scottish babies are significantly more advanced than American ones, but that the definition of an extension was not clearly defined. This problem also occurred in other experiments testing Bower's findings.

In a partial replication of Bower's (1972) study, (not previously described), Dodwell, Muir, and DiFranco (1976) observed 18 infants aged 1 to 3 months in the presence of either a 3-dimensional graspable object or a 2-dimensional picture of it. Bower had reasoned that if infants could already discern the third dimension (without much experience) they would not reach for a 2-dimensional picture of an object. Unlike Bower, who found a high rate of reaching to the object and no reaches to the picture, Dodwell et al. found some reaching in both conditions, but no differences except in the total number of visual orientations which were higher for the object.

In an attempt to eliminate any possible differences in criterion measures, the videotapes from this study were reanalyzed by DiFranco, Muir, and Dodwell (1978) using a less restricted criterion for what constituted a reach (in terms of distance moved) and a much more detailed analysis of the various components of reaching behavior. With the less strict criterion for a directed reach, a significant difference was indeed obtained between the object and picture response, but the results were still very different from Bower's report that no reaches were directed towards the picture. The fine-grain analysis of reach components revealed no differences between the two conditions, but did illuminate the great variation in individual styles both between and within babies. Interestingly, the authors contend that the infants who reached most frequently shared a dominant pattern of reaching, namely a full arm raise with shaped hand. This pattern, they argue, is consequently a more mature style of reaching. Unfortunately, by collapsing their data across a relatively large time frame (1-3 weeks), they may have masked any developmental trend.

In addition to the problem of using different criteria for defining a reach, two other factors are pertinent in determining whether infants do or do not reach more for a ball than a picture (Rader & Stern, 1982). First, the picture used in the Dodwell studies was small enough to function as an object. Second, Dodwell's subject population included a subset of older (2-3 week) babies, and since many neonatal responses disappear for a time it is possible that these older subjects biased the sample. Rader and Stern (1982) attempted to resolve the conflict between the Bower and Dodwell studies by using a large patterned picture of a ball and the younger age range for their 31 subjects. In addition, they added a control condition of a homogeneous blank picture card. Again, however, their definition of a reach, though clearly defined, was not exactly the same as either of the previous studies. Significant differences in reaching amount were found between both the ball and the picture vs the blank card, but no differences between the 2- and 3-dimensional stimuli. Thus, the Dodwell studies were supported, but the finding of a significant difference between either object and the baseline blank card did not coincide with the Ruff and Halton (1978) study which reported no differences between the baseline and object condition. The latter study did not use a blank card as a baseline, and it is quite probable that background objects raised the baseline rate of reaching. Of significance too, is the fact that the blank card also produced a fair number of reaches which were apparently not solicited by any visual stimuli. Rader and Stern conclude that neonatal reaching is an early behavior pattern whose frequency is increased by the presence of a patterned stimuli, i.e., visual contrast.

Finally, the Bower et al. (1970c) study of infants who expressed distress when they failed to touch a virtual object was replicated by Field (1977). Unfortunately, the use of 8 subjects at 3 median ages of 3.5, 5 and 7 months did not duplicate the neonatal aspect of the study. Also, Field did not fit goggles on his subjects, which means that any effect from the goggles, either of unfamiliarity or in the visual information (which differs slightly from normal), was not replicated either. Field had the subjects look at solid and comparable intangible images of objects both within and beyond arm reach. Emotional reactions and reaching behavior were found to be similar with both solid and image stimuli and hence did not support Bower's findings. However, closer inspection of the data reveal that only one 3-month and four 5-month babies actually placed their hand in the locus of the image. Furthermore, three out of the eight 7-month babies, all of whom did place their hand in the image locus, did show some surprise or frustration at this experience. Since Bower's results apply to infants up to 5 months of age and since the virtual image conditions of the two experiments were different, it is difficult to treat this study as a valid replication or to believe that the findings necessarily refute Bower's.

To summarize this period in the research on visually directed reaching, it is appropriate to state that by 1980, the existence of early sensory-motor coordination was regarded as an established fact by several researchers. The existence of rudimentary hand-eye coordination and the so-called "pre-reaching components'' (Trevarthen, 1974), i.e., aimed but unsuccessful reached, were documented. Of course, this alternative view to the traditional assumption of separate sensory and motor systems at birth was not believed by all. Indeed, the more astounding claims, such as innate knowledge of three dimensional space, were seriously challenged but no resolution over this issue has occurred. One important point, which should be made from reviewing the replication studies, is the impracticality of exact replication. Differences in subject ages, subject states, angle of support, environmental conditions, object/image stimuli, and observer criteria are all mediating factors.

RECENT RESEARCH AND THE DEVELOPMENTAL COURSE OF VISUALLY DIRECTED REACHING

Given the detailed descriptions of both reaching and antecedent behaviors (e.g., Halverson, 1933; White et al., 1964) in conjunction with the elegant, if controversial, observations of early hand-eye coordination (e.g., Bower et al., 1970a, 1970b, 1970c), how can we make sense of the developmental course of visually directed reaching? One approach is to distinguish clearly between those behaviors found before successful reaching (and grasping) first occurs and those which appear after this time.

Looking first at the grasping action, Bower (1979) reported that infants under 4 weeks exhibit a reach *with* grasp action where hand closure is temporally coincident with the end of the reach (sometimes just before or just after). After 5 months, the grasp is temporally uncoupled from the reach and always occurs approximately 400 ms after the reach has ended. Using sensitive pressure transducers in the objects, Bower also found that the grasp of the older infants was under tactual influence, suggesting that proprioceptive feedback was being used at the end of the reach to elicit the hand closure. In contrast, the neonates do not need physical contact to elicit the hand closure, it appears to come with the reach as a ''package''.

In looking at the reaching action, Bushnell (1985) suggested that behavioral components of prereaching and reaching may be distinguished in three ways. First, of course, prereaching is less accurate than reaching, although the degree of accuracy is a subject of contention (cf. Bower, 1974, reporting 40% hit rate of neonates to Dodwell et al., 1976 reporting 3%). A recent study by von Hofsten (1982) seems to confirm the existence of prereaching behavior and at the same time to explain part of the earlier confusion in results. Von Hofsten (1982) studied 14 infants between 5 and 9 days old in a semireclined position for eight 1-min periods with a brightly colored object being alternately present or absent. He found more movement activity while the object was absent, but no difference in the number of extended arm-hand movements between the two conditions.

Thus the increased tendency to extend the arm when the object was present was concealed by the decreased tendency to move the arm at all. Von Hofsten suggested that the earlier failures to show more reaches when the object was present (e.g., Ruff & Halton, 1978) were due to an interaction between the amount of forward extended movement and the general level of motor activity. In support of his findings, von Hofsten also noted that when the neonate actually fixated the object, the relative amount of extended arms was twice as high as the amount for nonfixated movement.

Bushnell (1985) makes a second distinction between prereaching and reaching on the quality of the movements and suggests that the visual system functions in two ways to direct reaching. Prereaching is characterized as ballistic, or visually elicited, whereas successful reaching is visually guided. That is, in prereaching the arm movement is "preprogrammed" or fully aimed at the target at the beginning of the movement. Regardless of the arm trajectory that follows, the essential property is that the course of movement is not purposefully altered during its performance or at completion. In contrast, reaching movements are characterized by a continuous monitoring process which adjusts the movement throughout its course in order to achieve success. These movements also may be aimed at the beginning, but the distinguishing feature is that they are capable of adjustment throughout the movement. As Bushnell points out, the critical experiment to argue that prereaching movements are ballistic is to compare prereaching to static objects with prereaching to objects which are moved after the start of the prereach. The experiment which most clearly approximates this condition was conducted by Bower & Wishart (1972) with 12 infants, 5 months of age. Here the lights were turned out before the infant reached for the object. Using an infrared camera technique, the infants were "seen" to accurately reach for the objects at least in the initial movement.

Additional evidence for neonatal ballistic movement appears to rest on the fact that prereaches characterized as "swipes" (White et al., 1964) or "flings" (Bower et al., 1970a) are rapid and unlikely to involve adjustments from feedback processes. The next question might be, are these prereaches actually aimed at the object? When von Hofsten (1982) examined the extensor movement of reaching with a 3-dimensional spatial-temporal analysis it was clear that movement performed during object fixation was aimed closer at the object than were other movements.

The third distinction, proposed by Bushnell (1985) is based on the underlying processes which allow accomplishment of a reach. For reaching to be successful either the "seen" object and the "felt" hand or the "seen" object and the "seen" hand must be matched or mapped onto one another. Evidence reviewed in the previous section of this paper suggests that young infants already have a primitive hand-eye, i.e., a visuoproprioceptive coordination because they can, for example, anticipate the touch of a 3-dimensional object. Older infants, however, accomplish hand-eye coordination by monitoring and progressively reducing the "gap" between the seen object and the seen hand; hence, the visually guided vs the visually elicited reach. If prereaching is visually elicited and visuoproprioceptively coordinated, what is the evidence for reaching being visually guided and visuovisually coordinated[4]?

Piaget's (1952) observations of looking to and fro from hand to object support the notion of visuovisual coordination, as do several other studies, described below, where experimenter manipulation interfered with the perception of the seen hand. Lasky (1977) observed the reaching of 50 infants between 2.5 and 6.5 months of age under normal vision and a mirror condition where the object could be seen but the hand was out of view. Infants of 3.5 to 4.5 months did not inhibit the reach in either condition, indicating that they did not utilize the sight of the hand during reaching. In contrast, infants of 5.5 to 6.5 months inhibited the reach or reached clumsily in the mirror condition, which suggests that they did rely on the sight of the hand while reaching. The older infants also became upset in the mirror condition, perhaps because they were "looking" for the hand which did not appear. It should be noted that if it was "absolutely" necessary for the hand to be seen, one would expect a complete inhibition of reaching in the no-visual-feedback condition.

Both Bower (1976) and McDonnell (1975) observed reaching between 4 and 10 months while the infants were wearing prism glasses which displayed the seen object and seen hand. If the infant was using seen object-seen hand coordination, the reaching would be successful, but if seen object-felt hand coordination was used, the reaching would be unsuccessful. Bower reported that infants younger than 6 months routinely missed the object, even after several attempts, while infants older than 6 months started their reach in the wrong direction but corrected it as soon as the hand came into view. These mid-reach corrective actions reveal not only that the seen hand was attended to but that the reaches were guided rather than ballistic. Conversely, the younger infants' failures to remedy their misses either within or between reaches support the view that prereaching is ballistic. McDonnell's results were slightly different in that all of his infants apparently corrected the trajectories of their reaches. (One might question whether the displacement in his prisms was less than that used by Bower.) However, the youngest infants' trajectories were the most deviant and often indicated an abrupt switch from a miss path to a hit path, which is consonant with an initial visually elicited arm reach suddenly being converted to a visually guided reach.

The fact that by 4 to 5 months of age reaching appears to be controlled with a seen object-seen hand coordination system which essentially guides the arm trajectory is an oversimplification. In reality, reaching behavior must always be elicited visually in order to start the movement. It is the appearance (or possibly the relative amount) of guided, corrective action that is the critical factor. Indeed we have already noted that 5-month-olds are capable of predictive aiming when, having viewed an object, they are left in the dark (Bower & Wishart, 1972). A tempting suggestion is that infants of this age may use either a predominantly aimed reach or a predominantly guided reach according to the environmental circumstances, i.e., being placed in the dark or made to wear a prism displacement lens!

In any case, this is not the end of the story, because after the infant can successfully reach it is obvious from the first and earliest study reviewed that the quality of the reaching movement increases in accuracy from zigzag movements to movements which do not deviate from the optimum path to the object (Halverson, 1933). Von Hofsten's (1979) quantitative analysis of the approach phase of 4- to 9-month-old infants' reaches provides further information on this developmental trend. The subjects were analyzed reaching for both still and moving objects by dividing the approach into movement elements, each of which denoted a change in direction. The number of movement elements decreased from 3-4 to 1-2 elements over the 5-month period. Furthermore, over the same time period, the duration, distance, and force of the first movement element increased so that a 9-month-old's reach consisted of a well-aimed, visually elicited portion with one or no corrections, i.e., visually guided portions.

McDonnell and Abraham (1979) studied perceptual adaptation in infants who repeatedly reached for objects while wearing laterally displacing prism glasses. They reasoned that adaptation should be minimal when reaching is visually guided, because no intercue discrepancy exists to motivate it, i.e., the seen object and seen hand are not displaced relative to one another. Generally, they observed that some adaptation did take place, but that the magnitude of the adaptation decreased between 5 and 7 months of age. This finding implies that the seen hand is relied on increasingly over this age period, as has been discussed earlier. However, the magnitude of adaptation increased again at 9 months of age. McDonnell (1979) interpreted this pattern of results as evidence that visually guided reaching "peaks" at around 7 months of age to be replaced by the more efficient ballistic style of reaching.

It is apparent that von Hofsten's and McDonnell's data do not agree on the "peak" of visually guided reaching, since von Hofsten's infants showed a steady trend toward ballistic reaching from the age of 4 months. Again, a plausible explanation might be that the infants in the McDonnell study were using more visually guided reaching than they might normally use, simply because of the demanding environmental conditions that they find themselves in. Von Hofsten, by studying a more natural, ecologically valid movement, has displaced the peak of visually guided reaching to 4 months (or earlier). The implications of this difference in experimental procedure are outlined briefly in the last section of the paper.

Finally, Lockman, Ashmead, and Bushnell (1984) observed the hand positioning and looking behavior of 5- and 9-month infants as they reached for horizontally and vertically oriented dowels. Infants of both ages usually looked at the dowel throughout the reach; however, on some occasions the infants stopped looking at the dowel before they touched it, even though they continued the reach and grasped the dowel. These instances of look-away reaches were significantly more frequent among the 9-month-olds than the 5-month-olds, and were no less accurate in their anticipatory hand orientation.

Thus, in each of the above three studies, infants aged 9 months and older had more ballistic qualities in their reaching and appeared to pay less attention to their hand than did younger infants down to 4 months of age. Drawing this conclusion in with other studies reviewed in this section, it is clear that a case can be made for a qualitative and quantitative distinction between prereaching, early reaching, and later reaching—all within the first 9 or 10 months of life.

A HEURISTIC FRAMEWORK FOR THE DEVELOPMENT OF VISUALLY DIRECTED REACHING: FUTURE DIRECTIONS IN RESEARCH

The current state of the research on visually directed reaching suggests a three-part developmental framework which appears to predict observable events (Bushnell, 1985). To reiterate briefly, it is suggested that the neonate comes with a rudimentary hand-eye coordination which is a visually elicited ballistic reach *with* grasp. However this action is seldom successful. By approximately 4 months, the infant is using a visually guided reach *and then* grasp system based on seeing both the object and hand, and incorporating error detection to achieve success. Remember that there is still the possibility that at least the first part of the reach may be aimed at this stage (Hofsten, 1979). By 9 months the visually guided system gives way again to a visually elicited, ballistic but accurate reach which only makes use of its error correction system when environmental circumstances demand.

The framework thus described is a useful tool for conceptualizing the developmental course of visually directed reaching because the three "stages" may be studied separately, or the transition points may be explored. Does the framework assist in the formation of a theory to explain visually directed reaching? The implicit theory under investigation is one which explains the *developmental* course of sensory-motor coordination. The framework stated here in terms of the absence or presence of aiming and guiding strategies might be an appropriate vehicle to study the mechanisms of development. It was never the intention of the author to write a theoretical position paper, and certain such a topic should be given more consideration than it will be here. Nevertheless, an attempt will be made to briefly outline some of the major issues and theoretical perspectives which could embrace the framework and direct future research.

How, then, may we explain the change from visually elicited to visually guided and back to visually elicited systems in reaching? At one level, the answer is tantalizingly simple. The infant switches from the early visually elicited system to a visually guided system because the latter is more successful in actually achieving the reach (Bower, 1974). Similarly, the visually guided system, although successful, is not so efficient in terms of speed and accuracy as a visually elicited ballistic movement, and so the infant switches to this system (McDonnell, 1979). However, this explanation does nothing to elucidate the neuromuscular mechanisms which are actually involved in this process.

At the motor control level the mechanisms under consideration are defined as open loop (ballistic) and closed loop (guided). The former consists of neuromuscular commands which are run off after initiation without reference to any sensory feedback, while the latter involve continuous matching of the neuromuscular commands with sensory feedback. Greene (1973) proposed a model of skilled performance where an environmental goal is first approximated under open loop control and then achieved with precision under refined closed loop control. This formulation was elaborated by Donnelly and Connolly (1983) into a simulated model for voluntary reaching, showing that a mixed control strategy appeared to work best in predicting infant behavior.

Knowing the mechanisms involved is one level of understanding, but there still is the developmental question of whether the change and refinement of the mechanisms is driven primarily by heredity, environment, or more likely some combination of the two. In addition, the change in the neuromuscular pathways themselves is also an important consideration. The traditional maturational explanation of the development of voluntary behavior involves the inhibition of reflex pathways by cortical supraspinal processes. This theory is not always accepted in the current literature (Keshner, 1982). Indeed some would argue that the subcortical, early pathways are the building blocks for later voluntary behavior, and that it would be wasteful of the human body to allow them to be inhibited (Easton, 1972).

Interestingly, data collected by von Hofsten (1984) in a longitudinal study of 23 infants from 1 week to 4 months of age appear to support the inhibition theory. Using his earlier described procedures, von Hofsten found that the amount of prereaching movements decreased significantly at 2 months of age, although the infants increased their attention to the object. The form also changes at this time from an open hand to a fisted one. This is followed by a period of relatively little hand-eye behavior, but later the extension movements reappear, and the hand starts to open when the object is seen. If these later movements are the beginning of visually *guided* reaching (even though this is earlier than other investigators place it), one could hypothesize that the early visual-perception system is a subcortically organized, unconscious mechanism that undergoes cortical inhibition as the visually guided hand-eye mechanisms mature and take over the system. Both von Hofsten (1984) and Bushnell (1985) argue for an integrated functioning of cortical and subcortical systems. Based on research by Kuypers (1962; Brinkman & Kuypers, 1973) they suggest that there are two motor systems concerned. The proximal system, organized at the brainstem level, is responsible for control of the gross movement of the arm and hand, and the distal system, organized at the cortical level, is responsible for the fine coordination of the hand. In this view, the rise of visually guided reaching would be contingent on the "kicking in" of the distal system at about 4 months when the infant has enough processing capacity to discern that the gap between the target and hand is informative (Bower, 1974).

Von Hofsten (1984) also has an alternative suggestion to the cortical inhibition theory in suggesting that it is arousal or the excitement of attending to the object which causes blocking of the movement by activating both antagonist and agonist muscles. In this case, the antagonist activation would have to be inhibited before normal reaching occurs.

In a more traditional view, Bushnell (1985) continues her explanation of development by speculating on the decline of visually guided reaching. She suggests that refinement and "overlearning" of the visually guided system eventually may lead to a response integration and an automating of the control so that the movement becomes ballistic again, freeing the attention span of the infant for cognitive development (Bushnell, 1985).

If the characteristics of earlier, neonatal ballistic movements can be proven to differ from those of the later, mature ballistic movements; then, the traditional inhibition hypothesis is difficult to refute. Bushnell herself tries to make this case by suggesting that her use of the word integration between distal and proximal systems means superimposition of the distal over the proximal. An alternative argument would be that the neuromuscular pathways originally used in the early, ballistic aims are the same ones used later, but with the added refinement of closed loop error detection mechanisms and cortical initiation. This line of thought leads to serious questions regarding the role of traditionally defined reflexes. Space does not permit an expansion of the recent controversial notions that such reflexes have little to do with the development of visually directed reaching, although other endogenous neural circuits *are* implicated (Donnolly & Connolly, 1983; McDonnell, 1979). These notions lead to the second alternative which is that the proximal and distal systems develop independently without either inhibitory or refining interaction.

While the neurophysiological mechanisms are awaiting a more definitive exposition[5], much research over the last 15 years has been derived from newer conceptions of development. Indeed two theoretical perspectives, one dealing with perception and the other with action, have been very influential in this respect. The importance of ecological validity, for example, in von Hofsten's work, and the early significance of the expanding optical array, for example, in Bower's work, both derive from a Gibsonian perspective of direct perception.

Direct perception implies that visual input is adequate in specifying the nature of objects or events and that this does not require elaboration by cognitive processes. Because it is the *environment* that *affords* action, the study of perception must involve the study of the animal-environment system (Gibson, 1966). Thus, in the case of visually guided reaching, researchers must consider the nature of the stimulation, i.e., the characteristics of the stimulus itself, in addition to the background information and other seemingly extraneous influences. This point is well recognized when we consider the variation in findings between researchers purportedly observing the same phenomena, but where the stimulus and/or environment were clearly not constant functions. Rather than trying to determine that infants do not show "reaches" at an early age, we should be investigating the "conditions" which afford or do not afford reaching, and henceforth inferring information about underlying processes.

Three studies, briefly reviewed, serve as an illustration of this approach. Willatts (1979) looked at how the object's *position* affected reaching. He found that the 4-month-olds manipulated and fixated less when the object was in an unfamiliar position, whereas the 5-month-olds exhibited no change. Willatts suggested that younger children had not completely "learned" object permanence (a cognitive skill) and that this affected their performance in reaching.

Two studies by von Hofsten also manipulated the object, this time by moving it across the field of vision. Von Hofsten is probably the first researcher to use a moving object stimulus, which is not surprising if one remembers that early researchers considered that young infants could not coordinate hand and eye movements with a stationary object, let alone a moving one. In fact, a moving object provides increased optical array information over a static one, and therefore it would seem logical to argue that, if a primitive coordination does exist, it may well be better stimulated by a moving object. Sure enough, von Hofsten and Lindhagen (1979) found that by 3 months of age, when an infant could master reaching for stationary objects, she would also successfully reach for moving ones. Furthermore, von Hofsten (1980) noted that 4.5-month-old infants appeared to predict where the moving object was going to be quite well indicating good perception, while 6-month-old infants tended to use a nonpredicting chase strategy, relying on their increasing motor skill and greater use of error detection systems.

Von Hofsten (1980) suggests that his data show the perception system to be ready, or "tuned," before the action system, although both are linked at the beginning. Certainly although there has been more attention paid to the infant's perception, we should not lose track of the action end of the system. Both Reed (1982) and Clark (1986) suggest that a marriage of the Gibsonian perspective of perception with the Bernsteinian perspective on action systems is a worthwhile approach.

The Bernsteinian perspective also is based on the absence of a cognitive processor, but not, of course, of a cognitive initiator. In this view, the multis-egmental human body solves the problem of its many degrees of freedom by constraining muscles to act coalitionally with few, maybe one, cognitive com-mand. In addition, the system must have flexibility to adjust to different envi-ronmental situations (Bernstein, 1967). Development of an action system is conceived of in three stages. First, coordination is achieved by constraining free variables into behavioral units. Second, control is achieved by the process of assigning values to the variables in the function. Third, skill is achieved by assigning optimum variables in that function (Kelso, 1982).

From research reviewed in section two it could be argued that the system is "coordinated" for visually directed reaching at birth. Of course, this is not to suggest that the control or flexibility of this structure is in place; indeed it is the study of how such control and skillful flexibility is gained that is of consummate interest. A useful hypothesis would be that control is gained by the addition of closed loop mechanisms to the early open loop coordination. Skillful flexibility of reaching would then occur by integrating the two sets of mechanisms together.

This hypothesis is not testable in a direct empirical fashion because this would necessitate an invasive neurophysiological approach not permissible with human subjects. However, recent work in the investigation of coordination and control in humans has centered on the analysis of kinematic, kinetic, and electromy-ographic variables. The logic is that those variables which remain constant or invariant under various conditions are "coordination" variables and those which change are considered "control" variables (see, for example, Kelso & Tuller, 1984). Thus, a method for looking at the changes from coordinated through controlled and ultimately skillful reaching would involve longitudinal 3-dimen-sional space, time, force (and EMG) analyses in search of invariant and variant factors. An interesting question, combining the perception and action perspec-tives, would be whether different environmental stimuli afford different coor-dinative structures (invariant factors) and/or different methods or rates of gaining control over the early primitive system?

A final postscript concerns individual differences. Whereas most research has grouped subjects only by age, it is by no means certain that the underlying mechanisms of hand-eye coordination are universal. For example, anthropo-metric differences may affect the amount or shape of movements. Perhaps even more importantly, we do not know whether the environment affords information in the same way to all normal people. The identification of individual behavioral styles (DiFranco et al., 1978) and of individual strategies for hand orientation (Hofsten & Fazel-Zandy, 1984) are examples of research which illustrate this consideration. One way of accounting for these differences in developmental studies would be to group infants by their reaching proficiency rather than their chronological age. Alternatively, longitudinal case studies of a few individuals, with carefully monitored information concerning anthropometric chacracteristics and experience, might yield important information concerning individual pathways of development. Indeed work with blind babies has already shown the importance of motivation for the development of motor behavior (Adelson & Fraiberg, 1974).

SUMMARY

The field of research on the development of visually directed reaching is currently very active, if somewhat controversial. Recent research has turned toward elucidating underlying processes rather than describing the overt changes in motor behavior as was prevalent in the early research. However, this is not to suggest that descriptive nonexperimental research has no place in the field. Indeed, the quantitative descriptions of "ecologically valid" reaching by von Hofsten contributes equally well to our understanding as the experimental research of Bower or McDonnell. Only by comparing behavior in a variety of conditions can we come to a complete understanding of the sensory-motor interaction which subserves visually directed reaching.

The fourth section of the paper was a brief excursion into the possible underlying processes of reaching and, in particular, their development. A "phaselike" framework for the development of reaching was presented. Based on the results of reviewed research, this framework appears to be a heuristic tool for researchers. Finally, it was suggested that appropriate research strategies would do well to be derived from theoretical perspectives which take into account the environmental/organismic interaction and individual differences resulting from experience, anthropometric factors, or insult to the nervous system.

REFERENCES

Adelson, E., & Fraiberg, S. (1974). Gross motor development in infants blind from birth. *Child Development, 45*, 114–126.

Bernstein, N. (1967). *The coodination and regulation of movements*. London: Pergamon Press.

Bower, T. G. R. (1972). Object perception in infants. *Perception, 1*, 15–30.

Bower, T. G. R. (1974). Development of infant behaviour. *British Medical Bulletin, 30*, 175–178.

Bower, T. G. R. (1976). Repetitive processes in child development. *Scientific American, 235*, 38–47.

Bower, T. G. R. (1979). *Human Development*. San Francisco: W. H. Freeman & Co.

Bower, T. G. R., Broughton, J. M., & Moore, M. K. (1970a). Demonstration of intention in the reaching behaviour of neonate humans. *Nature, 228*, 679–681.

Bower, T. G. R., Broughton, J. M., & Moore, M. K. (1970b). The coordination of visual and tactual input in infants. *Perception & Psychophysics, 8*, 51–53.

Bower, T. G. R., Broughton, J. M., & Moore, M. K. (1970c). Infant responses to approaching objects: An indicator of response to distal variables. *Perception & Psychophysics, 9,* 193–196.

Bower, T. G. R., & Wishart, J. G. (1972). The effects of motor skill on object permanence. *Cognition, 1,* 165–172.

Brinkman, J., & Kuypers, H. G. J. M. (1972). Splitbrain monkeys: Cerebral control of ipsilateral and contralateral arm, hand and finger movements. *Science, 176,* 536–538.

Bruner, J. S., & Koslowski, B. (1972). Visually preadapted constituents of manipulatory action. *Perception, 1,* 3–14.

Bushnell, E. W. (1985). The decline of visually guided reaching during infancy. *Infant Behavior and Development, 8,* 139–155.

Clark, J. E. (1986). The perception-action perspective: A commentary on von Hofsten. In M. G. Wade & H. T. A. Whiting (Eds.), *Motor Development in Children: Aspects of Coordination and Control* (pp. 197–206). Dordrecht: Martinus Nijhoff.

Clark, J. E., & Phillips, S. J. (1986). *The effect of walking speed on the interlimb temporal organization of infant walkers.* Manuscript submitted for publication.

DiFranco, D., Muir, D. W., & Dodwell, P. C. (1978). Reaching in very young infants. *Perception, 7,* 385–392.

Dodwell, P. C., Muir, D., & DiFranco, D. (1976). Responses of infants to visually presented objects. *Science, 194,* 209–211.

Donnelly, M. C., & Connolly, K. J. (1983). Motor development: A hypothesis and a simulation concerning voluntary reaching in infancy. *Human Movement Science, 2,* 15–33.

Easton, T. A. (1972). On the normal use of reflexes. *American Scientist, 60,* 591–599.

Field, J. (1977). Coordination of vision and prehension in young infants. *Child Development, 48,* 97–103.

Fox, R., Aslin, R. N., Shea, S. L., & Dumais, S. T. (1980). Stereopsis in human infants. *Science, 207,* 323–324.

Gesell, A., & Ames, L. B. (1947). The development of handedness. *Journal of Genetic Psychology, 70,* 155–175.

Gibson, J. J. (1966). *The senses considered as perceptual systems.* Boston: Houghton Mifflin.

Greene, P. H. (1973). Problems of organization of motor systems. In R. Rosen & R. Snell (Eds.), *Progress in Theoretical Biology,* (Vol. 2 pp. 303–338), New York: Academic Press.

Halverson, H. M. (1931). An experimental study of prehension in infants by means of systematic cinema records. *Genetic Psychology Monographs, 10,* 107–287.

Halverson, H. M. (1933). The acquisition of skill in infancy. *Journal of Genetic Psychology, 43,* 3–47.

Halverson, H. M. (1937a). Studies of the grasping responses of early infancy: I. *Journal of Genetic Psychology, 51,* 371–392.

Halverson, H. M. (1937b). Studies of the grasping responses of early infancy: II. *Journal of Genetic Psychology, 51,* 393–424.

Halverson, H. M. (1937c). Studies of the grasping responses of early infancy: III. *Journal of Genetic Psychology, 51,* 425–449.

Hofsten, C. von. (1977). Binocular convergence as a determinant of reaching behavior in infancy. *Perception, 6*, 139–144.

Hofsten, C. von. (1979). Development of visually directed reaching: The approach phase. *Journal of Human Movement Studies, 5*, 160–178.

Hofsten, C. von. (1980). Predictive reaching for moving objects by human infants. *Journal of Experimental Child Psychology, 30*, 369–382.

Hofsten, C. von. (1982). Eye-hand coordination in the newborn. *Developmental Psychology, 18*, 450–461.

Hofsten, C. von. (1984). Developmental changes in the organization of prereaching movements. *Developmental Psychology, 20*, 378–388.

Hofsten, C. von., & Fazel-Zandy, S. (1984). Development of visually guided hand orientation in reaching. *Journal of Experimental Child Psychology, 38*, 208–219.

Hofsten, C. von., & Lindhagen, K. (1979). Observations on the development of reaching for moving objects. *Journal of Experimental Child Psychology, 28*, 158–173.

Kelso, J. A. S. (1982). *Human Motor Behavior*. Hillsdale, NJ: Lawrence Erlbaum Associates.

Kelso, J. A. S., & Tuller, B. (1984). A dynamical basis for action systems. In M. S. Gazzaniga (Ed.), *Handbook of Cognitive Neuroscience* (pp. 321–326). New York: Plenum Press.

Keshner, E. A. (1982). Reevaluating the theoretical model underlying the neurodevelopmental theory. *Physical Therapy, 61*, 1035–1040.

Kuypers, H. G. J. M. (1962). Corticospinal connections: Postnatal development in the rhesus monkey. *Science, 138*, 678–680.

Lasky, R. E. (1977). The effect of visual feedback of the hand on the reaching and retrieval behavior of young infants. *Child Development, 48*, 112–117.

Lockman, J. J., Ashmead, D. H., & Bushnell, E. W. (1984). The development of anticipatory hand orientation during infancy. *Journal of Experimental Child Psychology, 37*, 176–186.

McDonnell, P. M. (1975). The development of visually guided reaching. *Perception & Psychophysics, 18*, 181–185.

McDonnell, P. M. (1979). Patterns of eye-hand coordination in the first year of life. *Canadian Journal of Psychology, 33*, 253–265.

McDonnell, P. M., & Abraham, W. C. (1979). Adaptation to displacing prisms in human infants. *Perception, 8*, 175–185.

Piaget, J. (1952). *The origins of intelligence in children*. New York: Norton.

Rader, N., & Stern, J. D. (1982). Visually elicited reaching in neonates. *Child Development, 53*, 1004–1007.

Reed, E. (1982). An outline of a theory of action systems. *Journal of Motor Behavior, 14*, 98–134.

Roy, E. A., Starkes, J., & Charlton, J. (1986). The contribution of the neurosciences to understanding the development of reaching. In M. G. Wade & H. T. A. Whiting (Eds.), *Motor Development in Children: Aspects of Coordination and Control* (pp. 443–456). Dordrecht: Martinus Nijhoff.

Ruff, H. A., & Halton, A. (1978). Is there directed reaching in the human neonate? *Developmental Psychology, 14*, 425–426.

Trevarthen, C. (1974). The psychobiology of speech development. *Neurosciences Research Program Bulletin, 12*, 570–585.

White, B. L., Castle, P., & Held, R. (1964). Observations on the development of visually-directed reaching. *Child Development, 35*, 349–364.

Willatts, P. (1979). Adjustment of reaching to change in object position by young infants. *Child Development, 50*, 911–913.

Wohlwill, J. F. (1973). *The study of behavioral development*. New York: Academic Press.

NOTES

[1] I will not repeat results which overlap between any two studies. This will result in an "additive" model which may not do justice to the authors in terms of the inclusiveness of their results. Of course, if authors differ on their major findings, these will be pointed out and hypotheses forwarded to account for the discrepancies.

[2] By enriching the environment of institutionalized infants they hoped eventually to compare the rate of development with a similar group of infants not receiving such enrichment. However, this study was their control group, which makes it somewhat surprising that they appeared to develop faster than the uninstitutionalized infants in the Halverson study.

[3] From looking at the original article the age range appears to be 6 to 20 days old. In this 1974 article Bower refers to 3 to 6 days old. It is unclear which Bower reference is correct?

[4] From an ecological viewpoint the adaptation of early intersensory coordination patterns would seem to have obvious significance in facilitating communication with the caregiver. However, it is equally obvious that some aspects of the system such as the grasp reflex have lost their adaptive significance. Perhaps the grasp reflex was more tightly linked with the visual system in the past and in this sense we are becoming less well adapted?

[5] The neurophysiological information is largely available from the animal research. Interested readers are directed to Roy, Starkes, and Charlton (1986) as a starting point for the integration of animal and human research in relation to neurophysiological development.

11.

PREHENSILE DEVELOPMENT: A CONTRAST OF MATURE AND IMMATURE PATTERNS

Diane Manchester

University of Oregon

ABSTRACT

Prehension in human infants is compared with mature prehensile patterns. Prehension is not an isolated movement of the upper extremity. Rather, prehension is a coordination of posture and movement involving the trunk, head, eyes, and upper extremity. Prehensile development reflects a progression from discontinuous movement patterns toward mature, fluent prehension. Visuomotor coordination is evident even in neonates. Thus, in the Gibsonian approach, some level of visual perception is guiding this behavior in a meaningful way. The infant-environment interaction defines an internal representation of the movement goal. This representation guides the control and coordination of immature prehensile behavior.

Prehension requires the development of coordination of multiple body segments, as well as the maturation of requisite perceptual and motor abilities. Research on human infant prehension (e.g., Bushnell, 1985; Hofsten, 1979; Hofsten & Fazel-Zandy, 1984) reveals a progression from immature toward mature control and coordination. Yet in much of the developmental literature, little, if any, discussion of the mature prehensile pattern is included. The intent of this paper, therefore, is to juxtapose information regarding mature and immature prehensile patterns. These patterns will be analyzed with respect to current psychological constructs of control and coordination of goal-directed movements (e.g., Arbib, 1980, 1985; Mounoud & Hauert, 1982). These constructs will be

165

interpreted in the context of Gibson's (1979) ecological approach. That is, movement is molded by complex interactions between the individual and the environment rather than by a discrete stimulus-discrete response causality. As Reed (1982) proposed in his theory of action systems, organisms do not merely respond to stimuli at their receptors. Instead, they respond to objects and events in their environment. Application of these ideas to infant development is important because of the adaptive goal-directed activity which has been observed in neonates and young infants (Bower, 1972, 1977, 1982; Bower, Broughton, & Moore, 1970; Hofsten, 1980, 1982, 1984; Trevarthen, 1974, 1975). These observations contrast with the concept that neonates and young infants up to 2 to 3 months of age act in a purely reflexive manner (Halverson, 1931).

At any point in time, infant prehensile ability is contingent upon nervous system maturation, anatomical changes, biomechanical constraints of growing motor effectors, and the manner in which these factors interact with the environment. This interaction allows elaboration of an internal representation of the movement goal. Although this representation may be rudimentary in neonates, mature prehension appears when the representation is "complete" with respect to parameter specification of target properties and of the kinematics of the movement. If the internal representation is "incomplete," then motor programming of a movement is maladjusted, and actions show discontinuities (Mounoud & Hauert, 1982). Indeed, discontinuous movements of the head and eyes (Bullinger, 1983; Goodkin, 1980; Kremenitzer, Vaughan, Kurtzberg, & Dowling, 1979; Regal, Ashmead, & Salapatek, 1983; Roucoux, Culee, & Roucoux, 1983) and of the arm (Halverson, 1931; Hofsten, 1979; McGraw, 1943) have been observed in infants when they orient to a visual target. These discontinuities suggest that some intermittent or discrete feedback process (Crossman & Goodeve, 1963; Keele, 1968) may be governing prehensile accuracy in young infants. In contrast, recent research of adult reaching movements (Biguer, Jeannerod, & Prablanc, 1985; Biguer, Prablanc, & Jeannerod, 1984; Pélisson, Prablanc, Goodale, & Jeannerod, 1986; Prablanc, Pélisson, & Goodale, 1986) supports the idea that mature reaching is governed by "on-line" correction processes (i.e., "pseudocontinuous" processing of arm trajectory error information). This processing depends upon an accurate internal representation of the target. This representation is updated by information from the retina and from the body segments during reaching movement.

Thus, prehensile development may be viewed as a progression from immature, discontinuous patterns toward mature, fluent prehension. At any point in time, these patterns reflect the status of the interaction of the infant with the environment and the maturity level of body systems. The abilities of the infant to operate within multiple frames of reference (e.g., eye relative to head, head relative to trunk, trunk relative to environment) and to perceive intrinsic (e.g., size, shape, color) and extrinsic (e.g., depth, orientation) features of a target object define an accurate internal representation of the movement goal. This representation is incomplete in infancy, which precludes smooth control and coordination of the body segments involved in prehension.

Prehension is not viewed here as an isolated movement of the upper extremity. Rather, prehension is seen as coordination of posture and movement involving the trunk, the head, the eyes, and the upper extremity. That is, mature prehension involves trunk stabilization or assistive rotation; eye movement to fixate a target; head orientation in establishment of gaze position (i.e., sum of head and eye movements); arm and forearm movements and orientation toward the target; and anticipatory shaping of the hand responsive to target parameters. Accordingly, the ontogeny of prehension is the progressive organization of postural and movement coordination. The infant develops the ability to control posture and movement of the involved body segments in a complementary manner (Reed, 1982). In order to reach successfully to a visual target, the position of the target must be translated into body-centered coordinates. The central nervous system must be able to monitor the frames of reference: eyes relative to the head; head relative to the trunk; and trunk relative to the environment (Biguer, Prablanc, & Jeannerod, 1984). During the period from 2 to 17 weeks of age, infants develop the ability to function within these frames of reference (Owen & Lee, 1986). Infants progress from a ''whole-body'' spontaneous orientation pattern (Trevarthen, 1974, 1975) to a coordination of trunk, head, and eyes which allows effective use of the arms and hands with respect to a visual object (Owen & Lee, 1986).

Because many developmental studies focus upon the behavior of the upper extremity *or* the head *or* the eyes rather than multisegmental integration, this paper will be divided accordingly. To understand the behavior toward which the infant is progressing, mature prehension will be examined first. An examination of infant prehensile behavior will follow. Both mature and immature prehension will be interpreted in terms of psychological constructs and the development of an internal representation of the movement goal. It is argued here that prehensile maturation reflects the elaboration of this representation, contingent upon the expansion of perceptual capacities and motor abilities.

MATURE PREHENSILE PATTERN-UPPER EXTREMITY

A two-phase model of mature prehension has been postulated (Jeannerod, 1981; Paillard, 1980, 1982; Paillard & Beaubaton, 1976). The first phase (transportation phase) involves the ballistic transport of the upper extremity toward a target. The second phase (homing-in phase) involves final guidance of the movement to ensure correct placement of the hand on the target. For the transportation phase, open-loop motor control is hypothesized, although more recent research (e.g., Biguer et al., 1985; Pélisson et al., 1986; Prablanc et al., 1986) may question this assumption. Open-loop control means a fairly rapid, visually triggered response that brings the hand into the vicinity of a target. For the homing-in phase, visual guidance may be used to correct arm trajectory and hand orientation.

In his study of human adult prehension, Jeannerod (1981) quantified the kinematics of the movement. He distinguished arm transport from hand shaping, which he termed the manipulation component. The following patterns were noted: On the arm position profile (Fig. 1), there appears a breakpoint of deceleration. This low-velocity period never exceeds one-third of the duration of the movement and may reflect the "homing-in" phase mentioned earlier. In addition, during arm transport, the hand opens to a maximum aperture and then closes in anticipation of contact with the target (manipulation component). The timing of this maximum hand aperture is constant despite amplitude of the grip. Jeannerod also found that the velocity pattern of the manipulation component (including hand opening and grasp formation) depends upon the size and the shape of the target. Finally, a temporal coincidence appears between the break-point of deceleration of arm transport and the beginning of finger closure. This phenomenon is independent of object size or movement amplitude.

Figure 1 illustrates, in general, the kinematic profile of mature prehension. The position curve is somewhat sigmoidal in shape. From this curve, as well as from the velocity curve, it is evident that there is an initial high-velocity, distance-covering phase followed by a deceleratory phase. Thus, arm transport shows distinct phases. The manipulation component, too, shows phases of high-velocity hand-opening followed by lower-velocity finger closure. The important point is that in mature reaching there appears to be temporal coordination between the transportation and manipulation components. That is, finger closure is temporally coordinated with the deceleration breakpoint of arm transport.

To explain this temporal coordination, Arbib (1980, 1985) has presented the idea of coordinated control programs of internal schemas. This theoretical base applies to target-oriented movements in which tasks must be performed in a particular order. For example, in successful prehension, the reach must precede the grasp and the grasp must precede manipulation. As Jeannerod's (1981) research has shown, the ability to preshape the hand simultaneously with arm transport is achieved in mature prehension. Within Arbib's (1985) internal schema conception, perceptual schemas may be embedded within motor schemas. An activated perceptual schema continuously monitors environmental interactions and is tuned to spatial relationships within the immediate environment. For example, the perceptual schema can monitor the parameters of a visual object and can gain access to the routines for interaction with the object (i.e., the motor schema). In prehension, successful localization of a visual object then activates schemas for recognition of size and orientation of the object. The perceptual schema then can affect concurrent activation of the two motor schemas: arm

Figure 1

Kinematic Profile of Adult Prehension

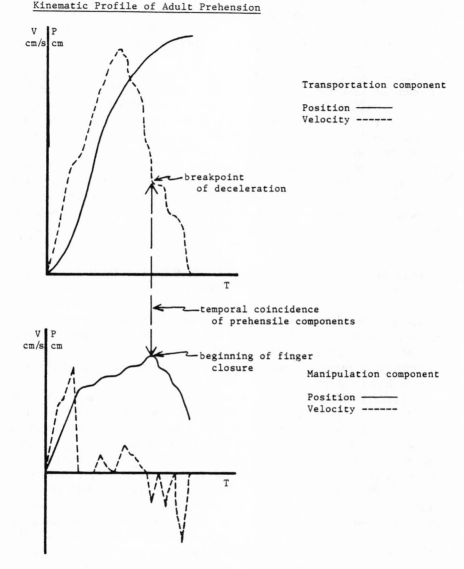

FIG. 1. Adapted from Jeannerod, M. (1981). Intersegmental coordination during reaching at natural visible objects. In J. Long & A. Baddeley (Eds.), *Attention & performance IX* (pp. 153–169). Hillsdale, NJ: Lawrence Erlbaum

transport and hand preshaping. Finger separation and orientation are guided by the output of the appropriate perceptual schemas. The final stage of grasping involves shaping the fingers under the control of tactile feedback. In summary, the internal schema allows sensing of an initial environmental state and building the representation of a goal, which then determines a single movement designed to achieve that goal.

Consequently, mature prehension is a fluent movement in which the arm transport and manipulation components are temporally coordinated to success-fully grasp a visual object. Forearm rotation to orient the hand and preshaping of the fingers appropriate to target object parameters occur concurrently with arm transport. With a mature prehensile system, an individual has some central representation of the goal and of the action which will achieve the goal. The central representation is continuously updated based upon the environmental state, upon the physical interactions which change the state of the body, and upon internal processes (e.g., long-term memory). Although the head and eye components of prehension are not included specifically in Arbib's concept, it is easy to envision their inclusion in such a schema framework.

MATURE PREHENSILE PATTERN—THE ROLES OF THE HEAD AND OF THE EYES

Reaching toward a visual target may be seen as a goal-directed response involving the trunk, head, eyes, and upper extremity. Studies of adult prehension have been done regarding head movement, eye movements (saccades), and the coordination of these components with arm movement in reaching (Biguer, Jeannerod, & Prablanc, 1982, 1985; Bizzi, 1981).

Bizzi (1981) studied eye-head coordination in monkeys and human adults. In order to foveate a visual target, three factors are important: (a) computation of the retinal error; that is, the angle between the foveal line of sight and the target; (b) movement of the head compatible with the amplitude of the eye saccade; and, (c) maintenance of fixation by compensatory eye movements because head movement (due to inertia and velocity differences) lags behind eye movement.

Using electromyographic (EMG) data, Bizzi observed (in monkeys) the se-quencing of eye and neck muscle activity and movement in response to a sudden, unexpected appearance of a target. The overt movements reflected the sequence of eye saccade followed by head movement (20–30 ms later). However, the EMG records showed that eye muscles contracted 20 ms after the beginning of neck muscle activity. Bizzi's explanation is that the contraction time of the neck muscles and the inertial properties of the head result in the discrepancy between the overt movement sequence and the order of muscle activation.

Extending the study of sequencing to include arm movement, Biguer et al.

(1982, 1985) examined humans in a visually elicited pointing task. Subjects (usually centrally fixated) had to orient and point to a small, light-emitting diode turned on within their peripheral visual fields. Similar to Bizzi, Biguer et al. found a discrepancy between the sequencing of overt eye, head, and arm movements and the order of muscle activation. While mean latencies of overt movements ascended in the order of eye, then head, then arm, EMG activation for the eye, neck, and biceps brachii muscles were nearly synchronous. EMG latencies for the neck and biceps brachii muscles always fell in the range of 200 to 220 ms. Because of this virtually synchronous muscle activation, Biguer et al., hypothesized that humans possess a synergy of central representation which involves parallel generation of commands to the segments involved in normal reaching. Such parallel generation of commands would allow faster mobilization of the multiple body segments involved in the reaching movement. Further, they hypothesized that this central representation utilizes information regarding target location within some body-centered map of visual space. This hypothesis seems to be compatible with Arbib's (1980, 1985) internal schema concept. That is, the requisite perceptual schema may be embedded within the motor schemas for head and for eye movements, as well as for arm transport and hand preshaping.

With respect to eye saccades and head movements in adults, the following trends may be summarized. Adults usually fixate a target via a primary, slightly hypometric saccade, followed by one secondary corrective saccade (Biguer et al., 1984; Regal, Ashmead, & Salapatek, 1983). Biguer et al. (1982, 1984) noted a slight but significant increase in saccade latency with target eccentricity. In addition, adult saccades are high velocity (i.e., averaging 800°/sec) and ballistic in nature (Aslin & Salapatek, 1975). With respect to head movement in adult subjects, the amplitude of head rotation increases with eccentricity of the visual target. However, the amplitude of the head movement is hypometric with respect to the target (Biguer et al., 1984, 1985; Regal et al., 1983). Regarding gaze, or the sum of the eye and head movements, Biguer et al. (1984, 1985) found that 60% of the distance to the target is covered by the head movement and that the remaining 40% of the distance is covered by the saccadic movement of the eyes. The axis of the head thus is hardly ever aligned with the target. The role of these body segments with respect to accuracy in reaching will be discussed later.

In summary, mature prehension is characterized by well-coordinated movements of the head, eyes, and upper extremity toward a visual target. The neural commands to the individual body segments may be generated in parallel so as to affect appropriate temporal coordination. Position profiles of the arm, the head, and the eyes indicate that movements of these segments are smoothly and accurately directed toward a visual target and seldom contain more than one correctional movement. Arbib's (1980, 1985) internal schema concept gives some theoretical basis for the temporal coordination of multiple body segments in mature prehension. Specifically, multiple motor schemas can be activated concurrently by the same perceptual schema. Accuracy of the movement is assured by the continuous tuning of the perceptual schema to internal and external environmental parameters.

The issue of accuracy becomes important developmentally because even neo-nates have been shown to exhibit some degree of precision in their reaching (Bower, 1972, 1977, 1982; Bower, Broughton, & Moore, 1970; DiFranco, Muir, & Dodwell, 1978; Dodwell, 1983; Hofsten, 1982). It may be helpful, therefore, to compare factors which determine accuracy in mature and immature reaching.

MATURE PREHENSION—CONTROL OF ACCURACY

Accuracy in prehension implies that once a target object has been localized, its location translated into body-centered coordinates, and its salient features detected, the proximal shoulder/arm musculature transports the hand toward the target and the distal forearm/hand musculature effects proper orientation and preshaping of the hand to achieve successful grasp. Because grasping in mature prehension is usually successful on first attempt, some feedback mechanisms must be operating during the movement to achieve the goal. One question to ask is whether this feedback is monitored intermittently (discrete control) or whether continuous, "on-line" corrections are occurring.

In the study of reaching and pointing in adults, the idea of continuous, "on-line" corrections occurring during movement toward the target is supported. The questions asked are: What information is derived from head and eye movements to enhance reaching accuracy (Biguer et al., 1984, 1985)? What is the role of retinal and oculomotor feedback in target localization (Prablanc et al., 1986; Pélisson et al., 1986)? And what underlying physiological mechanisms may be involved in continuous control of movement (Keller, Slakey, & Crandall, 1983)?

In a paradigm requiring adult subjects to point to light-emitting diode (LED) targets at 10°, 20°, 30° and 40° eccentricities from central fixation, Biguer et al. (1984, 1985) monitored the effect of head movement upon pointing accuracy. These movements were performed without vision of the moving hand. When subjects' heads were not allowed to move, pointing was hypermetric relative to the target (constant error being + 1.07° for a 10° target and + 3.23° for a 40° target). This hypermetria was statistically significant for targets of at least 30° eccentricity. Likewise, absolute error increased with target eccentricity, showing significance for targets at 40° eccentricity. When subjects' heads were allowed to move, there was no significant effect of eccentricity upon accuracy. Constant error hovered around − 0.5° for all targets. Thus, when subjects were tested in the "head-free" condition, pointing accuracy was enhanced, particularly for targets of, at least, 30° eccentricity. Biguer et al. concluded that more information about target position in body-centered space is available when the head *and* the eyes are allowed to move. The head-eye-upper extremity motor complex can operate in normal synergy. Further, kinesthetic information may be utilized in the head-free condition to assist calibration of the body frames of reference. In addition, there may be a critical angular displacement (e.g., 30° eccentricity) of the eyes or of the head beyond which pointing error increases dramatically. Finally, these researchers assume that information about gaze position which affects the motor programming of the upper extremity occurs after the limb begins to move. Because of the nearly synchronous EMG activation of the various segments, incorporation of feedback from gaze position must occur *during* the reaching movement. Therefore, in the head-free condition, position of the head is being continuously monitored and provides information to the motor schema for the upper extremity. This result is interesting in view of the Biguer et al. (1984, 1985) finding that the axis of the head seldom is aligned with the target. The absolute position of the head seems to be less important to accuracy than the interaction of head and eye movements or gaze position.

In addition to feedback derived from head movement, target location information may be obtained from retinal error information (i.e., distance of the target from the fovea) and from proprioceptive information from oculomotor muscles during fixation of a target. To explore these sources of feedback, Prablanc et al. (1986) used the paradigm of Biguer et al. (1984; 1985) described earlier. However, the head was not allowed to move. Pointing accuracy was compared across four visual conditions which manipulated the amount of feedback information available to the retina and/or via the oculomotor muscles. One of the conditions (Condition 4) allowed preprogramming of the hand movement. For this condition, hand movement did not begin until the first saccade toward the LED target was completed, at which time vision of the hand and of the target was precluded. Results indicated that pointing accuracy improved as target duration was increased. When the target was illuminated throughout the movement (Condition 3), pointing error was minimized. In this situation, retinal error *and* oculomotor reafference were available to control the trajectory of the arm movement. Because subjects were more accurate in Condition 3 than in Condition 4, Pélisson et al. concluded that ongoing retinal or oculomotor information allows correction of movement execution errors. Again, as in the work of Biguer et al. (1984; 1985), the idea of continuous error correction regarding target location was supported.

To more directly test the idea of continuous error correction in reaching and pointing movements, Pélisson et al. (1986) asked the question: Can these corrections accommodate a change in target location if this change occurs *during* the arm movement? The assumption is that after the initial saccade of the eyes, updated information of target location is available to tune the trajectory of the arm. The experimental design involved translocation of the LED target during the high-velocity portion of the initial saccade, when subjects were unaware consciously that a change had occurred (double-step paradigm). Also, the translocation always occurred after hand movement was initiated. The distribution of pointing responses in this double-step condition was compared to the distribution of responses for a single-step condition in which the target location remained unchanged. Results showed that the distributions of responses for the two conditions were statistically different for all subjects. Subjects could alter arm trajectory without conscious awareness of target translocation. Further, because this change required no additional central processing time, reprogramming of the movement was not occurring. Instead, Pélisson et al. propose a "pseudocontinuous" control of the movement based upon retinal error information. This conclusion is supported by the absence of any inflection point on the arm trajectory profiles which would indicate a discrete correction in the double-step condition.

In summary, accuracy of reaching in adults is improved when the head *and* the eyes are free to move. When retinal error and extra retinal (e.g., oculomotor) feedback are available *throughout* a reaching movement, accuracy is enhanced. Further, target translocation information is accommodated *during* a reaching movement without evidence of a discrete correction or reprogramming of the movement. Therefore, "pseudocontinuous" control may be occurring. As will be discussed later, this "pseudocontinuous" control of movement may be distinct from the mode of control used by infants.

Although this paper will not explore in depth the physiological basis for this "pseudocontinuous" control, research on the role of the cerebellum in "saccadic" eye movements (Keller et al., 1983) may have implications for this control. In this study, the following model is supported. A local feedback circuit generates an error signal (based upon a centrally created efferent copy of eye position) when the eyes are not located in their orbits at the desired position. This "desired" position is based upon the centrally recreated position of the target in orbital coordinates, presumably derived from retinal information. The motor error signal affects the firing of burst neurons which are located within the brain stem saccadic generator. These neurons synapse upon oculomotor neurons and can affect saccadic output. Usually these burst neurons are inhibited by a pool of tonically discharging pause cells. However, higher visual or volitional brain centers inhibit the pause cells when a saccade is initiated. Therefore, there is a "window" in time during which the burst cells are disinhibited and are able to receive motor error input. The burst cells are active until the motor error is reduced to a small value. During their activity, the burst cells inhibit the pause cells. But then as burst cell activity falls with reduction of the motor error, the pause cells resume their tonic discharge and again inhibit the burst cells. Thus, a type of reciprocal inhibition is occurring in this burst cell-pause cell circuit. Keller et al. hypothesize that electrical stimulation within the posterior vermis of the cerebellum can affect eye movement during that "window" in time when the saccade has begun and the pause cells are inhibited. In their reseach on monkeys, these researchers found that intrasaccadic stimulation of the posterior vermis altered these saccades (e.g., causing significant hypometria in horizontal saccades), which were already partially complete at the neural level. Thus, cerebellar input (possibly via intermediate nuclei) to the burst neurons during the temporal "window," in turn, affects the spatial parameters of saccadic output. The burst neurons are active until the centrally created efferent copy of eye position corresponds to the internal representation of target position. The evidence that ongoing saccades may be corrected based upon motor error information correlates well with the behavioral research (Pélisson et al., 1986; Prablanc et al., 1986). As Prablanc et al. found, a reaching movement is more accurate when retinal and oculomotor feedback regarding target location is available throughout the movement. This feedback may affect the ongoing saccade alteration suggested by Keller et al. (1983). The Keller research, of course, does not address the perceptual-motor mechanism governing arm movement. It may be speculated, however, that this temporal "window" mechanism may update a perceptual schema which, in turn, has access to the motor schema for the upper extremity (e.g., per Arbib's 1985 construct). Parallel generation of neural commands to body segments was suggested by Biguer et al. (1982, 1985). This parallel structure may apply not only to movement initiation, but also to ongoing error correction. The role of the cerebellum in these processes is important in terms of prehensile development. Questions which will be addressed later include: At what point is cerebellar function mature? And does cerebellar immaturity affect infant reaching behavior?

The foregoing discussion emphasizes the effects of visual information upon reaching accuracy. Ongoing kinesthetic tuning of the movement may complement these effects. As Biguer et al. (1985) suggest, kinesthetic information from the neck may adapt to negligible levels when the head is in a fixed position. But when the head is free to move, additional frame-of-reference (i.e., eye relative to head relative to trunk) information is available to tune the reaching movement. Further, because ongoing movements can be controlled without visual feedback of the moving hand, a comparison of visual information regarding target position and nonvisual information regarding hand position may occur (Prablanc et al., 1986).

To summarize, mature prehension is a fluent movement pattern including orientation of the head and eyes to a visual target, movement of the upper extremity toward that target, and coincident shaping of the hand sensitive to target object parameters. For the upper extremity, the arm transport component consists of an initial acceleratory and a final deceleratory phase. The manipulation component consists of smooth opening and closing of the hand. The onset of hand closure appears to be temporally linked to a breakpoint in deceleration in the arm transport component. Accuracy of reaching movements in the mature individual may be governed by "pseudocontinuous" control involving visual error information from the retina, as well as kinesthetic feedback from oculomotor, neck and, upper extremity muscles. Physiological research supports a cerebellar role in transmitting motor error information to burst neurons in the brainstem. These burst neurons then affect the spatial characteristics (and, therefore, accuracy) of ongoing saccades. The implications of this neural mechanism for control of the upper extremity remain speculative. But the idea of a temporal "window" during which error information may be incorporated at the neural level to affect an ongoing movement is intriguing when compared to the behavioral research (e.g., Pélisson et al, 1986).

IMMATURE PREHENSILE PATTERNS

While mature prehension may be governed by this apparent continuous control of upper extremity trajectory, infant prehensile patterns lack this smooth coordination and control. Two somewhat paradoxical questions may be asked regarding infant prehension. First, what factors contribute to this lack of smooth coordination and control? Second, how can we explain evidence of visual control of arm movements in neonates (Bower, 1972, 1977, 1982; Bower et al., 1970; Hofsten, 1980, 1982, 1984; Trevarthen, 1974)?

The first question could be answered by citing factors intrinsic to the infant: an immature nervous system undergoing progressive myelination; a neuromuscular control system in which the involved body segments mature at different times; rapidly changing anatomy and resultant biomechanical constraints; an immature perceptual system. Traditionally, neonates were viewed as lacking intersensory coordination. Specifically, sight, hearing, and touch were unrelated activities and became integrated through the experience or actions of the infant over time (Piaget, 1952, 1953, 1954; Bushnell, 1981; Butterworth, 1983; Hofsten, 1983). The second question, however, requires focusing upon extrinsic factors (i.e., the environment) and a more contemporary view of infant coordination. Infant perception and behavior are now viewed by many authors (Butterworth, 1983; Clark, 1986; Hofsten, 1983; Kugler, Kelso, & Turvey, 1982) in the context of Gibson's (1979) ecological approach. From birth, a structured sensory environment provides the infant with information regarding self-perception relative to that environment. According to Gibson, this perception serves behavior, and behavior is controlled by perception. Therefore, the observation that neonates do not grasp visual objects does not imply that arm movements cannot be visually controlled. Current thought is that early prehensile movement is exploratory (and not manipulative), with sensory organs preadapted to extract environmental information from the beginning of life (Hofsten, 1983). Perception, thus, can be meaningful to behavior from birth rather than being a random array of modality-specific sensations.

Therefore, from birth, prehensile patterns may reflect the current status of the infant-environment interaction. Intrinsic maturation factors interact with the extrinsic structured sensory environment. This "environment" may be broadly defined to include forces produced by the movement itself. In terms of psychological constructs, infants, even neonates, possess an internal representation of the movement goal. This viewpoint allows explanation of visual control of arm movements in neonates. The sophistication of this representation may depend upon the level of interaction of intrinsic and extrinsic factors at any point in development. The elaboration of an infant's internal representation of the movement goal may be defined by two factors. One factor is the appearance of more continuous movement trajectories of the upper extremity, eyes, and head. The second factor is the appearance of anticipatory behavior in forearm orientation and hand shaping appropriate to the target object.

IMMATURE PREHENSILE PATTERNS—UPPER EXTREMITY

The arm trajectory in neonates and young infants has been called ataxic (McGraw, 1943) and zigzag (Halverson, 1931; Hofsten, 1979). The trajectory appears to be governed by discrete, intermittent feedback. The ability to move the hand to the vicinity of the target with a single ballistic unit as seen in adults implies a well-developed representation in body-centered coordinates of the extrinsic characteristics (e.g., distance, direction) of the target. Young infants (up to about 36 weeks of age) do not demonstrate this ability. Likewise, the ability to orient and shape the hand consistent with intrinsic properties of the target object (e.g., dimensions, shape) implies a well-developed representation of these qualities. While mature prehensile patterns, as described earlier, incorporate these features, infants greatly improve hand orientation capabilities between the ages of 5 and 9 months (Hofsten & Fazel-Zandy, 1984; Lockman, Ashmead, & Bushnell, 1984) and hand shaping for a pincer-type grasp develops between 9 and 12 months of age (Gesell, 1946; Halverson, 1931).

TRAJECTORY OF THE UPPER EXTREMITY

In the classic work of Halverson (1931), he noted the circuitous approach of the arm toward a visual target. Halverson filmed infants in age groups between 16 and 52 weeks (cross-sectional study). The target object was a 1-in cube. The observed forms of approach were backhand, circuitous and, straight. The most circuitous approaches occurred in the lower age groups, with 20-week-old infants showing the least direct approach. None of the 16-week-old infants in Halverson's study completed the approach to the cube. By the ages of 36 to 40 weeks, an immature form of a straight approach was observed. These age groups tended to begin with a straight approach, but then digressed laterally. Corrections in trajectory brought the hand back into line with the cube. In terms of vertical trajectory, Halverson observed that infants 20 to 24 weeks of age showed a series of submovements of the arm with a raise-project-lower pattern. By the ages of 40 to 52 weeks, infants could achieve a single, fluent thrust in which they could raise the arm and simultaneously direct its course. In summary, Halverson noted angular, zigzag approaches in the younger infants (16 to 20 weeks of age), with a dominance of abductive/adductive movements at the shoulder and an inability to move the arm fluently (see also Boyd, Albert, Vogtle, Gustke, & Hakala, 1984).

While Halverson's study and other research (e.g., Bower et al., 1970; Field, 1977; Trevarthen, 1974, 1975) offer largely qualitative assessment of infant prehension, von Hofsten and his coworkers have quantitatively analyzed the kinematics of infant reaching movements (e.g., Hofsten, 1979, 1980, 1982, 1984; Hofsten & Fazel-Zandy, 1984; Hofsten & Lindhagen, 1979). Von Hofsten (1979) studied infants longitudinally between the ages of 12 and 36 weeks while they were seated in a semireclining seat, from which they could reach for a colorful toy positioned at nose height. The paradigm included stationary as well as moving targets. Like Halverson (1931), von Hofsten observed a series of submovements within a single reaching attempt. Each submovement or ballistic unit was comprised of one acceleratory and one deceleratory phase, with the opportunity for feedback of hand relative to target position to be monitored at the end of each unit. This discontinuous feedback structure differs from the mature pattern of a smooth, ongoing feedback mechanism. However, with age, infants showed a progression toward fewer movement elements per reach. Reaches consisting of only one or two elements increased from 22% at 15 weeks of age to 75% at 36 weeks. Thus, a trend toward more mature reaching with fewer movement elements can be seen.

In conjunction with fewer movement elements with age, von Hofsten found that the duration of movement elements changed with age depending upon the position of the element within the reach. Infants at 15 weeks of age tended to reach with movement elements which were equal in duration (350–400 ms). With increasing age, the first element lengthened to about 500 ms while subsequent units shortened to about 250 ms. Thus, a trend toward a larger initial ballistic movement within each reach is apparent. Coupled with temporal reorganization of the movement elements with increasing infant age, a larger proportion of the initial distance to the target is covered in the first element. In addition, the maximum acceleration of infant reaches shifted toward the first part of the first movement element. Thus, a greater emphasis is placed upon the first movement element in moving the hand to the vicinity of the target. The apparent need for frequent discrete feedback (especially early in the movement) is diminishing. From a psychological viewpoint, these trends could indicate that the infant's internal representation of the movement goal is becoming better defined during the age range of 12 to 36 weeks. Because this representation is more "complete" at movement onset for the older infants, the first movement element may be preprogrammed to better approximate the "best" approach toward the target. Specification of relative force and duration parameters in the appropriate muscles is better matched with the movement goal. In mature prehension, the initial acceleratory ("ballistic") portion of the movement moves the hand at least two-thirds of the initial distance to the target (see Table 1). The final "guided" phase allows final adjustment of the forearm and hand to target object parameters. In von Hofsten's (1979) study of infants, the first movement element appears to become more comparable to the mature pattern (acceleratory portion) with respect to distance covered, proportion of movement duration, and acceleration.

In summary, both Halverson (1931) and von Hofsten (1979) observed zigzag trajectories in the reaching movements of infants. In the age range of 12 to 20 weeks, in particular, reaching consists of a series of discrete movement elements.

Table 1
Characteristics of Reaching Approach Phase in Infants and Adults

	Infants[a]	**Adults**[b]
Trajectory	**Zigzag**	**Sigmoidal**
Movement elements	1 to 5	1
Distance covered during acceleratory portion of first movement element	With age, increases to 75% of total distance	$\geq$ ⅔ of total disance
Duration of first movement element	With age, changes from equal to significantly greater duration than subsequent movement elements	Encompasses single ballistic phase
Acceleration	Maximum becomes redistributed to *first part* of the first movement element with increasing age	First phase of movement is acceleratory

[a]Observed by von Hofsten, C. (1979). Development of visually directed reaching: The approach phase. *Journal of Human Movement Studies, 5,* 160-178, in infants 12 to 36 weeks of age.
[b]Observed by Jeannerod, M. (1981). Intersegmental coordination during reaching at natural visible objects. In J. Long & A. Baddeley (Eds.), *Attention & performance IX* (pp. 153-169). Hillsdale, NJ: Lawrence Erlbaum.

Digressions from a straight path to the target occur laterally as well as vertically. The vertical digressions indicate that infants may have difficulty compensating for the force of gravity (Hofsten, 1979). Thus, specification of appropriate muscle forces must be matched not only to the target location per se, but also to the counteracting force of gravity for fluent movement to occur.

The presence of discrete movement elements in infant reaching may imply a strategy of successive approximations (Crossman & Goodeve, 1963; Keele, 1968; Langolf, Chaffin, & Faulke, 1976; Schmidt, 1982). This movement strategy consists of two processes: an open-loop, distance-covering phase which alternates with a feedback phase during which the size and direction of the aiming error is evaluated. Breaks between successive open-loop segments should result in discontinuities in the arm trajectory and velocity profiles. For adults in a Fitts' type of tapping task, such discrete control is not evident (Langolf et al., 1976). However, for rapid movements, the processing time for these successive approximations would exceed the observed movement times. But in infant reaching movements, the movement elements are of sufficient duration (at least 250 ms) to allow this feedback strategy. One assumption of the successive approximations strategy is that the average time for the initial movement element and for each corrective movement is equal. While this assumption holds true for the 15-week-old infants, the first movement element became proportionally larger for the older infants in von Hofsten's (1979) study. Thus, we may be seeing a shift away from the strict successive approximations strategy with age. Again, this shift may be indicative of a more elaborate internal representation of the movement goal and an enhanced ability of the infant to function wihin the intrinsic (e.g., eye relative to head) and extrinsic (trunk relative to environment) frames of reference. As will be discussed later, expanding function of the crebellum also may contribute to this shift.

In summary, the zigzag trajectories characterizing reaching movements in young infants (approximate age range of 12 to 36 weeks) may reflect a successive approximations control strategy. However, a shift toward the mature pattern of an initial ballistic, distance-covering phase transporting the arm to the target vicinity is apparent. Expanding perceptual capacities contributing to an internal representation of the movement goal may enable this shift. More fluent arm transport also develops with the effective use of distal forearm and hand musculature and the coordination of proximal and distal forearm and hand muscles.

ANTICIPATORY FOREARM ORIENTATION AND HAND-SHAPING

For an individual to act in an anticipatory manner in a goal-directed movement, an adequate internal representation of the movement goal must exist to allow preprogramming of movement parameters (Mounoud & Hauert, 1982). In an infant whose representation is incomplete, anticipatory forearm orientation and hand shaping may be limited. In addition, the underlying neuromuscular organization must be developed sufficiently to allow effective use of distal musculature and to allow its coordination with proximal arm musculature.

A brief overview of the development of this proximal-to-distal control may be helpful. In neonates, spontaneous forward extensions of the arms are often accompanied by opening of the hand (Hofsten, 1982, 1984; Trevarthen, 1974). This hand opening contrasts with the fisted posture resulting from the passive traction reflex (Twitchell, 1965), but does not necessarily reflect a differentiated response of proximal and distal musculature. Until the age of 2 months, this spontaneous behavior is thought to serve an exploratory rather than manipulative function (Hofsten, 1982). After 2 months of age, however, hand opening is seen during forward extensions of the arm when an infant visually fixates a target object. This hand opening reflects adaptive behavior in preparation for manipulation (Hofsten, 1984). According to von Hofsten, a dissociation of arm and hand movements is occurring at this age. This dissociation may correlate with the advent of cortical control over the distal musculature, although proximal and distal muscles are not yet coordinated. This concept is supported by work of Kuypers (1962, 1964) and Brinkman and Kuypers (1972). These researchers studied split-brain monkeys and found evidence that neural pathways descending from the brainstem primarily control proximal limb musculature, and a direct corticospinal pathway affects distal musculature. This latter pathway results in a high degree of fractionation of finger movements. Specifically, the area of the frontal lobe of the cerebral cortex which controls hand movements significantly increases in thickness during the first 15 months of life. Also, myelination of the pyramidal tract is incomplete until about 2 years of age. Thus, fine motor control of hand movements may be developed and refined during this period (Williams, 1983). The subcortical and cortical pathways mature at different times whereby proximal muscle control occurs prior to distal muscle control. At 2 to 3 months of age, proximal muscles show relative increases in growth and strength (Trevarthen, 1974, 1975). Even at 16 to 20 weeks of age, proximal musculature dominates with little elbow flexion or extension or independent hand movement. By 28 weeks of age, however, more flexibility at the elbow, increased hand rotation, and orientation of the thumb for opposition are evident (Halverson, 1931). Grasp formation becomes better controlled in transition from a crude, whole hand grasp at 18 weeks to a pincer-type grasp at 34 weeks. This grasp formation is now under increased influence of visual guidance (Hofsten & Fazel-Zandy, 1984).

In summary, discrepancy exists among research studies as to the exact advent of proximal-distal musculature coordination. But, generally, the progression appears to be as follows. Until 2 months of age little proximal-distal dissociation of function occurs. Though some dissociation occurs at this time, proximal muscles dominate in strength and control. By 28 weeks, distal muscles are more effective in forearm and hand orientation. And by 34 weeks, a pincer-type grasp appears. At this point, the approach toward the target loses its angularity and refinement of shoulder-elbow joint coordination is apparent.

Thus, by about 34 weeks of age, the underlying neuromuscular capabilities which would enable anticipatory forearm orientation and hand shaping are present. By 40 weeks of age, proximal and distal muscles are approximately equal in efficiency (Gesell, 1946). If the appropriate perceptual abilities and frame-of-reference "mapping" are also present, fairly fluent goal-directed movement should be possible. Recent research will be described to give a more detailed account of these indices of anticipatory behavior: forearm orientation and hand shaping.

Anticipatory manual adjustments during infant reaching movements require visuomotor coordination. Visually detected object parameters may be translated into appropriate prehensile action. Proper orientation of the hand is essential for efficient grasping. To investigate the degree to which infants could orient their hands to a target rod, von Hofsten and Fazel-Zandy (1984) studied 15 infants from 18 to 34 weeks of age (longitudinal study). The final 540 ms period prior to object contact was analyzed. Results showed that for all age levels infants adapted hand orientation to target orientation to some degree. Except at 18 weeks of age, infants improved the adjustment of hand relative to target orientation during the analyzed portion of the reach. At 18 weeks of age, most adjustments were made after contact with the rod. The maturation of the distal motor system contributes to the precision of hand orientation. But conclusions as to age effects were unclear. Specifically, these researchers noted that hand adjustment prior to movement or during the early part of the reach were at least as important as adjustments during the analyzed 540-ms period. Presetting hand orientation early in the movement and making adjustments during the final approach phase were alternative strategies represented at all ages studied. Certain infants maintained a predominant strategy over time. Regardless of strategy, however, anticipatory forearm/hand orientation is occurring between the ages of 18 and 34 weeks.

Lockman et al. (1984) also studied anticipatory hand orientation in infants reaching for a dowel. They analyzed reaches for 5-month-old and 9-month-old infants (16 subjects per group). Reaching movements were divided into segments: beginning, middle, touch, and grasp. Results showed that 9-month-old infants oriented their hands appropriate to target orientation earlier in a reaching movement than 5-month-old infants. Nine-month-old infants achieved proper hand orientation prior to tactual contact with the dowel, and 5-month-old infants achieved proper alignment at the "grasp" point. These researchers concluded that 9-month-old infants can orient their hands more effectively on the basis of visual information than the younger infants. Although Lockman et al. stated that 5-month-old infants have the motor ability for this orientation, Halverson (1931) did not observe significant hand rotation (supination to pronation or semipronation to full pronation) in infants until 28 weeks of age. So some question exists as to the degree of distal control at 5 months of age.

Two additional observations were noted by Lockman et al. (1984). First, the two age groups differed in the visual control of the movement. The younger infants usually looked at the dowel from the beginning of the reach to the point of contact. In contrast, older infants could look *briefly* at the stimulus and still perform the appropriate manual adjustments. Second, the 9-month-old infants achieved appropriate hand orientation whether the dowel was presented at the midline or to the side. However, the 5-month-olds achieved closer hand relative to dowel orientation when the dowel was presented to the side. Therefore, the body/environment coordinate system may not be as well developed in the younger infants. This difference may apply particularly to "mapping" capabilities for the distal muscles. Thus, in the older infants, a brief assessment of object orientation is meaningful within their more fully developed frame-of-reference system. This factor, combined with greater proximal-distal muscular efficiency and coordination, allows more effective programming of hand orientation in the older infants.

In summary, the ability to orient the hand properly to grasp a visual object is refined during the period of about 18 to 38 weeks of age. This refinement in visuomotor coordination may be linked to maturation of distal muscle control and proximal-distal muscle coordination; to development of the infant's frame-of-reference system; and, in general, to elaboration of some central perceptual-motor programming structure. Emerging cortical control of movement is affecting the control of distal musculature. Cortical influence also affects the ability of older infants to briefly visually assess target object parameters and then glance away as the reach is completed. Although this "visual release" action is not expected until about 15 months of age, cortical dominance over movement is expected at about 8½ months of age (McGraw, 1943). Therefore, the "visual release" behavior may reflect an increasing ability to centrally preprogram a reaching movement.

Anticipatory behavior also may be indexed by hand shaping and finger adjustment appropriate to visual object parameters. Bower et al. (1970) observed anticipatory hand shaping under visual control in infants as young as 6 days old. In addition, Trevarthen (1974) noted finger extension and flexion coupled to arm extension and withdrawal relative to a target object in infants of 1 to 2 weeks of age. These neonatal abilities are not well quantified, however, and a clear definition of "anticipatory hand shaping" is missing. Other research (McGraw, 1943) indicated that infants of 5 to 8 months of age show compulsive, repeated finger extension and flexion upon movement initiation. Upon final approach to the target, however, the hand often would be fisted (Field, 1977). McGraw concluded that these hand movements and arm transport are isolated activities.

Such behavior contrasts, of course, with mature temporal coordination between the transport and manipulation components (Jeannerod, 1981). Although 4-month-old infants can reliably contact an object, backhand approaches are prevalent. Grasping at this age, if present, is slow and awkward (Hofsten & Fazel-Zandy, 1984). Accordingly, Halverson (1931) noted a progression from a primitive squeeze grasp at 20 weeks of age to more oppositional (thumb and forefinger) grasps beginning at 36 to 40 weeks of age. Although no precise description of infant hand shaping emerges from these studies, anticipatory parameters including dimension of hand aperture, timing of hand opening, and force of the grasp may be discussed.

Hand aperture, or finger-thumb separation, has been studied in infants 7 to 15 days of age (Bower, 1972). The question was asked: Can infants adjust hand aperture appropriate to target object size? Objects included rods (0.5 cm and 2.5 cm in diameter) and balls (3.5 cm and 7.0 cm in diameter). Bower's results showed that finger-thumb separation (or interhand separation in two-handed reaches) increased monotonically with object size. Bower invoked a Gibsonian (1979) explanation that these infants can translate environmenal stimuli into effective action toward the stimulus object. Two factors regarding Bower's results should be considered, however. First, the *form* of hand shaping for the rod vs the ball was not documented and may be different. Halverson (1931) noted that a slender target object allows fortuitous (not anticipatory) opposition of the thumb and fingers in infants 4 to 20 weeks of age. These infants never demonstrated opposition with a target cube. Thus, knowledge of whether thumb movement is abductive/adductive or oppositional relative to the objects in Bower's study may be important in interpreting the extent to which the stimuli shape the behavior. Second, in Bower's study, the finger-thumb (or interhand) separation exceeded target diameter for the smaller rod and for the larger ball. For the other two objects, effector separation approximated or was slightly less than object diameter. These results contrast to the finer tuning seen in mature prehension. In adults, hand aperture increases with target size but always exceeds target diameter (Jeannerod, 1981). In summary, anticipatory behavior as indexed by hand aperture may be occurring even in neonates. However, fine tuning of aperture dimension and of independent finger adjustment may not appear until 6 to 12 months of age. This fine tuning may be contingent upon pyramidal tract maturation (Williams, 1983) and emerging cortical control (Trevarthen, 1974).

The timing of hand opening in a reaching movement, like hand aperture, is an index of anticipatory behavior. In mature prehension, the hand opens to a maximum aperture and then closes upon approach to the target object. These actions are temporally coordinated with arm transport (Jeannerod, 1981). In 20-week-old infants, Bower (1982) has observed anticipatory hand movement. The hand opens and closes prior to object contact. These movements, therefore, are not tactually controlled. In contrast, Bower observed that in neonates hand closure occurred upon object contact (i.e., offset time = Ø). With age, the offset time increases steadily. That is, hand closure occurs earlier in the reach. By 20 weeks of age, the average offset time is 450 ms, which indicates more successful anticipation and visual control of the grasp. Thus, the timing of final hand closure in a reaching movement appears to be age dependent and linked to increasing visual control of the movement.

The force of grasp is another anticipatory parameter. In mature prehension, grasping force is specified in anticipation of the weight of the target object. During the first year of life, grasping force seems to follow an "all-or-none" law. In infants, grasping force is disproportionate to the pressure necessary to hold and lift an object (Halverson, 1931; McGraw, 1943). Mounoud and Hauert (1982) have studied infants' anticipation of object weight. Their results showed that infants 6 to 8 months of age use a global nonspecific preprogramming strategy with respect to object weight. Prehension is rigid, with stiffened joints resulting from cocontraction of agonist and antagonist muscles. The grasp is functionally adapted to grasp objects of different weights. But prediction of specific weights among various objects is not evident at this age. However, a partial preprogramming strategy appears between 9 and 13 months and progresses toward specific preprogramming of force at 14 to 16 months. These older infants predict weight variations, and grasping force is proportionate to the calculated weight.

To summarize, anticipatory hand shaping has been observed in neonates. Primitive grasping behavior, however, may not appear until around 20 weeks of age. Further, thumb-forefinger opposition is not apparent until about 36 to 40 weeks of age. In reviewing information on the anticipatory parameters of hand aperture, timing of hand closure and grasping force, some trends emerge. While adjustment of hand aperture to object size may be occurring in neonates, anticipatory hand closure becomes more evident at about 20 weeks of age. Further, predictive force specification may not be well developed until 14 to 16 months of age. This progression supports the contention of Lockman et al. (1984) that the development of visuomotor coordination should be discussed with respect to specific object features (e.g., size, weight) rather than in a more global manner.

In terms of the upper extremity, research on prehension supports the idea that the internal representation of intrinsic and extrinsic object features is "incomplete" in infants (Mounoud & Hauert, 1982). The status of this representation reflects interaction between current perception of environmental parameters and neuromuscular maturation. For example, the zigzag trajectory of the arm and apparent successive approximations strategy suggest that young infants (especially in the 3 to 5 month age range) are unable to accurately preprogram target location. At the same time, these infants lack compensatory postural control of their arms relative to gravity. Likewise, anticipatory hand orientation and shaping are dependent upon emergent cortical control of distal muscles and increasing visual guidance of reaching in infants 5 to 9 months of age. During the first year of life, the progressive proximal-to-distal muscle coordination is reflected in fewer discrete movement elements. Response integration becomes possible. This integration means that the entire prehensile sequence is initiated based upon assessment of target parameters prior to movement (Bushnell, 1985). An accurate central representation which links perception with the body-centered coordinate system precludes intermediate assessments during the movement. The next question to ask is: Does this conception apply to eye and head movements in infants?

IMMATURE PREHENSILE PATTERNS—THE ROLES OF THE HEAD AND OF THE EYES

The relationship of eye and head movements to arm movements in infants has not been studied systematically as in adults. However, when orienting to a visual stimulus, eye and head movements in young infants show discontinuities reminiscent of the multiple movement elements found in infant arm trajectories (Aslin & Salapatek, 1975; Hofsten, 1979; Regal, Ashmead, & Salapatek, 1983). Further, compared to adults, head movement may be more important than eye movement in gaze shift in infants (Bullinger, 1983; Owen & Lee, 1986; Regal et al., 1983).

Like adults, the amplitude of head rotation in infants increases with target eccentricity. However, unlike adult, infant head movements often show multiple

Figure 2

Multiple Head Movement Components

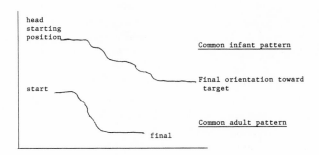

FIG. 2. Adapted from Regal, D. M., Ashmead, D. H., & Salapatek, P. (1983). The coordination of eye and head movements during early infancy: A selective review. *Behavioral Brain Research, 10,* 125–132

movement elements (Fig. 2). Regal et al. (1983) have studied head movements in infants of 1, 3 and 5 months of age. Infants oriented to visual targets at 10°, 20°, 30°, and 40° eccentricity. These researchers observed that multiple movement elements increased in number with target eccentricity, but decreased in number with age. Thus, as with arm trajectories, young infants show discontinuities in head movements when orienting to a visual target.

Some similarities exist between head movement patterns and eye saccades in infants. For example, Regal et al. (1983), as well as Roucoux, Culee, and Roucoux (1983), have noted that target fixation in infants is sometimes achieved via a series of small saccades (Fig. 3). In contrast, adults usually fixate a target via a primary, slightly hypometric saccade, followed by one secondary corrective saccade. Regal et al., by monitoring eye movements using electrooculographic (EOG) techniques, showed that multiple saccades increased with target eccentricity and decreased with age. For instance, among 3-month-old infants, 33% of infants used multiple saccades at 10°, while 75% of infants used multiple saccades at 40° eccentricity. Among the 5-month-old group of infants, only 20% used multiple saccades at 10° and 62% at 40° target eccentricity. Thus multiple saccades decreased in number with age, presumably reflecting a trend toward the more mature pattern of fixation.

The amplitude of saccadic units within an eye movement has been studied in 1- and 2-month old infants (Aslin & Salapatek, 1975). Each saccadic element, whether single or in a series, was approximately equal in amplitude for a given target distance. But, as target distance increased, the amplitude of each saccadic unit increased. So, each saccadic element to a 20° target was about twice as large

Figure 3

Multiple Eye Movement Components

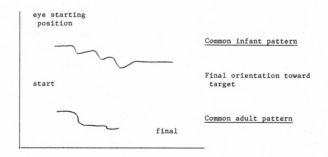

FIG. 3. Adapted from Regal, D. M., Ashmead, D. H., & Salapatek, P. (1983). The coordination of eye and head movements during early infancy: A selective review. *Behavioral Brain Research, 10*, 125–132

as each element to a 10° target. *Within* a given target eccentricity, however, saccadic elements were about equal in amplitude, as indexed by EOG potential. Therefore, young infants apparently program saccade amplitude based upon target eccentricity (or initial retinal error) and then reapply that amplitude until the target is localized. Saccade amplitude is not being revised based upon target location information available between movement elements.

The presence of these multiple elements in both head and eye movements in young infants supports the idea that their internal representation of the movement goal is incomplete. In adults, an initial saccade traverses about 90% of the angular distance to a target. In infants, only about 50% of this distance is traversed by the initial saccade. Thus, the preprogramming of location is limited in these infants. However, a successive approximations model of feedback (Crossman & Goodeve, 1963; Keele, 1968) for head and eye movements may be questionable. For example, the amplitude of saccadic elements apparently is not being updated periodically. However, other parameters (e.g., velocity, duration) which were not reported by Aslin and Salapatek (1975) may have shown sensitivity to intermittent feedback. In addition, intersaccadic intervals were longer for 1-month-old than for 2-month-old infants. Thus, some feedback processing may be occurring during these intervals and may be sensitive to effects of maturation (nervous system and/or cognitive). Future research of infants possibly could address these questions more systematically with paradigms which manipulate the amount of visual feedback available during the gaze shift to a peripheral target.

Head movement in orienting to a visual target is important in young infants (from birth to 5 months of age) for both moving and stationary targets (Bullinger, 1983; Owen & Lee, 1986; Regal et al., 1983). Head turning and eye rotation (including compensatory back rotation) are normally combined in a coordinated pattern to produce head-and-eye saccades for scanning the visual environment. This saccadic scanning is inefficient in infants less than 3 months old. After this time, neck muscles gain strength and tracking of moving targets is achieved in this saccadic manner. By 9 months of age, whole-body postural stabilization may be coordinated with the coupled oscillation of the head and eyes (Trevarthen, 1974). Thus, functional orienting to visual objects can be achieved by a relatively immature visuomotor system (Owen & Lee, 1986).

In fact, 3-day-old infants can track a moving target with their heads (Bullinger, 1983). Experimentally, these infants' heads were released from a starting position and allowed to accelerate to a general orientation consistent with target position. Their heads would then oscillate to a final position reflecting target location. Likewise, Owen and Lee (1986) also found that in 14-week-old infants, head movement is important in compensating for body rotation and tracking moving targets. By 25 weeks of age, head movement trajectory is smooth and head-target coupling reaches adult levels. In contrast, at this age, eye movements are still jerky and eye-target coupling has not reached adult levels. In addition, infants, particularly at 14 weeks of age, lacked prospective head control. That is, head movement which slightly anticipates target movement is not present as in the adult (Owen & Lee, 1986). Thus, although these infants can achieve functional orienting to a visual target, anticipatory capacity and smooth head-eye coordination have not yet matured.

This immaturity of head-eye coordination also is supported by work of Regal et al. (1983). These researchers studied infants of 1, 3, and 5 months of age. Infants oriented to targets at 10°, 20°, 30°, and 40° eccentricity. Results showed that, compared to adults, head movements in these infants assumed even a greater proportion of gaze shift (proportion unreported). Further, head movement in some infants occurred prior to eye movement, particularly at greater target eccentricities. For example, among 3- and 5-month-old infants, 5% of the infants followed this pattern at 10° eccentricity. At 40° target eccentricity, however, 35% of these infants followed the head-prior-to-eye pattern (though compare Goodkin, 1980). This pattern contrasts with the mature pattern (Biguer et al., 1982, 1984, 1985; Bizzi, 1981) in which neural commands to the head and eyes are synchronous, but inertial properties of the head result in an eye-prior-to-head movement pattern. This sequencing difference suggests that the central coordinative structure invoked for adults (e.g., Arbib, 1980, 1985) may not be operating in young infants.

In summary, in infant head-eye coordination, two major trends emerge. First, head and eye movements show discontinuities in young infants. These "sub-movements" are reminiscent of the multiple ballistic components in arm trajectory observed by von Hofsten (1979). Although current research does not provide clear evidence, discrete, intermittent feedback control (Crossman & Goodeve, 1963; Keele, 1968) may be operating in infant head-eye orientation to a visual target. With respect to amplitude of eye saccades in young infants, however, this parameter appears to be insensitive to updated information of retinal error (i.e., distance from line of sight to target). Second, head movement is more important in gaze shift in infants (especially birth to 6 months of age) than in adults. Specifically, a larger proportion of gaze shift is attributed to head movement. Further, in some infants, the head-eye sequencing pattern is distinct from the mature pattern. Thus, although young infants may achieve functional orientation to visual targets, neonates may be utilizing "prefunctional," subcortical coordination (Owen & Lee, 1986; Trevarthen, 1974). As cortical influence over these body segments emerges, smooth, synergistic control of the head and eyes is possible. By approximately 1 year of age, children show a mature pattern of saccades and target acquisition (Roucoux et al., 1983). Thus, during the first year, progressive coordination of the trunk, the head, the eyes, and the upper extremity occurs. Accuracy in prehensile movements is not necessarily dependent upon this "whole-body" coordination. But the control of accurate reaching in infants is distinct from mature prehensile control.

IMMATURE PREHENSION—CONTROL OF ACCURACY

In mature prehension, a model of "pseudocontinuous" movement control has been invoked (Biguer et al., 1985; Pélisson et al., 1986; Prablanc et al., 1986). Such control involves ongoing kinesthetic feedback from the neck and the moving arm, as well as retinal feedback and oculomotor reafference or efference copy. Although the oculomotor signal alone can slightly improve pointing accuracy, this signal coupled with foveal input of target location can improve performance substantially (Prablanc, Echallier, Jeannerod, & Komilis, 1979; Prablanc, Echallier, Komilis, & Jeannerod, 1979). What role do these feedback sources have in immature prehension? In recent years, the extent of neonatal reaching accuracy has been controversial (Bower, 1972, 1977, 1982; Bower et al., 1970; Bower, Dunkeld, & Wishart, 1979; DiFranco et al., 1978; Dodwell, 1983; Dodwell, Muir, & DiFranco, 1979; Hofsten, 1982, 1984; Ruff & Halton, 1978; Trevarthen, 1974). For example, Bower (1972) has observed target object contacts in 40% of reaches by infants 7 to 15 days of age. Ruff and Halton (1978), however, observed contacts in only 7% of reaches by infants in this age group. Nevertheless, sufficient evidence exists to conclude that some level of visuomotor coordination exists in very young infants (Lockman & Ashmead, 1983). In fact, reaching accuracy appears to be controlled to some degree by visual, oculomotor, and kinesthetic feedback.

The importance of visual fixation in infant prehension has been emphasized by von Hofsten (1979, 1982, 1984). The effect of fixation upon reaching accuracy in neonates (5 to 9 days of age) has been studied (Hofsten, 1982). Von Hofsten compared the number of forward arm extensions toward a slowly moving target among different visual behaviors observed in the infants. These behaviors included fixation (F), nonfixation (NF), eyes closed (CL), and indeterminate gaze (IG). The number of forward extensions in the F condition were twice the number for each of the other three categories. Further, in the F condition, the initial distance (infant to target) was reduced to a significantly greater extent (64% vs 54% each for CL + NF and for IG). Regarding accuracy, approach angles were smallest in the F condition (e.g., 32.1° for F vs 54.3° for CL). Therefore, fixation of the target resulted in more frequent and more accurate reaching behavior.

These results are important in the context of the ecological approach (Gibson, 1979) and in isolating factors which contribute to reaching accuracy in neonates. First, although the visual acuity of the infant is approximately 1/30 of adult acuity, fixation of the target elicited more frequent arm extensions and apparently allowed better assessment of the infant-to-target distance. Thus, in the Gibsonian approach, some level of visual perception is guiding these infants' behavior in a meaningful way. Physiological support for this behavior is cited by Maurer and Lewis (1979). Specifically, two visual neural pathways may be functional at birth: the retinal (Y cell)-superior colliculus pathway and the retinal (X cell)-

lateral geniculate nucleus-visual cortex pathway. Although the visual cortex is immature at birth, research on evoked responses shows that some level of geniculocortical activity is present by 1 month of age. At birth, the cortical path may be partially functioning so that some feature detection can occur. In fact, the X-retinal ganglion and lateral geniculate cells are sensitive to high spatial frequency information. Partial functioning of this pathway would contribute to the accuracy of the observed neonate reaching responses to visual targets. Second, extraretinal or oculomotor cues available during fixation of the target may assist the accuracy of forward extensions in neonates. As observed in adults (Prablanc et al., 1979; Prablanc et al., 1986), retinal and extraretinal cues regarding target location may complement each other even in the immature system. Because the superior colliculus and brain stem nuclei involved in oculomotor activity appear to be functional at birth (Keller et al., 1983; Maurer & Lewis, 1979), oculomotor information regarding target location may be utilized by neonates.

To ensure that the fixation/accuracy effect was not the result of head orientation, von Hofsten (1982) measured approach angles when the infant's head was directed at the target in the nonfixated and the indeterminate gaze conditions. He found that approach angles were larger (i.e., less accurate forward extensions) when the head was oriented toward the target. Therefore, he concluded that head orientation does not seem to determine accuracy of the forward extensions. This result corresponds to the conclusion from the research of adults (Biguer et al., 1984, 1985): that the absolute position of the head is not important to reach accuracy. However, the question of whether accuracy of reaching improves in a head-fixed vs a head-free condition in infants remains unanswered. In fact, kinesthetic afference may contribute to infant reaching accuracy. For example, von Hofsten (1982) invoked Bruner's (1973) interpretation of kinesthetic influence. That is, the hand is directed by a locational command via articular proprioception and kinesthesis from the upper extremity. Owen & Lee (1986) extend this idea as follows. They maintain that visual guidance of upper extremity movement requires prior establishment of the frames of reference (eye relative to head, head relative to trunk and trunk relative to upper extremity) by proprioception. Also, the mechanoreceptors of the joints and muscles allow continuous feedback of the movement. But these receptors, in turn, need periodic tuning by vision. While young infants (up to about 5 months of age) can function without vision of their arms, performance without vision deteriorates by about 5 months of age. Owen and Lee (1986) suggest that visual tuning of proprioception begins at this age. This chronology fits with Bushnell's (1985) concept of prehensile control in infants. She defines the basis of prereaching as the "seen target/felt hand." Specifically, prior to 4 months of age, infants rely on prewired, visuoproprioceptive spatial coordination. At 4 months of age, reaching becomes visually guided and more accurate. The "seen target/felt hand" basis for prereaching correlates with von Hofsten's (1982) observation that neonates did not compare hand relative to target position to achieve accuracy (Piaget, 1953). Thus, neonates may have been relying more upon proprioception, or the "felt-hand," while fixating the target.

Control of reaching accuracy in young infants may be summarized as follows. Fixation of the target object contributes to elicitation of reaching behavior and to accuracy of the arm trajectory. This visual fixation effect was observed not only in neonates but also in older infants (12 to 36 weeks of age) (Hofsten, 1979). Visual fixation of the target may allow infants to utilize retinal and extraretinal (oculomotor) cues for movement control. In addition, the role of proprioception may be twofold. First, proprioception may establish the body frames of reference in the young infant. Second, proprioception may provide ongoing control of arm trajectory, particularly important for infants of less than 5 months of age. Between 5 and 9 months of age, visual "tuning" of proprioception occurs. Beyond 9 months of age, infants use less visual guidance and are more able to accurately preprogram the movement (Bushnell, 1985). By this age, discontinuities in arm trajectories have been "smoothed," and more mature patterns are evident. Subcortical control of reaching may predominate in young infants. By 9 months of age, however, cortical influence may allow the observed preprogramming abilities. In addition, perceptual abilities are developed so that a fairly complete central representation of the movement goal and body-centered frames of reference exists.

DISCUSSION

Mature and immature prehensile patterns have been discussed with respect to the sophisication of an internal representation of the movement goal. Mounoud and Hauert (1982) explore the idea that action programs exist at birth, which then vary according to the status of this internal representation. At each developmental stage, new procedures are established based upon new built-in representations. Movement parameters are calculated on the basis of these representations. These calculations anticipate specific situational characteristics including object properties (e.g., size, weight) and action properties (e.g., duration, velocity, amplitude). The extent to which appropriate anticipation occurs is reflected in the movement characteristics. Discontinuous movement characteristics are indicative, therefore, of an "incomplete" internal representation. Thus, prehensile development may be viewed in terms of movement discontinuity and anticipatory capabilities. These factors then become indices of the elaboration of the internal representation of the movement goal.

Movement discontinuities are observed in upper extremity, head, and eye movements when infants orient to a visual target. Trajectories of the upper extremity are zigzag, containing multiple movement elements. During the period from about 3 to 9 months of age, however, a transition toward fewer movement elements and smoother trajectories is apparent. Likewise, with head and eye movements in infants, multiple movement elements also are observed. In the age range of 1 to 5 months, however, the number of multiple movement elements decreases. Trajectories more often assume the mature pattern of a primary movement followed by one corrective element. Thus, for these body segments, the infant acquires enhanced ability to preprogram target location parameters. A shift from respecifying movement parameters during the movement (i.e., successive approximations) to a more anticipatory mode is occurring. The internal representation is being refined in terms of distance and time parameters. In addition, the visuomotor system undergoes calibration. Owen and Lee (1986) define this calibration as the scaling of perceptual information relative to the spatial and temporal dimensions of actions. Through practice, infants discover the relationship between visual "units" with the units of their bodies (e.g., arm length) and of their actions (e.g., speed of the reach). Therefore, the "smoothing" of arm transport is enabled by refinement of the internal representation calibrated in accurate body-centered coordinates.

Anticipatory capabilities in infants also index the status of the internal representation. For example, anticipatory hand orientation relative to a visual object is improved during the period from 5 to 9 months of age. In addition, in this period, infants develop the ability to assess object parameters at movement onset and then glance away while completing the movement. Again, these infants demonstrate an increasing ability to preprogram their movements. Likewise, development of the manipulation component reveals the transition from gross to fine control. Neonates have some ability to adjust hand aperture to object size. However, infants begin to show more mature anticipatory patterns of hand opening/closing at about 5 months of age. At this time, the movement goal is perceived as a separate, manipulable unit toward which manipulatory action can be directed (Hofsten & Spelke, 1985). Further, anticipatory specification of grip force appropriate to the object is developed even later, at 14 to 16 months of age. Thus, a progression of prehensile abilities in which sensitivity to various object parameters (e.g., size, weight) occurs at different times is evident.

The discontinuities and paucity of anticipatory control in the behavior of young infants differ from the mature prehensile pattern. The mature pattern is characterized by relatively smooth trajectories of the upper extremity, head, and eyes when reaching for a visual target. In the adult, these body segments may be activated in parallel as part of a central synergy. Further, the mature temporal coordination of the transportation and manipulation components may not be present during the first year of life, although this has not been quantitatively studied in infants. Like adults, infants may utilize retinal, extraretinal (oculomotor), and kinesthetic feedback to some degree to achieve reaching accuracy. Yet the underlying neural substrates responsible for the mature versus immature prehensile patterns may differ.

For example, the role of the cerebellum in reaching accuracy was suggested based upon the Keller et al. (1983) research. Whereas in adults the cerebellum may be important to correction of eye saccades based upon retinal error relative to a visual target, research indicates that the visual-cerebellar link may be poor until 2 to 3 months of age. However, some cerebellar influence upon the oculomotor system is present by 2 months of age because anomalous eye movements are not seen (Goodkin, 1980). According to Halverson (1931), the cerebellum accounts for 6% of the total brain weight at birth. By 1 month of age, this value is 10%. During the first year of life, the increasing size and function of the cerebellum parallel the increasing control of musculature by the cerebral cortex. The importance of cortical control over distal forearm and hand musculature was discussed earlier. In addition, the coordination of multiple body segments to achieve skilled prehension reflects cortical control. The importance of the parietal cortex to prehensile coordination has been emphasized (Jeannerod, 1984). In studying prehension in a patient with parietal lobe damage, Jeannerod observed the following behaviors. First, temporal coordination between the transportation and manipulation components was disrupted. Second, anticipatory finger posturing was lacking. Although the spatial accuracy of arm transport was not affected, the manipulation component was altered. That is, a palmar, rather than fingertip, grasp was used. These behaviors are reminiscent of the patterns seen in young infants. Thus, in infants, the advent of anticipatory hand shaping and temporal coordination of the prehensile components may indicate the emerging function of the parietal cortex. While the behavior of older infants (at least 5 months of age) may reflect this emerging cortical control, reaching in young infants may be controlled primarily by subcortical structures (e.g., superior colliculus and brain stem).

Until prehension comes under substantial cortical control, the application of Arbib's 1985 construct is meaningless. The temporal framework suggested by Arbib can only apply to a mature system in which the parietal cortex, in particular, is functioning. Nevertheless, young infants demonstrating prereaching behavior are responding to objects in their environment in a meaningful way. The visual pathways enabling this behavior may be functional to some extent at birth (Maurer & Lewis, 1979). Although older infants (approximately 3 to 9 months of age) may be using a successive approximations strategy in reaching for visual objects, very young infants may be relying upon innate coordinative patterns (Hofsten, 1984) to govern their prereaching behavior. This behavior may be ballistic and unaffected by intermittent feedback (Bower, 1977; Bushnell, 1985). Apparently at about 7 weeks of age, however, restructuring of these coordinative patterns may be occurring. At this time, a decrease in reaching activity occurs, followed by a dramatic increase in forward arm extensions and finger-opening activity (Hofsten, 1984). Again, nervous system maturation may underlie these changes. In addition, these infants may be reaching a "critical point" in their anatomical growth. Biomechanically, the former movement pattern becomes untenable and a new pattern is required (Kugler et al., 1982). Whether the impetus for transitions in behavior are neurally or biomechanically based, maturational changes may be viewed as part of the "environment" to which the infant must adjust. The changes in this environment contribute to the updating of the infant's internal representation of the movement goal.

To better define the transitions of infant prehensile behavior, systematic, quantitative study in several areas would be helpful. Evaluation of hand shaping needs to be more defined, particularly in very young infants. Spatial, as well as temporal, characteristics of this shaping are important. In addition, the question raised by Hofsten and Fazel-Zandy (1984) regarding alternative timing strategies of hand orientation remains unanswered. That is, is it appropriate to say that anticipatory hand orientation improves between 5 and 9 months of age? Or is there use of alternative strategies across ages such that some infants orient their hands early in the movement while others delay this orientation? Finally, a more detailed study of the effects of visual fixation and retinal/extraretinal feedback during reaching in infants would be helpful. Such study could ascertain whether intermittent feedback is utilized, thus causing the discontinuous trajectories of the prehensile segments. As a more detailed picture of infant prehension emerges, programming strategies during development may become more clear.

REFERENCES

Arbib, M. A. (1980). Interacting schemas for motor control. In G. E. Stelmach & J. Requin (Eds.), *Tutorials in motor behavior* (pp. 71–81). New York: North Holland.

Arbib, M. A. (1985). Schemas for the temporal organization of behavior. *Human Neurobiology, 4*, 63–72.

Aslin, R. N., & Salapatek, P. (1975). Saccadic localization of visual targets by the very young human infant. *Perception and Psychophysics, 17*, 293–302.

Biguer, B., Jeannerod, M., & Prablanc, C. (1982). The coordination of eye, head, and arm movements during reaching at a single visual target. *Experimental Brain Research, 46*, 301–304.

Biguer, B., Jeannerod, M., & Prablanc, C. (1984). The contribution of coordinated eye and head movements in hand pointing accuracy. *Experimental Brain Research, 55*, 462–469.

Biguer, B., Jeannerod, M., & Prablanc, C. (1985). The role of position of gaze in movement accuracy. In M. I. Posner & O. S. M. Marin (Eds.), *Attention and performance XI* (pp. 407–424). Hillsdale, NJ: Lawrence Erlbaum Associates.

Bizzi, E. (1981). Eye-head coordination. In J. M. Brookhart & V. B. Mountcastle (Eds.), *Handbook of physiology, section 1: The nervous system, Vol. II, motor control, part 2* (pp. 1321–1336). Bethesda, MD: American Physiology Society.

Bower, T. G. R. (1972). Object perception in infants. *Perception, 1*, 15–30.

Bower, T. G. R. (1977). *A primer of infant development*. San Francisco, CA: W. H. Freeman.

Bower, T. G. R. (1982). *Development in infancy*. San Francisco, CA: W. H. Freeman.

Bower, T. G. R., Broughton, J. M., & Moore, M. K. (1970). The coordination of visual and tactual input in infants. *Perception & Psychophysics, 8*, 51–53.

Bower, T. G. R., Dunkeld, J., & Wishart, J. G. (1979). Infant perception of visually presented objects. *Science, 203*, 1137–1138.

Boyd, C. E., Albert, J., Vogtle, L. K., Gustke, L., & Hakala, M. W. (1984). Kinesiological analysis of the upper extremity during grasp in the three-month-old. *Physical and Occupational Therapy in Pediatrics, 4*, 51–67.

Brinkman, J., & Kuypers, H. G. J. M. (1972). Splitbrain monkeys: Cerebral control of ipsilateral and contralateral arm, hand and finger movements. *Science, 176*, 536–539.

Bruner, J. S. (1973). Organization of early skilled action. *Child Development, 44*, 1–11.

Bullinger, A. (1983). Space, the organization and objects, their cognitive elaboration in infants. In A. Hein & M. Jeannerod (Eds.), *Spatially oriented behavior* (pp. 215–222). New York: Springer-Verlag.

Bushnell, E. W. (1981). The ontogeny of intermodal relations: Vision and touch in infancy. In R. D. Walk & H. L. Pick, Jr. (Eds.), *Intersensory perception and sensory integration* (pp. 5–35). New York: Plenum Press.

Bushnell, E. W. (1985). The decline of visually guided reaching during infancy. *Infant Behavior and Development, 8*, 139–155.

Butterworth, G. (1983). Structure of the mind in human infancy. In L. P. Lipsitt (Ed.), *Advances in infancy research* (Vol. II, pp. 1–29). Norwood, NJ: Ablex.

Clark, J. E. (1986). The perception-action perspective: A commentary on von Hofsten. In M. G. Wade & H. T. A. Whiting (Eds.), *Motor development in children: Aspects of coordination and control* (pp. 197–206). Dordrecht: Martinus Nijhoff.

Crossman, E. R. F. W., & Goodeve, P. J. (1963). Feedback control of hand movement and Fitts' law. *Proceedings of the Experimental Society*, Oxford.

DiFranco, D., Muir, D. W., & Dodwell, P. C. (1978). Reaching in very young infants. *Perception, 7*, 385–392.

Dodwell, P. C. (1983). Spatial sense of the human infant. In A. Hein & M. Jeannerod (Eds.), *Spatially oriented behavior* (pp. 197–213). New York: Springer-Verlag.

Dodwell, P. C., Muir, D. W., & DiFranco, D. (1979). (Retort to Bower, Dunkeld, & Wishart reference), *Science, 203*, 1138–1139.

Field, J. (1977). Coordination of vision and prehension in young infants. *Child Development, 48*, 97–103.

Gesell, A. (1946). The ontogenesis of infant behavior. In L. Carmichael (Ed.), *Manual of child psychology* (Vol. I, pp. 335–373). New York: Wiley.

Gibson, J. J. (1979). *The ecological approach to visual perception*. Boston: Houghton Mifflin.

Goodkin, F. (1980). The development of mature patterns of head-eye coordination in the human infant. *Early Human Development, 4*, 373–386.

Halverson, H. M. (1931). An experimental study of prehension in infants by means of systematic cinema records. *Genetic Psychology Monographs, 10*, 107–285.

Hofsten, C. von. (1979). Development of visually directed reaching: The approach phase. *Journal of Human Movement Studies, 5*, 160–178.

Hofsten, C. von. (1980). Predictive reaching for moving objects by human infants. *Journal of Experimental Child Psychology, 30*, 369–382.

Hofsten, C. von, (1982). Eye-hand coordination in the newborn. *Developmental Psychology, 18,* 450–461.

Hofsten, C. von. (1983). Foundations for perceptual development. In L. P. Lipsitt (Ed.), *Advances in infancy research* (Vol. II, pp. 241–264). Norwood, NJ: Ablex.

Hofsten, C. von. (1984). Developmental changes in the organization of prereaching movements. *Developmental Psychology, 20,* 378–388.

Hofsten, C. von, & Fazel-Zandy, S. (1984). Development of visually guided hand orientation in reaching. *Journal of Experimental Child Psychology, 38,* 208–219.

Hofsten, C. von, & Lindhagen, K. (1979). Observations on the development of reaching for moving objects. *Journal of Experimental Child Psychology, 28,* 158–173.

Hofsten, C. von, & Spelke, E. S. (1985). Object perception and object-directed reaching in infancy. *Journal of Experimental Psychology: General, 114,* 198–222.

Jeannerod, M. (1981). Intersegmental coordination during reaching at natural visible objects. In J. Long & A. Baddeley (Eds.), *Attention & performance IX* (pp. 153–169). Hillsdale, NJ: Lawrence Erlbaum.

Jeannerod, M. (1984). The contribution of open-loop and closed loop modes in prehension movements. In S. Kornblum & J. Requin (Eds.), *Preparatory states and processes* (pp. 323–337). Hillsdale, NJ: Lawrence Erlbaum.

Keele, S. W. (1968). Movement control in skilled motor performance. *Psychological Bulletin, 70,* 387–403.

Keller, E. L., Slakey, D. P., & Crandall, W. F. (1983). Microstimulation of the primate cerebellar vermis during saccadic eye movements. *Brain Research, 288,* 131–143.

Kremenitzer, J. P., Vaughan, H. G., Jr., Kurtzberg, D., & Dowling, K. (1979). Smooth-pursuit eye movements in the newborn infant. *Child Development, 50,* 442–448.

Kugler, P. N., Kelso, J. A. S., & Turvey, M. T. (1982). On the control and co-ordination of naturally developing systems. In J. A. S. Kelso & J. E. Clark (Eds.), *The development of movement control and coordination* (pp. 5–78). New York: Wiley.

Kuypers, H. G. J. M. (1962). Corticospinal connections: Postnatal development in the Rhesus monkey. *Science, 138,* 678–680.

Kuypers, H. G. J. M. (1964). The descending pathways to the spinal cord, their anatomy and function. In J. C. Eccles & J. C. Shade (Eds.), *Organization of the spinal cord* (pp. 151–188). Amsterdam: Elsevier.

Langolf, G. D., Chaffin, D. B., & Foulke, J. A. (1976). An investigation of Fitts' Law using a wide range of movement amplitudes. *Jounal of Motor Behavior, 8,* 113–128.

Lockman, J. J., & Ashmead, D. H. (1983). Asynchronies in the development of manual behavior. In L. P. Lipsitt (Ed.), *Advances in Infancy Research* (Vol. II, pp. 113–136). Norwood, NJ: Ablex.

Lockman, J. J., Ashmead, D. H., & Bushnell, E. W. (1984). The development of anticipatory hand orientation during infancy. *Journal of Experimental Child Psychology, 37,* 176–186.

Maurer, D., & Lewis, T. L. (1979). A physiological explanation of infants' early visual development. *Canadian Journal of Psychology/Review of Canadian Psychology, 33,* 232–252.

McGraw, M. B. (1943). *The neuromuscular maturation of the human infant.* New York: Columbia University Press.

Mounoud, P., & Hauert, C-A. (1982). Development of sensorimotor organization in young children: Grasping and lifting objects. In G. E. Forman (Ed.), *Action and thought—From sensorimotor schemes to symbolic operations* (pp. 3–35). New York: Academic Press.

Owen, B. M., & Lee, D. N. (1986). Establishing a frame of reference for action. In M. G. Wade & H. T. A. Whiting (Eds.), *Motor development in children: Aspects of coordination and control* (pp. 287–308). Dordrecht: Martinus Nijhoff.

Paillard, J. (1980). The multichanneling of visual cues and the organization of a visually guided response. In G. E. Stelmach & J. Requin (Eds.), *Tutorials in motor behavior* (pp. 131–146). New York: North Holland.

Paillard, J. (1982). The contribution of peripheral and central vision to visually guided reaching. In D. J. Ingle, M. A. Goodale, & R. J. W. Mansfield (Eds.), *Analysis of visual behavior* (pp. 367–385). Cambridge, MA: MIT Press.

Paillard, J., & Beaubaton, D. (1976). Triggered and guided components of visual reaching: Their dissociation in split-brain studies. In M. Shahani (Ed.), *The Motor system: Neurophysiology and muscle mechanism* (pp. 371–384). Amsterdam: Elsevier Scientific.

Pélisson, D., Prablanc, C., Goodale, M. A., & Jeannerod, M. (1986). Visual control of reaching movements without vision of the limb. II. Evidence of fast unconscious processes correcting the trajectory of the hand to the final position of a double-step stimulus. *Experimental Brain Research, 62*, 303–311.

Piaget, J. (1952). *The origins of intelligence in children*. New York: Norton.

Piaget, J. (1953). *The origin of intelligence in the child*. London: Routledge & Kegan Paul.

Piaget, J. (1954). *The construction of reality in the child*. New York: Basic Books.

Prablanc, C., Echallier, J. E., Jeannerod, M., & Komilis, E. (1979). Optimal response of eye and hand motor systems in pointing at a visual target. II. Static and dynamic visual cues in the control of hand movement. *Biological Cybernetics, 35*, 183–187.

Prablanc, C., Echallier, J. E., Komilis, E., & Jeannerod, M. (1979). Optimal response of eye and hand motor systems in pointing at a visual target. I. Spatio-temporal characteristics of eye and hand movements and their relationship when varying the amount of visual information. *Biological Cybernetics, 35*, 113–114.

Prablanc, C., Pélisson, D., & Goodale, M. A. (1986). Visual control of reaching movements without vision of the limb. I. Role of retinal feedback of target position in guiding the hand. *Experimental Brain Research, 62*, 293–302.

Reed, E. S. (1982). An outline of a theory of a action systems. *Journal of Motor Behavior, 14*, 98–134.

Regal, D. M., Ashmead, D. H., & Salapatek, P. (1983). The coordination of eye and head movements during early infancy: A selective review. *Behavioral Brain Research, 10*, 124–132.

Roucoux, A., Culee, C., & Roucoux, M. (1983). Development of fixation and pursuit eye movements in human infants. *Behavioral Brain Research, 10*, 133–139.

Ruff, H. A., & Halton, A. (1978). Is there directed reaching in the human neonate? *Developmental Psychology, 14*, 425–426.

Schmidt, R. A. (1982). *Motor control and learning: A behavioral emphasis*. Champaign, IL: Human Kinetics.

Trevarthen, C. (1974). The psychobiology of speech development. *Language and brain: Developmental aspects. Neuroscience Research Program Bulletin, 12*, 570–585.

Trevarthen, C. (1975). Growth of visuomotor coordination in infants. *Journal of Human Movement Studies, 1*, 57.

Twitchell, T. E. (1965). The automatic grasping responses of infants. *Neuropsychologica, 3*, 247–259.

Williams, H. G. (1983). *Perceptual and motor development.* Englewood Cliffs, NJ: Prentice Hall.

AUTHOR NOTE

I gratefully acknowledge the assistance of Dr. Steven Keele and Dr. Marjorie Woollacott for their comments on a draft of this article.

12

DEVELOPMENT OF OBJECT INTERCEPTION

Kathleen Williams

Kansas State University

ABSTRACT

Object interception encompasses a broad range of simple and complex motor actions, from anticipating the "movement" of a row of lights in order to push a button at the appropriate time to arriving at the correct place on a tennis court to return an overhead smash. Despite differing levels of complexity, any interception task involves spatial-temporal tracking of an object, decision-making about how and when to respond, and body positioning or repositioning in order to successfully meet the object. It is well documented that older children and adults perform these types of tasks more proficiently than younger children. Applied and basic research dealing with the development of object interception is reviewed to demonstrate the convergence in the results of these studies, despite widely differing experimental tasks and paradigms.

Object interception may be loosely defined as the ability to be at the right place at the right time in order to make an appropriate motor response. More specifically, object interception involves the processes of visually tracking an object over time and through space, positioning the body or body parts accurately to receive an object, and decision-making about when and how to respond. The types of tasks encompassed under this rubric may be placed on a continuum, depending upon the extent to which each of these processes is involved. At one end of the continuum are tasks like charging the net in tennis to return a drop shot. Complex responses like these require a high degree of tracking, positioning, and decision-making. At the other end of the continuum, pressing a button to intercept a "blip" on an oscilloscope screen or Bassin Timer minimizes spatial demands, and emphasizes temporal requirements. Somewhere between these two extremes are activities like playing catch with a 3- or 4-year-old. The thrower tosses the ball gently to a very stationary youngster. Spatial and temporal tracking demands are present, as are decisions about what specific response should be made. Most adult throwers, however, minimize the amount of positioning or repositioning that must be done by these developmentally young performers. While these tasks differ dramatically in their response demands, they have a common anticipatory element: To be successful, performers must anticipate *where* and *when* to make their response.

Over the last 10 to 15 years, developmentalists have become interested in studying interception tasks from both basic and practical perspectives. Some researchers have been interested primarily in describing the overt movement patterns used by performers as they progress from their first rudimentary attempts at specific movement skills (e.g., catching—Seefeldt, Reuschlein, & Vogel, 1972; punting—Roberton & Halverson, 1984). Others (Payne, 1982) have examined age or task complexity differences in order to add to our knowledge about teaching methodologies or task appropriateness. Investigators interested in more basic information have attempted to discover what processes underlie successful object interception and how they may change over time (Haywood, 1977; Shea, Krampitz, Northam, & Ashby, 1982).

The purpose of this review is to synthesize these different types of information about object interception. This synthesis will be divided into three parts. First, process-oriented or descriptive investigations will be summarized. These studies generally involve some type of catching task and often try to offer practitioners specific information relating to skill learning. Second, experimental studies, using tasks with minimal response demands, will be reviewed. These investigations provide much of our information about the mechanisms underlying specific changes which occur as children (or adults) become more competent movers and anticipators. They have yielded information about age differences in sensory and motor processing. Finally, two currently popular models for explaining the changes described will be discussed. Motor programming and a dynamic model of movement production will be described briefly. Their power to explain adequately the observed aged differences in interception skills will be examined.

PROCESS DESCRIPTIONS OF INTERCEPTION SKILLS

Until recently, most of the research related to the ontogenesis of interception skills consisted of process descriptions of change. Overt movement configurations were detailed from the time a skill first emerged to when it reached its most advanced or complex form. Some developmental sequences detail patterns of change without specifying *when* or *if* that change would occur for every individual. For example, investigators carefully described what novice performers looked like as they attempted to catch a tossed ball. They detailed the actions of more proficient performers as they attempted skills like kicking or striking a stationary or moving object. Other investigators have chronicled the emergence of movement skills with the explicit goal of providing guidelines for "normal" development for parents and practitioners. These lists of motor skills, from their simplest to most complex, were intimately tied to the ages at which certain skills were observed to emerge in (generally) 50% or more of a subject sample.

The bulk of the validation studies for developmental sequences have been performed in two laboratories, at Michigan State University and at the University of Wisconsin. The Michigan State group (see review in Branta, Haubenstricker, & Seefeldt, 1984; Seefeldt et al., 1972) described sequences for catching, kicking and striking based on mixed longitudinal data. Langendorfer (1982) and Roberton and Halverson (1984) have hypothesized, and in some cases partially validated, sequences of change in interception skills from cross-sectional and longitudinal samples. Although some specific sequences differ substantially from one investigator to another, they all illustrate trends from less preparation or anticipation of what is necessary for optimal success to a more accurate anticipation of events and a preparation for action. For example, Roberton (Roberton & Halverson, 1984) hypothesized the sequence of changes which occur in various body parts as individuals gain competence in punting (Table 1). She divided the body into two movement components, the arm and leg action. Additionally, she hypothesized that preparation (ball release) and action (ball contact) phases change at different rates. Therefore, the arm action component was subdivided into two phases. When validated, this developmental sequence would describe the sequence of changes that occurs as punters become competent performers.

There are numerous textbooks which catalogue the available research about hypothesized and validated developmental sequences of change. Wickstrom's (1983) text is the most exhaustive synthesis of this work, including unpublished theses and dissertations.

Another body of literature, also descriptive, chronicled the emergence of interception skills with an emphasis on the age of attainment. These investigations emphasized success or failure during a performance. There was little attempt to link success with "form", or process, as described by developmental sequences. If form was considered at all, it was of secondary importance, since normative standards were of primary interest. For example, McCaskill and Wellman (1938) and others (Gutteridge, 1939) used a 50% success rate to determine the age by which a criterion level of proficiency was expected. They ordered skills from simple to complex and then estimated motor ages, based upon when half of the children at that age successfully completed the task. For example, by 44 months, 50% of the children McCaskill and Wellman (1938) tested were able to catch a large, 9½-inch ball.

Table 1
Hypothesized Developmental Sequences for Punting

Arm Component: Ball Release

Step 1.   Hands are at the sides of the ball. Ball tossed upward from both hands after support foot has landed.

Step 2.   Hands are at the sides of the ball. Ball dropped from chest height after support foot has landed.

Step 3.   Hands are at the sides of the ball. Ball is lifted upward and forward from the waist. It is released at or just prior to support foot landing.

Step 4.   One hand is rotated to the side and under the ball. Other hand is on top of the ball. Hands carry the ball on a forward and upward path during the approach. Ball is released at chest level as the final approach stride begins.

Arm Component: Ball Contact

Step 1.   At ball contact, arms drop bilaterally from ball release to a position on each side of the hips.

Step 2.   After ball release, arms bilaterally abduct. The arm on the side of the kicking leg may pull back as that leg swings forward.

Step 3.   After ball release, the arms bilaterally abduct during flight. At contact, the arm opposite the kicking leg has swung forward with that leg. The arm on the side of the kicking leg remains abducted and to the rear.

Leg Component

Step 1.   No step or one short step is taken. Kicking leg swings forward from a position parallel to or slightly behind the support foot. Knee may be totally extended by contact or, more frequently, still flexed 90 degrees with contact above or below the knee joint. Thigh is still moving forward at contact. Ankle tends to be flexed.

Step 2.   Several steps may be taken. The last step onto the support leg is a long stride. The thigh of the kicking leg has slowed or stopped forward motion at contact. The ankle is extended: The knee has 20 to 30 degrees of extension still possible by contact.

Step 3.   Child may take several steps, but the last is actually a leap onto the support foot. After contact, momentum of the kicking leg pulls the child off the ground in a hop.

Note. From M. A. Roberton and L. E. Halverson (1984). *Developing children: Their changing movement* (pp. 122-123). Philadelphia: Lea & Febiger.

Catching: Influential Environmental Factors

Many recent studies have emphasized age differences in catching skill. In particular, investigators examined the relationship between environmental variables (like ball size or distance thrown) and developmental level. Some researchers (e.g., Issacs, 1980; Payne & Koslow, 1981) used rating scales based on developmental sequences (like Hellweg, 1972) to quantify descriptions of catching performance. The results of these and other, similar investigations are consistent. For the most part, children catch larger balls more often than smaller ones, especially at younger ages (Gutteridge, 1939; Isaacs, 1980; McCaskill & Wellman, 1938; Payne, 1982; Payne & Koslow, 1981); older children use "better form". That is, older children make hand catches, rather than trapping the ball against their bodies. Smaller balls are more successful at bringing out this pattern, even in young children (DuRandt, 1985; Isaacs, 1980).

In addition to their important descriptions of age changes in motor skills, some of these studies have begun to shed light on the types of factors that contribute to improved control. For example, Ridenour (1974) found that object speed was important in determining flight direction, whereas object size was not. She also found that objects moving toward the midline were most easily detected by the youngsters in her study.

Ball trajectory is another factor that has an impact on successful catching (Table 2). DuRandt (1985) found that different aged children were most successful at catching balls thrown at different trajectories. Although 4-year-olds were generally poor catchers (averaging only a 20% success rate), they caught *most* often when the ball had a low trajectory; on the other hand, a throw with a medium arc resulted in more catches by older children.

The influence of ball color was examined by several investigators. It appears to be an important perceptual factor involved in catching success. Unfortunately,

Table 2
Mean Success Rate (%) in Catching Balls of Different Trajectories

	Age Groups		
Trajectory	**4 years**	**6 years**	**8 years**
Low	24.31	42.48	77.19
Medium	17.96	47.29	83.67
High	16.02	39.75	82.73

Note. From R. DuRandt (1985). Ball catching proficiency among 4-, 6-, and 8-year-old girls. In J. E. Clark & J. H. Humphrey (Eds.) *Motor development: Current selected research* (p. 39). Princeton, NJ: Princeton Book Co.

because of differences in how color was manipulated, its precise importance is unclear. Isaacs (1980) found that 7-year-old children caught their preferred ball color using the best form. Morris (1976) found that children caught blue and yellow balls better than white ones (he did not ask children which color they preferred). The size of this effect decreased with age, suggesting to Morris that lesser skilled catchers were more influenced by color. Contrast between background and ball also affected catching. In general, the greater the contrast between the two, the greater the catching proficiency. This was not true when white balls were used, however, suggesting an interaction between the attention-getting qualities of a color and the background against which the child is working. These data demonstrate the importance of the context in which the skill is being performed—a fact that is being taken into account by more and more developmentalists (Clark, 1987; Roberton, 1987; Thelen, 1987).

A final, but perhaps most important factor in catching success is the use of available response time. Children appear to become more efficient and effective in its use with increasing age. In her classic study of age differences in interception skill, Harriet Williams (1967) found a fascinating interplay between temporal and spatial accuracy. In that investigation, first- to sixth-graders had to predict where and when a projected ball would land. Williams (1967) found that the youngest children began their responses as quickly as the oldest children she tested. These first-graders were spatially and temporally inaccurate, however. Williams stated that these youngsters moved "as quickly and as far as [they] could in the 'time alloted' (p. 8)". By fourth grade (9 years), children erred in the opposite direction—they waited and watched the ball for inordinate amounts of time, resulting in spatially accurate, but *very late* responses. Finally, around 11-12 years, the children coordinated their ability to move to the correct landing spot both quickly and accurately.

Findings of a study by Pelligrini (1979) were consistent with Williams's (1967), although she used a different approach and paradigm. Pelligrini required 7- to 11-year-olds to observe projected balls for either 200 or 300 ms before they could begin to move to catch them. She found that children's catches were better if they waited longer (300 ms) before moving into position. The youngest children tested benefitted most from waiting. These results suggested that the children were able to extract information that they did not "normally" receive—information that 7-year-olds in Williams's study might have used to improve their accuracy.

The investigations reviewed to this point relied principally on descriptions of the course of development for selected interception skills. Developmental sequences for skills like punting and catching trace specific actions from their onset to their highest level of competence. Researchers studying the ontogenesis of catching are beyond this first level of description and have begun to determine what environmental factors (like trajectory, ball size, and color) can influence the level of skill observed. Although several of these studies indirectly explored processing differences across the ages investigated, none directly sought to uncover underlying mechanisms which control the ability to successfully intercept and receive an object. The next section of this review will examine that body of research, primarily experimental in nature, which is beginning to discover these mechanisms of control.

EXPERIMENTAL INVESTIGATIONS OF OBJECT INTERCEPTION

Experimental studies of object interception, often called coincident or coincidence anticipation, generally use tightly controlled stimulus inputs and minimal response requirements. A stimulus can consist of viewing a "blip" on an oscilloscope or TV screen, or the lights on a Bassin runway. Somewhat more complex tasks include watching a ball or other object as it drops down a chute or moves along a trackway. Stimuli are varied by changing their speed. Subjects' responses to these stimuli are very simple, generally a button push or release made by the hand or foot. At most, a simple arm movement, reminiscent of a linear positioning task, might be used. Despite the minimal response requirements of these tasks, patterns of age differences found in these studies have been consistent with those catching studies cited earlier.

Regardless of task specifics, differing displays, or stimulus velocities, many of these investigations yielded an unsurprising age effect. At all speeds, older children or adults perform more accurately than young children. Of greater interest, however, is an initially unexpected age and velocity interaction (Fig. 1), found when stimuli range from slow to moderately paced. The youngest children (here 5 years old) responded progressively earlier to slow moving stimuli. It was not until 7 and 9 years of age that slowing stimuli down resulted in smaller errors. On the other hand, subjects of all ages responded increasingly later to faster stimulus speeds. This interaction was found across a number of different investigations, with a variety of simple movements, from a button press (Haywood, 1977) to a linear arm movement (Shea et al., 1982; Williams, 1985, in press; Wrisberg & Mead, 1983), a simple catching movement (Isaacs, 1980), or video game (Ball & Glencross, 1985). Wade (1980) found similar results when he tested young, mentally retarded children as they performed an arcade-type interception task. Early responses to slow-moving stimuli remained following training (Wrisberg & Mead, 1983) and were amplified in subjects who were trained using relatively fast stimulus velocities.

There have been some inconsistencies in this general pattern of results. For example, Dunham (1977) tested 7- to 12-year-olds and found age main effects, but no stimulus speed by age interaction. The speeds he used, however, were faster than those used by many investigators. Subjects tested by Bard, Fleury,

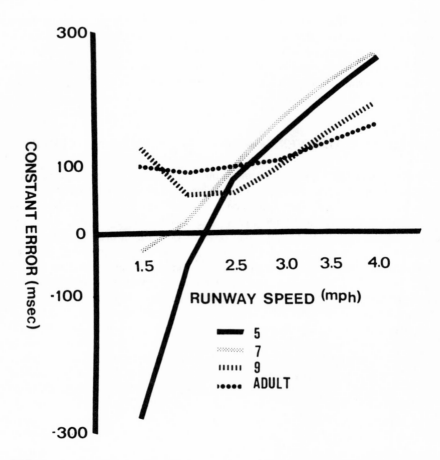

FIG. 1. Constant errors (in ms) for 5-, 7-, 9-year-old boys and adult males responding to stimuli traveling between 1.5-4.0 mph. (reprinted from "Age Differences on a Coincident Anticipation Task: Influence of Stereotypic or 'Preferred' Movement Speed", Kathleen Williams, *Journal of Motor Behavior, 17*(4), 394, 1985. Reprinted with permission of the Helen Dwight Reid Educational Foundation. Published by Heldref Publications, 4000 Albemarle St. N.W., Washington, D.C. 20016. Copyright © 1985.)

Carriere, and Bellec (1981) performed more accurately in relation to a faster stimulus at all ages, i.e., there was no interaction between age and velocity.

Investigators often have used these types of timing paradigms to test hypotheses about how changes in responses evolve. Shea and his colleagues (1982) were among the first to hypothesize an information processing solution to children's less accurate performances. Since children process information more slowly than adults, Shea reasoned that increasing response time should improve their performances. Available response time can be increased by slowing stimuli down or by lengthening the distance over which a stimulus may be viewed (holding speed constant). Both techniques have been used with adults, but varying stimulus speed has remained the most popular means for manipulating response times with children.

Shea's information processing hypothesis seemed reasonable, based on other investigations that reported improved performances when subjects had more time to respond (e.g., Gallagher & Thomas, 1980). As illustrated in Fig. 1, however, the reverse effect occurred. Young subjects actually performed more poorly when they viewed slower moving stimuli; only the direction of their errors changed. So, although response time probably is a limiting factor at some (especially faster) speeds, the "answer" is clearly more complex, given the robust nature of the age by velocity interaction.

Other factors have been tested for their influence on anticipatory response accuracy. Thomas, Gallagher, and Purvis (1981) proposed that the length of reaction times might influence timing accuracy, since initiating responses more quickly results in increased time for meeting other task demands. They used a relatively fast stimulus speed (10 mph) in their study, making response times very short. Faster reaction times would be advantageous when responses had to be made very quickly, as in their study. So, although reaction times probably do influence accuracy at faster stimulus speeds, they seem unlikely to contribute much to accuracy at slower speeds.

Other investigators have examined response complexity for its influence on timing accuracy. Bard et al. (1981) compared two tasks, one requiring throwing a ball coincident with the "motion" of a lighted array, the other a button press. They found differences only in the magnitude of errors. Errors were larger for the more complex accuracy and timing task. Stadulis (1985) compared the results of a Bassin task with one where subjects had to intercept a ball rolling down a chute. Although he equated stimulus speeds and display lengths as nearly as possible, results were not quite so straightforward as in the Bard et al. (1981) study. For example, typical age effects occurred for the "rolling ball" experiment, while none were found for the Bassin task. As in other experiments however, Stadulis' subjects were most accurate at the fastest velocities for both tasks. Finally, no age by stimulus speed interaction occurred for the Bassin timing task; a significant interaction, similar to the one reported earlier (Shea et al., 1982; Williams, 1985) was found in the rolling ball task.

With few exceptions, there is at least one clear consistency between lab and field investigations of anticipatory timing. Young children often initiate or complete their responses too early. What is it about task requirements that gives young children this difficulty? What is it that makes youngsters find it so hard to wait or "hold back" (Halverson & Roberton, 1966) when that is required for an appropriate response?

Williams (1985, in press) and others (Shea et al., 1982) have demonstrated that young children not only fail to "hold back", but their responses also show little, if any, attempt to adapt to external stimulus demands when movement times or movement speeds are used for comparison. Very young children use movements that are primarily stereotypic and made at a "preferred" movement speed (Williams, 1985). Five-year-olds used the same arm movement speed across a range of five to six different stimulus velocities (Williams, 1985, in press). Consequently, the only time these children responded accurately was when (and if) their preferred speed happened to coincide with the speed of the array. Comparing actual arm movement speeds with available response times illustrates this point clearly (Fig. 2). When there was either more or less available response time (at slower or faster stimulus speeds), 5-year-olds moved either too fast or too slowly, respectively. Stimulus and response speeds matched very well at 5-year-olds' preferred speeds, however. In contrast, older subjects made a closer match at more speeds, demonstrating their adaptability to a range of stimuli.

Kinematic characteristics of subjects' responses to anticipatory timing tasks also were examined (Williams, 1985, in press). Results of these investigations give a slightly different picture of how young children responded. At all stimulus velocities, most subjects made an initial ballistic, or distance-covering movement, followed by a series of one or more corrections (Fig. 3). Although all responses consisted of these two phases, there were several important age differences in how responses could be partitioned into the two parts. There were no differences among groups of children in the number of corrections they made during slow movements, but 5-year-olds made more corrections when they responded to fast movements. On the other hand, adults made *fewer* corrections than 5-year-olds when moving to fast speeds. In addition, 5-year-olds had a longer (duration) correcting phase to their movements than older subjects. This result was important when the magnitude of subjects' corrections is considered. Both Williams (1985) and Salmoni (1983) reported corrections of greater magnitude made by young children than by adults. In other words, 5-year-olds' greater number of corrections of higher magnitude resulted in increased response times for faster stimuli. More important than these specific details was that movements examined at one level of analysis (e.g., movement times) seemed to be stereotypic. When investigated at another level (e.g., their kinematics), some adaptation became apparent. Five-year-olds *did* attempt to make adjustments. Their apparent problem was in modulating those adjustments appropriately.

So, what changes are taking place from the time when children respond in ways that are relatively independent of stimulus characteristics to the time when they can make responses that are intimately coordinated with its spatial-temporal characteristics? We certainly do not have all the answers yet, but we are getting closer.

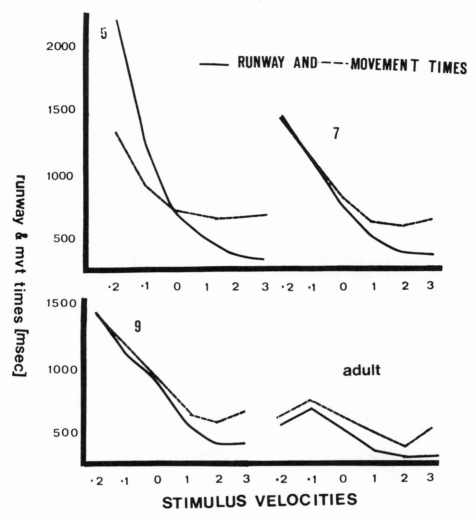

FIG. 2. Comparisons of runway and movement times for 5-year-olds (upper left), 7-year-olds (upper right), 9-year-olds (lower left), and adults (lower right) for stimulus velocities averaged relative to baseline preferred speeds (0). Stimuli are incremented (+1, +2) and decremented (−1, −2) in .8 mph units from the baseline. (reprinted from "Age Differences on a Coincident Anticipation Task: Influence of Stereotypic or 'Preferred' Movement Speed", K. Williams, *Journal of Motor Behavior, 17*(4), 402, 1985. Reprinted with permission of the Helen Dwight Reid Educational Foundation. Published by Heldref Publications, 4000 Albemarle St. N.W., Washington, D.C. 20016. Copyright © 1985.)

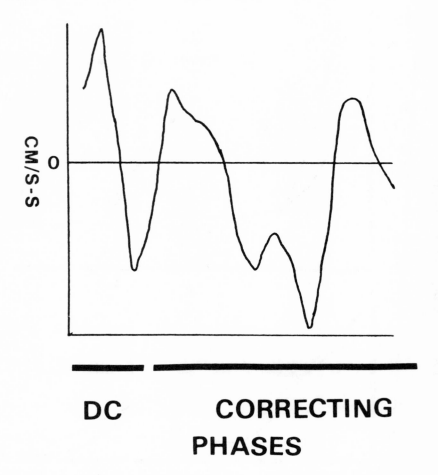

FIG. 3. Distance-covering (DC) and correcting segments of a smoothed acceleration curve (arbitrary units). This curve was derived from the x-coordinates of a simple, horizontal arm movement

Investigators have typically examined only one part of the input-output inter-action at a time. For example, information processors emphasized what type of information entered the system, and what went on internally as it was processed. Others (e.g., Williams, 1985, in press) have focused on the output and tried to make inferences about what goes on internally. Currently, there is no coherent picture detailing how inputs influence outputs. On the perceptual side, we know that many changes occur throughout childhood. For example, young children generally pick out only one or two familiar elements in a display and act upon them, often stereotypically. Seigler (1981) suggested that children may limit inputs in order to simplify problems. Perhaps young catchers react to the thrower's moving arm since they cannot anticipate the ball's trajectory or arrival time. On the other hand, by 9 or 10 years of age, children begin to ignore irrelevancies and to key in on the important aspects of a visual display. They also become faster information processors. They can quickly shift their attention from the hand/arm at release, to follow the ball's path. They also are beginning to make appropriate adjustments in their body position.

Clearly, other changes also must occur. Children must learn how to control the movements they make, once they decide to make them. It is one thing to visually track a ball from the thrower's hand. It is another to coordinate and control the movements necessary to get into proper position for catching. While the movements which children make in their positioning attempts (and final successes) have been extensively described, the mechanisms which underlie the evolution of their coordination and control remain to be discovered. In the final section of this review, two models will be described that have the potential for explaining how timing ability emerges over time.

MODELS OF INTERCEPTION SKILL

Currently, two models are undergoing extensive scrutiny for their power to explain various aspects of motor coordination and control. Motor programming, for example, has been offered by some theorists (e.g., Schmidt, 1982) as a solution. Another alternative is a dynamic model of movement control (Kelso & Tuller, 1984). Both models will be examined briefly for their ability to explain the age differences observed to occur in interception skills.

Proponents of motor programming models (Pew, 1974; Schmidt, 1985) suggest that movement patterns are coded and stored as a template somewhere in the nervous system. In order to make any movement, the appropriate program must be selected and "run off". Although there is some disagreement over the amount of detail contained in the encoded message, there is consensus that the program holds information essential for movement production. Clearly, motor programs cannot be so specific as to require a different program for each unique movement. Such a requirement would result in storage and retrieval problems that were a common criticism of closed-loop theories of motor control (Adams, 1971). The most current thinking (Schmidt, 1985) is that particular values are supplied to the appropriate program each time a specific action is required. Reparameterizing motor programs for each new movement would give them sufficient flexibility to account for similar actions that needed to be performed at different speeds, durations, or magnitudes. At least two aspects of motor programs have yet to be satisfactorily explained, however: How the program is "built" as a motor skill is learned, and why (apparently) centrally stored motor programs are necessary, given increasing evidence that much of movement is generated at lower spinal and reflex centers (Hasan & Enoka, 1985; Kelso, Holt, Rubin, & Kugler, 1981).

A dynamic model avoids some of the problems of motor programming because it uses muscular dynamics and reflex activity (e.g., stretch reflexes: Hasan & Enoka, 1985) to explain movement production. This model posits that muscles are controlled as functional collectives. Within these groupings, one or two parameters are set, and specific movement topographies (configurations) emerge as an outcome of those specifications. Muscular configurations adjust to changing environmental conditions automatically.

A simple mass spring system has been used to model how muscular adjustments occur. The system consists of a spring, weighted at one end and fixed at the other. The spring's specific characteristics are determined by setting length and stiffness parameters. Stretching (moving) and releasing the spring will result in its oscillation; eventually, however, the spring will return to its original position (how long the attainment of an equilibrium state will take is based on the specific combination of length and stiffness—see Turvey, Fitch, & Tuller, 1982 and Tuller, Turvey, & Fitch, 1982, for an excellent tutorial on these concepts). Muscle groups are hypothesized to equilibrate to established endpoints in a similar fashion. New endpoints can be set by varying parameters like muscle length and stiffness.

Although the mechanisms of parameterization are not entirely clear, this model has at least two developmental implications. First, if there were an experiential basis for setting the musculature, children would be expected to perform less competently than adults since they have had less experience in "selecting" parameters. Second, there is at least one study (Davis & Kelso, 1982) which suggests that there might be developmental differences in the frictional (stiffness) properties of muscle. If either (or both) of these conditions held, children's parameterization of the musculature might be less accurate than older subjects'. Then, youngsters would have greater difficulty stopping or slowing movements once initiated. The result would be the ballistic-type movements described in so many of the studies reviewed (Haywood, 1977; Shea et al., 1982; Williams, 1985).

Even though the overt appearance of the movements made by young children was ballistic, experiments by Williams (1985, in press) demonstrated that at least some youngsters attempted to make adjustments. Their attempts at response modification were observed only when the kinematics were examined. These types of corrections might signify attempts at reparameterization. Since this whole area of study is only beginning, these suggestions are purely speculative. They give us a starting point, however, for exploring structural explanations for changes in movement control.

In summary, interception skills have been examined from several perspectives. Process descriptions of motor skills like catching and punting were summarized. These included hypothesized and validated developmental sequences of interception skills and examinations of environmental factors which might influence the observed level of skill. Experimental investigations which provide clues regarding the underlying mechanisms of control also were synthesized. Both types of research are beginning to give us a cohesive picture of children who proceed from making responses that are relatively stereotypic to adapting their actions when it is appropriate. We are only beginning to speculate about the reasons these changes occur. That is where our future research must take us.

REFERENCES

Adams, J. A. (1971). A closed loop theory of motor learning. *Journal of Motor Behavior, 3*, 111–150.

Ball, C. T., & Glencross, D. (1985). Developmental differences in a coincident timing task under speed and time constraints. *Human Movement Science, 4*, 1–15.

Bard, C., Fleury, M., Carriere, L., & Bellec, J. (1981). Components of the coincidence-anticipation behavior of children aged from 6 to 11 years. *Perceptual and Motor Skills, 52*, 547–556.

Branta, C. F., Haubenstricker, J., & Seefeldt, V. (1984). Age changes in motor skills during childhood and adolescence. In R. L. Terjung (Ed.), *Exercise and sport sciences reviews* (Vol. 12, pp. 467–520). Lexington, MA: D. C. Heath & Co.

Clark, J. E. (1987). The perception-action perspective: A commentary on von Hofsten. In M. G. Wade & H. T. A. Whiting (Eds.), *Motor skill acquisition in children: Aspects of coordination and control* (pp. 197–206). Dordrecht, The Netherlands: Martinus Nijhoff.

Davis, W. E., & Kelso, J. A. S. (1982). Analysis of "invariant characteristics" in the motor control of Down's Syndrome and normal subjects. *Journal of Motor Behavior, 14*, 194–212.

Dunham, P. (1977). Age, sex, speed, and practice in coincidence-anticipation performance in children. *Perceptual and Motor Skills, 45*, 187–193.

DuRandt, R. (1985). Ball catching proficiency among 4-, 6-, and 8-year-old girls. In J. E. Clark & J. H. Humphrey (Eds.), *Motor development: Current selected research* (pp. 35–44). Princeton, NJ: Princeton Book Co.

Gallagher, J. D., & Thomas, J. R. (1980). Effects of varying post-KR intervals upon children's motor performance. *Journal of Motor Behavior, 12*, 41–46.

Gutteridge, M. V. (1939). A study of motor achievements of young children. *Archives of Psychology, 244*, 1–178.

Halverson, L. E., & Roberton, M. A. (1966). *A study of motor pattern development in young children*. Report to the Research Section of the National Convention of the American Association for Health, Physical Education and Recreation, Chicago, IL.

Hasan, Z., & Enoka, R. M. (1985). Isometric torque-angle relationship and movement-related activity of human elbow flexors: Implications for the equilibrium-point hypothesis. *Experimental Brain Research, 59*, 441–450.

Haywood, K. M. (1977). Eye movements during coincident anticipation performance. *Journal of Motor Behavior, 9*, 313–318.

Hellweg, D. (1972). *An analysis of perceptual and performance characteristics of the catching skill of 6-7 year old children.* Unpublished doctoral dissertation, University of Wisconsin, Madison.

Isaacs, L. D. (1980). Effects of ball size, ball color, and preferred color on catching by young children. *Perceptual and Motor Skills, 51*, 583–586.

Kelso, J. A. S., Holt, K. G., Rubin, P., & Kugler, P. N. (1981). Patterns of human interlimb coordination emerge from the properties of non-linear, limit cycle oscillatory processes: Theory and data. *Journal of Motor Behavior, 13*, 226–261.

Kelso, J. A. S., & Tuller, B. (1984). A dynamical basis for action systems. In M. Gazzaniga (Ed.), *Handbook of cognitive neuroscience* (pp. 321–356). New York: Plenum Press.

Langendorfer, S. (1982). *Developmental relationships between throwing and striking: A prelongitudinal test of motor stage theory.* Unpublished doctoral dissertation. University of Wisconsin, Madison.

McCaskill, C. L., & Wellman, B. L. (1938). A study of common motor achievements at the preschool ages. *Child Development, 9*, 141–150.

Morris, G. S. D. (1976). Effects ball and background color have upon the catching performances of elementary school children. *Research Quarterly, 47*, 409–416.

Payne, V. G. (1982). Simultaneous investigation of effects of distance of projection and object size on object reception by children in grade 1. *Perceptual and Motor Skills, 54*, 1183–1187.

Payne, V. G., & Koslow, R. (1981). Effects of varying ball diameters on catching ability of young children. *Perceptual and Motor Skills, 53*, 739–744.

Pelligrini, A. M. (1979). *Visual cues for movement initiation in the organization of catching skills.* Unpublished master's thesis, University of Illinois.

Pew, R. W. (1974). Human perceptual-motor performance. In B. Kantowitz (Ed.), *Human information processing: Tutorials in performance and cognition.* New York: L. Erlbaum.

Ridenour, M. V. (1974). Influence of object size, speed, and direction on the perception of a moving object. *Research Quarterly, 45*, 293–301.

Roberton, M. A. (1987). Developmental changes in the relative timing of locomotion. In M. G. Wade & H. T. A. Whiting (Eds.), *Themes in motor development* (pp. 82–95). Dordrecht, The Netherlands: Martinus Nijhoff.

Roberton, M. A., & Halverson, L. E. (1984). *Developing children—Their changing movement.* Philadelphia: Lea & Febiger.

Salmoni, A. W. (1983). A descriptive analysis of children performing Fitts' reciprocal tapping task. *Journal of Human Movement Studies, 9*, 81–96.

Schmidt, R. A. (1982). *Motor control and learning: A behavioral emphasis.* Champaign, IL: Human Kinetics Press.

Schmidt, R. A. (1985). The search for invariance in skilled movement behavior. *Research Quarterly for Exercise and Sport, 56*, 188–200.

Seefeldt, V., Reuschlein, S., & Vogel, P. (1972). *Sequencing motor skills within the physical education curriculum.* Report to the National Convention, American Association for Health, Physical Education and Recreation.

Seigler, R. (1981). Developmental sequences within and between concepts. *Monographs of the Society for Research in Child Development, 46,* (Serial No. 189).

Shea, C. H., Krampitz, J. B., Northam, C. C., & Ashby, A. A. (1982). Information processing in coincident anticipation tasks: A developmental perspective. *Journal of Human Movement Studies, 8,* 73–83.

Stadulis, R. E. (1985). Coincidence-anticipation behavior of children. In J. E. Clark & J. H. Humphrey (Eds.), *Motor development: Current selected research* (Vol. 1, pp. 1–18). Princeton, NJ: Princeton Book Co.

Thelen, E. (1987). Development of coordinated movement: Implications for early human development. In M. G. Wade & H. T. A. Whiting (Eds.), *Motor skill acquisition in children. Aspects of coordination and control* (pp. 107–124). Dordrecht, The Netherlands: Martinus Nijhoff.

Thomas, J. R., Gallagher, J. D., & Purvis, G. J. (1981). Reaction time and anticipation time: Effects of development. *Research Quarterly for Exercise and Sport, 52,* 359–379.

Tuller, B., Turvey, M. T., & Fitch, H. (1982). The Bernstein perspective: II. The concept of muscle linkage or coordinative structure. In J. A. S. Kelso (Ed.), *Human motor behavior: An introduction* (pp. 253–270). Hillsdale, NJ: L. Erlbaum.

Turvey, M. T., Fitch, H., & Tuller, B. (1982). The Bernstein perspective: I. The problems of degrees of freedom and context-conditioned variability. In J. A. S. Kelso (Ed.), *Human motor behavior. An introduction* (pp. 239–252). Hillsdale, NJ: L. Erlbaum.

Wade, M. G. (1980). Coincidence anticipation of young normal and handicapped children. *Journal of Motor Behavior, 12,* 103–112.

Wickstrom, R. (1983). *Fundamental motor patterns* (3rd ed.). Philadelphia: Lea & Febiger.

Williams, H. G. (1967). *The perception of moving objects by children.* Unpublished paper. University of Toledo.

Williams, K. (1985). Age differences on a coincident anticipation task: Influence of stereotypic or "preferred" movement speed. *Journal of Motor Behavior, 17,* 389–410.

Williams, K. (in press). Age differences in the contribution of selected kinematic characteristics to timing accuracy. *Journal of Human Movement Studies.*

Wrisberg, C. A., & Mead, B. J. (1983). Developing coincident timing skill in children: A comparison of training methods. *Research Quarterly for Exercise and Sport, 54,* 67–74.

AUTHOR NOTE

An earlier version of this paper was presented at the Annual Convention of the American Alliance for Health, Physical Education, Recreation, and Dance, Cincinnati, OH, April, 1986.

13

FACILITATING AQUATIC MOTOR DEVELOPMENT: A REVIEW OF DEVELOPMENTAL AND ENVIRONMENTAL VARIABLES

Stephen Langendorfer
Kent State University

Lawrence D. Bruya
Amy Reid
North Texas State University

ABSTRACT

Taking a developmental perspective, this paper reviews a number of important variables influencing aquatic skill acquisition including newly identified aquatic developmental sequences and several aquatic environmental factors. Developmental sequences for water entry, arm action, leg action, and body position have been hypothesized. Frequently overlooked environmental variables include depth, temperature, and humidity in addition to the more popular water clarity and chemistry factors. Another neglected factor in aquatics has been the role of large and small equipment in learning to swim. Equipment may successfully act to reduce fear in the young child. Finally, the learner-teacher interaction has been observed as an important factor in relation to the previous two variables. A conceptual model for teaching and research in aquatics is proposed to include these variables. A concerted developmental research effort is needed to bring aquatic practices in line with current educational and developmental theory and knowledge.

Throughout the twentieth century, national organizations such as the American National Red Cross (ARC) and the Young Men's Christian Association (YMCA) have provided leadership in swimming and aquatic programs in the United States (American Red Cross, 1968; Arnold & Freeman, 1972; deBabadillo & Murphy, 1973). These agency swimming programs have claimed remarkable success in reducing the rate of drowning in the population. The primary focus of these programs has been on teaching methods and behaviors. Recently, a spate of swimming texts have appeared with emphasis on the young child (Bory, 1971; Groscott, 1975; Miner, 1980; Murray, 1981; Newman, 1983; Prudden, 1974). These texts, too, have focused primarily on traditional teaching behaviors and activities. For the most part, both programs and texts have ignored the actual processes by which aquatic skills are acquired by the child.

This omission is not unique to aquatics, as Seefeldt has noted that many elementary physical education texts are "devoid of information to assist teachers in the analysis of the movements their programs are designed to elicit" (1980, pp. 314–315). Seefeldt also suggested that teachers of motor skills (presumably including aquatic specialists) need "1) a knowledge of developmental sequences . . . ; 2) the ability to identify the various levels of development . . . ; and 3) a knowledge of the activities and experiences that will assist the learner in moving to a mature level" (p. 318). The emphasis in swimming programs has focused on this third aspect of teaching. The two prerequisite teaching skills of knowledge and analysis largely have been ignored. This fact highlights the need to integrate aquatic programs and current motor development research literature. It also reinforces the call for further research addressing aquatic processes by young children (Langendorfer, 1986).

The purpose of this paper is to review current developmental aquatic research and to provide a pragmatic framework from within which further research could be conducted. Specifically, the paper will attend to hypothesized aquatic developmental sequences and to the identification of important environmental variables which may influence the acquisition of aquatic skills. A conceptual model for integrating various factors also will be proposed.

MOTOR SEQUENCES IN AQUATIC ASSESSMENT

There is ample evidence in the motor developmental literature that motor skills change over time, both in pattern and product scores (Roberton & Halverson, 1984). A number of studies have identified robust motor sequences for such skills as throwing (Roberton, 1977, 1978; Roberton & Langendorfer, 1980), striking (Harper & Struna, 1973; Langendorfer, 1987), hopping (Halverson & Williams, 1985; Roberton & Halverson, 1984), and rolling (Roberton & Halverson, 1984; Williams, 1980). There is evidence that aquatic skills progress similarly through ordered motor sequences (Erbaugh, 1978, 1980; Langendorfer, 1984a; McGraw, 1939; Oka, Okamoto, Yoshizawa, Tokuyama, & Kumamoto, 1978; Reid, Bruya, & Langendorfer, 1985).

McGraw (1935/1975, 1939) provided the first evidence for regular, ordered changes in infant aquatic behaviors. She demonstrated a shift from stereotypic "reflexive" swimming of the newborn to the "disorganized or struggling behavior" of the first year infant to the intentional or deliberate kicking and paddling motions of the older, water-experienced infant (McGraw, 1939). McGraw hypothesized that these aquatic changes reflected alterations in neural control structures. She claimed shifting neural control sites could be generalized to explain changes in other motor activities such as prone and erect locomotion, rolling, and sitting behaviors (McGraw, 1945/1963). Since she was not primarily interested in aquatic behavior, McGraw did not attempt to observe further changes in the intentional phase of swimming.

Recently, Erbaugh (1978, 1980) demonstrated sequential changes in intentional aquatic skills in preschool children. She developed an aquatic assessment instrument for preschoolers in which aquatic skills could be measured validly, reliably, and objectively (Erbaugh, 1978, 1980). Using this instrument, she noted a series of differences in aquatic motor patterns and accomplishments across age groups. For example, in the front locomotion category, the typical arm pattern of "inefficient paddling" action for the three-year-olds differed from the "efficient human stroke" and rudimentary attempts at "alternating overarm crawl" arm actions in five-year-olds. Similar kinds of differences were observed in other aquatic categories (Erbaugh, 1978, 1980).

Erbaugh (1981) subsequently observed longitudinal changes in aquatic movement patterns for young children between the ages of 3 and 5 years. In addition to changes in product scores such as distance able to be swum and amount of independence from teachers in water, she observed developmental changes in arm and leg patterns and body and head positions. Importantly, Erbaugh (1981) observed that some of these aquatic changes were sequential in nature. The young and less experienced three-year-olds predominantly moved through the water with a "leg-dominated" pattern while the older and more experienced five-year-olds used arm patterns, particularly with an "overarm crawl" pattern.

In a similar vein, a Japanese group (Oka et al., 1978) identified regular age-related shifts in the muscular organization and qualitative patterns of leg "kicking" motions as well as increased distance of locomotion across the preschool years. In particular, they noted a pattern shift from the "pedaling" swimming action of two-year-olds to a "flutter kick" action used predominantly by six-year-olds.

Langendorfer (1984a) has hypothesized changes in movement components (arm action, leg action, body position) for supine and prone aquatic locomotion. These observations appear remarkably consistent both with the Erbaugh and Japanese observations. The arm action sequence was hypothesized to shift from primitive rapid, short pulling motions to slower, but longer "action-reaction" paddling movements to an advanced aerodynamic "lift" or "sculling" action.

Similarly, leg actions were hypothesized to change from "plantar push" (i.e., pedaling) to "rapid dorsal splashing" to an advanced "efficient fluttering." Finally, he hypothesized decreases in horizontal body position angle in the water in both prone and supine locomotion actions.

Most recently, in a continuing longitudinal study, Reid and Bruya (1984; Reid, Bruya, & Langendorfer, 1985) proposed and then identified sequences in "entry to the water" skills. Categories in entry behaviors included movement pattern progressions, entry support progressions, equipment characteristics, starting positions, and degree of initial body part immersion. Frequency of occurrences based on 100 videotaped trials suggested that feet-first entries supported either directly by large equipment or teachers were the easiest methods for young children to use for initial entry into the aquatic environment. The data also suggested that the young children in the sample were more likely to enter after some body part was already wet or immersed in the water. The hypothesis from the data is that these frequently occurring behaviors are developmentally most primitive. Age and skill differences, however, have not yet been identified to confirm any developmental trends.

Research Directions for Assessing Aquatic Motor Sequences

Aquatic developmental sequences have begun to be identified, consistent with the urging of Seefeldt (1980). Unfortunately, these data have been acknowledged by few aquatic professionals and as such have not been included in current aquatic teaching or assessment techniques. Current aquatic assessment instruments (American Red Cross, 1968; Arnold & Freeman, 1971; deBarbadillo & Murphy, 1973) are traditional motor performance tests which emphasize product scores (e.g., length of breath holding; distance of prone glide). They also reflect the biases of the particular teaching techniques by representing specific teaching progressions rather than developmental changes in aquatic behavior. The developmental aquatic instruments which reflect developmental sequences and varying developmental levels (Erbaugh, 1978, 1980, 1981; Langendorfer, 1984a) need to be incorporated into the mainstream of aquatic assessment (Bruya, Franklin, Langendorfer, & Reid, 1984).

Seefeldt (1980) also suggested that activities and experiences used by teachers must provide developmental information to help swimmers move through the motor sequences. Current aquatic instruments and teaching techniques approach aquatic skill acquisition from an "error perspective" which does no fit with a developmental assessment perspective. The "error perspective" assumes that any behaviors not matching "mature" or biomechanically "correct" stroke patterns are "errors" and must be expunged by proper teaching. The problem with this perspective is that it ignores the existence of developmental sequences as well as age, readiness level, or current developmental status factors for each individual swimmer. The presence of motor sequences suggests that developmentally appropriate teaching techniques best individualize the expectations, activities, and drills by encouraging movement at developmental levels one beyond the current status exhibited by the individual (Roberton & Halverson, 1984; Seefeldt, 1980). Training programs for aquatic specialists must begin to emphasize observation and analysis skills oriented toward motor developmental changes (Reid, et al., 1985) as well as appreciation of cognitive and social developmental changes. Additionally, the identification of aquatic activities and equipment that provide challenges and opportunities for varying developmental solutions must be a major priority for aquatic specialists (Bruya, et al., 1984).

AQUATIC ENVIRONMENTAL VARIABLES

Children as well as adults come to the aquatic setting with a wide variety of personal aquatic histories. They may react positively based on successful experiences or, as a result of negative or insufficient experiences, they may show fear and trepidation. It is the contention of many experts (Ammons, 1984; Bruya, 1985b; Hutt, 1976; Shaw, 1976) that positive initial experiences promote superior learning and development. Likewise, the first aquatic experiences must be both gentle and happy as well as challenging and exciting. Such a positive impression most often is the responsibility of the supervising and care-giving adults. They also must be carefully planned prior to water entry. The likelihood of a positive experience is enhanced by careful selection of the major factors within the aquatic movement environment (Herkowitz, 1980; Seefeldt, 1980).

The major aquatic environmental factors identified in this review include water condition, facility design and large equipment structures, small manipulable equipment, and the child-adult (learner-teacher) interaction. Each of these factors will be reviewed and examined in relationship to their roles in aquatic skill acquisition. Several research directions for each also will be identified.

Variable 1. Water Condition

Physical water condition is the first major aquatic environmental factor considered here which may contribute to initial and lasting impressions on young children. Basically, four distinct water condition variables may affect young children's swimming: 1) water clarity; 2) water chemistry; 3) air/water temperature and humidity; and 4) water depth. The first three have received the most previous attention. In particular, water clarity and chemistry generally are subject to public health guidelines and have been discussed extensively in the literature (Thomas, 1972, 1976). Aside from unsanitary and poorly controlled pools and swimming areas which may deter reluctant participants, water clarity and chemistry probably have little immediate impact upon the acquisition of swimming skills (Langendorfer, 1986).

On the other hand, the temperature/humidity of the water and air has been a topic of continuing debate by preschool swimming personnel (Council for National Cooperation in Aquatics, 1985; Langendorfer, 1986; Langendorfer & Willing, 1985; Newman, 1983; Thomas, 1972). It may be a singularly important factor in the young child's adjustment to the water. Frequently, pools are multiuse facilities trying to accommodate the activity of numerous groups. A typical water temperature of 78–80°F (25°C) is comfortable for exercising adults but deviates drastically from the recommendations for children by most aquatic experts. For instance, the CNCA (1985) recommends a minimum of 82°F while various authors suggest minimums varying from 86° to 96°F (Murray, 1981; Newman, 1983; Thomas, 1976). Authors have reported particularly difficulty in teaching young children swimming and readiness skills at temperatures below 80°F (Newman, 1983; Timmermans, 1975). The immature thermoregulatory system of young children probably makes water temperature variations especially crucial for very young children and infants. There is even evidence that cool water may be a contributing factor in two reported cases of hyponatremia, or "water intoxication" in infants (Council for National Cooperation in Aquatics, 1985; Langendorfer, 1984b, 1985, 1986).

Equally important to water temperature is the relationship of air temperature to water temperature and the resulting relative humidity. Thomas (1976) recommends that air temperatures be maintained either 3–5°F higher than water temperatures or 85–87°F if the water temperature is 85°F or higher. He also recommends relative humidity between 75–85%. The resulting balance between air and water temperature in a pool environment creates high humidity which reduces water evaporation from the skin, reducing the chilling effect. In fact, one of the authors has noted that a temporary air temperature increase 5°F above water temperature to 87°F during the period of lessons has reduced complaints by instructors, young children, and the handicapped swimmers in one aquatic program.

One often neglected factor in acquisition of aquatic skills by young children is the depth of water in which the learning must occur. Like water and air temperature, pool depth usually is determined by the needs of adult users and is not adjustable for young swimmers. The availability of relatively shallow water becomes particularly important for the young nonswimmer since these same individuals are just beginning to master balance in a terrestrial environment. Lack of foot support and balance in a cool, viscous, buoyant medium like water can be a terror-evoking experience to the young child. The experience of many preschool swimming authors has suggested the importance of independence of movement in actually learning to swim (Arnold & Freeman, 1971; deBarbadillo & Murphy, 1973; Langendorfer, 1984a). In fact, Australian swimming instructors have noted the ease with which young children teach themselves to swim when they are in water in which they can stand (Bory, 1971; Timmermans, 1975). The next section will discuss means for artificially varying the water depth for young children.

Research Directions in Water Condition Factors

The controversy regarding water conditions largely is based upon varying opinions by many self-designated experts. Remarkably, little empirical research has been conducted regarding the effect of the water condition variables such as temperature and depth. A number of the concerns could readily be addressed and answered with simple research studies. For instance, the claim that water temperature contributes to hypothermia and other diseases could be decided simply by measuring body temperature changes resulting from swimming lessons in several different pool and air temperatures. Comparisons of changes in swimming skills for groups taught in deep and shallow pools also is a readily accomplishable study. The failure of swimming personnel to conduct relatively simple research studies of this nature before issuing opinions has perpetuated a number of myths and misunderstandings (Langendorfer, 1986).

Ongoing studies related to the effects of water variables on health and safety as well as skill acquisition of young children are needed drastically. The aquatic community needs to understand the effect of water and air temperatures and water depth upon young children trying to learn to swim. The studies are, by nature, developmental since many of the effects likely are related to age, body size (Erbaugh, 1986b), skill level, developmental status, or experience (Erbaugh, 1986a). A forum for the investigation, discussion, and dissemination of recent findings is being developed by the Council for National Cooperation in Aquatics through the newly published *National Aquatics Journal* and the National Advisory Committee on Aquatics for Young Children. This is a necessary and important first step.

Variable 2. Small Equipment in the Aquatic Environment

It can be noted that swimming instructors frequently use a variety of toys and small equipment as an aid in teaching swimming and aquatic play with young children in the water. For the purpose of this review, small equipment will be divided into three general categories: 1) flotation and body support; 2) aids to locomotion; and 3) toys and distractors. The first type of equipment includes the standard kickboard, pull buoy, inflatable arm cuffs, inner tubes, styrofoam "bubbles," and lifejackets or PFDs (personal flotation devices). Recently, several inflatable vests and swimming suits with foam inserts have appeared on the market which also fall into this category. Equipment in this category has been popular in many preschool swimming programs (deBarbadillo & Murphy, 1973). The efficacy of such equipment has been noted by Erbaugh (1986a) when the mean ages for acquisition of supported and unsupported children's swimming locomotion skill differed significantly.

The second type of small equipment overlaps the first category to the degree that flotation devices also aid locomotion specifically and other swimming skills generally (Erbaugh, 1981, 1986a). Items specific to the locomotion aid category include fins (also called "flippers"), hand paddles, and masks or goggles. Although these items are less frequently used for teaching young children, they have been suggested for older swimmers (American Red Cross, 1968; Arnold & Freeman, 1972).

Finally, a variety of other toys and aquatic equipment, both commercially available and homemade, often are observed in the young child's aquatic environment. For example, boats, balls, rings, poker chips, washclothes, watering cans, and submersible painted objects are a few of the suggested aquatic play items (Murray, 1981; Newman, 1983). Erbaugh (1987) described that in water play situations "toy-mediated play" was most commonly observed as compared to conventional (i.e., games) or physical play (i.e., parental contact, splashing, or roughhousing). It could be hypothesized that, in addition to flotation supports, aquatic toys and small equipment have some inherent motivating characteristics for young children that allow them to serve as distractors for the fearful or reluctant young child. Their relative familiarity in an otherwise unfamiliar environment also may contribute to their value and frequency of use.

Research Directions for Small Aquatic Equipment

Small aquatic equipment use may represent a significant variable in aquatic skill acquisition for young children, either as incentives and motivators or as physical supports to movement. At the present time, however, the use of small equipment in aquatics can be described more as an "art" by creative instructors than as a scientifically based teaching technique. The exploration of small equipment is an area ripe for empirical investigation.

A task analysis approach (Herkowitz, 1980, 1984; Morris, 1976) may provide one fruitful framework for investigation of small equipment. For instance, one "factor" from an aquatic task analysis for children learning to swim may include "types of support" with levels of complexity ranging from 1) no flotation device to 2) support by an adult to 3) support with a styrofoam "bubble" to 4) support from inflatable arm cuffs. Differences in learning time (number of lessons to criterion) could provide an empirical test for significant differences between types of support. Further testing for interactions between age, skill, or amount of experience by support type could illustrate important developmental trends or differences that could have very practical applications. In addition, different sizes and types of equipment could be compared for shifts in developmental patterns or rates of change (Erbaugh, 1986a; Reid et al., 1985).

Variable 3. Facilities and Large Equipment

Until recently the design of aquatic facilities and the use of large play equipment for promoting skill acquisition has been largely neglected in the aquatic literature. The development of a body of literature for the use of large contemporary play equipment in children's play environments has lead to explorations of play equipment in aquatic environments (Bowers, 1976; Bruya, 1985a, 1985b; Bruya & Buchanan, 1977, 1978; Fowler & Bruya, 1983; Hutt, 1976).

Findings in support of the value of contemporary play structures have recently been reported. First of all, it is reported that play structures actually magnify children's feelings of competence due to the number of choice and options available (Shaw, 1976). Events (i.e., individual parts of play structures) can provide children incentives for moving through the structure (Carter, Bruya, & Fowler, 1983; Fowler & Bruya, 1983). An accessible structure design also encourages use by children of varying ages and skill levels (see Table 1.). The concept of "linkage" promotes a unifying concept for diverse play structures and events placed in proximity to one another. Such a "linked" structure provides more complexity and play options than each of the individual events (Bruya, 1985b; Shaw, 1976). Additionally, the numerous options offered by contemporary play equipment for movement at varying developmental levels permits the child to approach the structure in unique ways as his/her perceptions change due to growth and experiences with the structure (Bruya, 1979; Bruya & Buchanan, 1977). Thus, play equipment seems to motivate children by providing incentives such as hierarchic motoric options and feelings of competence due to familiarity in the surroundings (Bruya & Buchanan, 1977, 1978).

As these design elements and resulting benefits to children's play were iden-

Table 1
Play Structure Design Elements for Use in the Aquatics Medium

DESIGN ELEMENTS FOR AQUATIC STRUCTURES*	
Linkage	Individual parts attached to create a larger single structure
Play Routes	Preferred directions that children follow when using the structure
Events	Those parts of the structure that attract and hold a child's attention and encourage movement

*Adapted from Bruya, 1985a

tified, it was suggested that they might be applied equally to aquatic play (Bruya, 1985b; Franklin & Bruya, 1983; Franklin, Bruya, & McWilliams, 1984). Hutt's investigation (1976) revealing that nursery school children spent more time investigating and playing with novel objects (i.e., equipment) suggested that large equipment in the water could present a similar type of "familiar novelty" which both would encourage and challenge young children to explore it (Bruya, 1985b; Reid & Bruya, 1984). In fact, Reid & Bruya (1984) verified that young children placed in an aquatic environment with complex configurations of equipment did indeed spend time slowly adapting to the water and acquiring rudimentary aquatic skills at an individualized pace. In addition, the presence of large equipment encouraged perserverance in practicing skills while decreasing negative behaviors such as crying and reluctance to participate (Reid et al., 1985).

Research Directions: Large Aquatic Equipment

The research studies dealing with large equipment in the aquatic environment have been limited in number and scope. While the initial findings have supported the positive value of aquatic play equipment, studies have been limited to preschool children receiving beginning experiences with the water. There is a need to explore age, skill, and gender differences in children's use of play structures. It is certainly unknown to what extent play structures can promote aquatic learning for older and more experienced swimmers. In addition, specific teaching techniques for individual pieces of equipment, for different equipment configurations, and for varied "linkage" designs must be studied. Integrating play structures with traditional "learn-to-swim" techniques and goals also will be needed.

Variable 4. Student-Teacher Interactions

The acquisition of swimming skills traditionally has been assumed to be a product of an instructor's intervention (ARC, 1968; Arnold & Freeman, 1972). Under this assumption, the aquatic learning process was seen to result primarily from efficient and appropriate instruction and feedback from a teacher. In addition, many persons assume an "error perspective," (i.e., that learning is a gradual process of eliminating improper movements) to be a fact. All too frequently the traditional methods of aquatic instruction have failed to acknowledge the existence of individual differences in learning rates, styles, and performances. In addition, the traditional aquatic instructor has little familiarity with the concepts of the active nature of learning and developmental processes, the existence of developmental sequences of changes, and pedagogical and learning principles from human movement, sport, and exercise.

Previous information in this review has suggested the existence of new perspectives for viewing aquatic skill acquisition. Specifically, developmental changes in aquatic skills as described by different investigators have been reported. Such regular, sequential, and gradual changes in aquatic motor skills differs appreciably from the traditional behavioristic and teacher-oriented perspectives. In addition, a number of previously neglected environmental variables such as water conditions and small and large equipment have been noted as important parts of the aquatic skill acquisition process.

Concomitant with these novel and differing perspectives on the aquatic learning process are some incumbent changes in student-teacher interaction styles. The previous information suggests that the emphasis in aquatics should be shifted from instruction by the teacher to learning by the child; from eliminating "errors" to eliciting developmentally more advanced behaviors and motor patterns; and from traditional teaching methods to play-leader guided discovery and exploration (Mossten, 1966).

Even fairly traditional pedagogical information suggests that varied teaching styles provide important considerations in the instructional setting (Mossten, 1966). In that light, it may be more appropriate for the teacher of young children to use an exploration or guided discovery style instead of the more common command style. As an example, problems may be proposed to children in relation to pieces of equipment (e.g., Can you duck under the kickboard? or Can you float on your back while holding the float on your chest?). Also, attention to major factors in aquatic environmental engineering may be an important addition to teaching swimming to young children (Herkowitz, 1980, 1984). Controlling such aspects as water depth or temperature, the use of flotation devices, or large play equipment all may be very important when structuring the aquatic learning environment. Erbaugh (1987) observed the frequency of toy-mediated play between parents and children. Apparently, as observed earlier in this paper, toys can serve important motivational roles in aquatic skill acquisition.

Research Directions: Student-Teacher Interactions

The whole relationship between aquatic instructor and student needs to be reevaluated in light of these attempts to ". . . make the content fit the needs of the children rather than making the children fit the progression" (Logsdon, 1984, p. 294). This presupposes that the aquatic instructor is willing to permit the students to ". . . create something and not . . . do something that has been predetermined" (Ammons, 1984, p. 455). Research in teacher behavior particularly from the movement education perspective (Barrett, 1984) will lead to important new directions in aquatic instructional techniques. These changes in pedagogical orientation also may lead to changes in the ultimate goal of aquatic education. Perhaps the primary purpose for aquatic instruction must change from learning swimming strokes to acquiring overall competence in "watermanship." Instructors will learn to accept and, indeed, encourage aquatic movement outcomes beyond traditional strokes and skills.

There is a need to develop new aquatic teaching curricula including problem statements and movement progressions that both structure and encourage aquatic learning. Learning progressions for enhancing entry skills, prone and supine locomotion skills, breath control, and advanced water safety skills must be developed and pilot tested. From a developmental perspective, such progressions must be examined for their utility with different age and skill levels. From a play perspective, new schemes and role models for aquatic play leaders must be introduced. Finally, teaching and interaction patterns for use with large and small equipment and from an environmental engineering perspective must be introduced to aquatic education.

A MODEL FOR AQUATIC SKILL ACQUISITION

The previous review has suggested the need for different ways of conceptualizing aquatic skill acquisition. Figure 1 presents a proposed "model" of one possible configuration of factors in aquatic education. The model suggests three levels of "independent" factors leading up to "outcome" or "dependent" factors. As suggested previously in this paper, an assessment of the learner's past history of experiences, motivation, and predisposition to the water plus the present status of aquatic movement patterns and skills provides a basis for subsequent instruction planning. In terms of instructional planning, the model suggests both "environmental" and "teaching" factors as the basis for teaching preparation. The manipulation of water conditions, use of small and large equipment, novel games, and activities constitute the major factors which the aquatic instructor must consider when setting or engineering the aquatic environment for each student. Obviously, typical class settings must include large numbers and varieties of such variables in order to accommodate expected individual differences. The final level of intervention factors in the model includes attention to teaching techniques and understanding of developmental needs. Finally, outcome factors are diversified to include a number of different possible levels and goals of aquatic learning. For instance, not only does aquatic learning lead to strokes, but also to "readiness" skills such as breath control and water entry and "watermanship" skills such as water safety, lifesaving, and advanced skills.

While the model is proposed as a pragmatic instructional device for aiding instructors in structuring the aquatic learning-teaching environment, it also can serve as a tool for planning basic aquatic research. We suggest that the factors at any level of the model can serve as either independent or dependent variables within a research study. For instance, a researcher might measure some level of learner history such as fear of the water (assessment factor) and determine the effect of that factor upon the rate or extent of eventual aquatic skill acquisition. In an empirical vein, a researcher might provide an intervention strategy to lessen

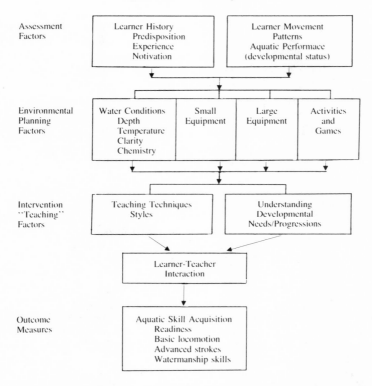

FIG. 1. A proposed model for classifying major factors in the acquisition of aquatic motor skills

fear and determine the correlational effects on improvement in skill acquisition. In addition, the researcher-teacher may be interested in modifying a planning factor such as water temperature or the presence of large equipment and subsequently determine whether fear continues to be displayed. Similar studies can and should be developed at all factor levels within the model in order to solidify our understanding the aquatic skill acquisition process.

The goal of this review paper perhaps can best be summarized by the following quote from Kate Barrett (1984) in her description of the purpose for creating an environment for learning movement:

A commitment to helping all children reach their potential for movement is a commitment to creating an environment that optimizes learning. Children cannot learn how to move unless this occurs. For this to happen children must be

safe,

on task successfully,

challenged,

and confident.

(Barrett, 1984, p. 347)

The purpose of this paper has been to promote a similar goal in aquatic environments: safe, successful, challenging, and developmentally appropriate activities, equipment, and teaching techniques to promote optimal aquatic skill acquisition.

REFERENCES

American Red Cross (1968). *Swimming and water safety textbook*. Washington, DC: The American National Red Cross.

Ammons, M. (1984). The challenge of teaching. In B. J. Logsdon (Ed.), *Physical education for children* (2nd ed., pp. 455–457). Philadelphia: Lea & Febiger.

Arnold, L. C., & Freeman, R. W. (Eds.) (1972). *Progressive swimming and springboard diving program*. New York: National YMCA Program Materials.

Barrett, K. (1984). The teacher as observer, interpreter, and decision-maker. In B. J. Logsdon (Ed.), *Physical education for children*. (2nd ed., pp. 295–355). Philadelphia: Lea & Febiger.

Bory, E. (1971). *Teaching children to swim*. New South Wales, Australia: Paul Hamlyn Pty Ltd.

Bowers, L. (1976). *Principles of design for playgrounds*. Tampa, FL: University of South Florida Film Library.

Bruya, L. D. (1979). The play environment as an effector of mobility and communication in deaf-blind children. In D. M. Compton, M. G. Burrows, & P. A. Witt (Eds.), *Facilitating play recreation, and leisure opportunities for deaf-blind children and youth* (pp. 81–99). Denton, TX: North Texas University Press.

Bruya, L. D. (1985a). Design characteristics used in playgrounds for children. In J. L. Frost & S. Sunderland (Eds.), *When children play* (pp. 215–220). Wheaton, MD: Association for Childhood Education International.

Bruya, L. D. (1985b). The effect of play structure format differences on the play behavior of preschool children. In J. L. Frost & S. Sunderland (Eds.), *When children play* (pp. 115–120). Wheaton, MD: Association for Childhood Education International.

Bruya, L. D., & Buchanan, H. E. (1977). *An evaluation of a play environment and the effect of changing structural complexity on the observed motor behavior of preschool age children*. (NTSU 35718), Denton, TX: North Texas State Research Grant.

Bruya, L. D., & Buchanan, H. E. (1978). The effect of changing structural complexity on the observed motor behavior of preschool age children. In C. B. Corbin (Ed.), *Symposium Papers: Teaching behavior and sport history* (Vol. 1, pp. 72–76). Washington, D.C.: American Alliance for Health, Physical Education, Recreation, and Dance Publications.

Bruya, L. D., Franklin, L., Langendorfer, S., & Reid, A. (November, 1984). *Establishing a preschool aquatics movement program*. Paper presented to the Preschool Aquatics Workshop *Opportunities in Aquatics*, Biennial Conference of the Council for National Cooperation in Aquatics, Forth Worth, TX.

Carter, C., Bruya, L. D., & Fowler, C. L. (June, 1983). *Positive effects as an indicator of play routes on a play structure*. Paper presented to the International Conference on Play and Play Environments, Austin, TX.

Council for National Cooperation in Aquatics (1985). Aquatic activity programs for children under the age of three. *National Aquatics Journal, 1*(2), 12–13.

deBarbadillo, J., & Murphy, M. M. (1973). *Teaching the very young to swim*. New York: Association Press.

Erbaugh, S. J. (1978). Assessment of swimming performance of preschool children. *Perceptual and Motor Skills, 47*, 1179–1182.

Erbaugh, S. J. (1980). The development of swimming skills of preschool children. In C. Nadeau, K. Newell, G. Roberts, & W. Halliwell (Eds.), *Psychology of motor behavior and sport—1979* (pp. 324–335). Champaign, IL: Human Kinetics.

Erbaugh, S. J. (1981). The development of swimming skills of preschool children over a one and one-half year period. *Dissertation Abstracts International, 42*, 2558A.

Erbaugh, S. J. (1986a). Effects of aquatic training on swimming skill development of preschool children. *Perceptual and Motor Skills, 62*, 439–446.

Erbaugh, S. J. (1986b). Effects of body size and body mass on the swimming performance of preschool children. *Human Movement Science, 5*, 1–12.

Erbaugh, S. J. (1987). Parent-child interactions during an informal swimming session. In J. E. Clark & J. H. Humphrey (Eds.), *Advances in motor development research* (Vol. 1, pp. 61–74). New York: AMS Press.

Fowler, C. L., & Bruya, L. D. (June, 1983). *A comparison of a play environment with play events with dependent measures of On, Off, Under, and Touching Equipment*. Paper presented to the International Conference on Play and Play Environments, Austin, TX.

Franklin, L., & Bruya, L. D. (June, 1983). *An aquatics curriculum based on play structure use*. Paper presented to the International Conference on Play and Play Environments, Austin, TX.

Franklin, L., Bruya, L. C., & McWilliams, M. (November, 1984). *Novel equipment used in aquatic programming*. Paper presented to the Preschool Aquatics Workshop #3, *Opportunities in Aquatics*, Biennial Conference of the Council for National Cooperation in Aquatics, Fort Worth, TX.

Groscott, J. K. (1975). *The basic swimming guide*. Mountainview, CA: World Publications.

Halverson, L. E., & Williams, K. (1985). Developmental sequences for hopping over distance: A prelongitudinal screening. *Research Quarterly for Exercise and Sport, 56*, 37–44.

Harper, C. J., & Struna, N. (April, 1973). *Case studies in the development of one-handed striking*. Paper presented to the National Convention of the American Association of Health, Physical Education, and Recreation, Minneapolis, MN.

Herkowitz, J. (1980). Developmentally engineered equipment and playspaces for motor development and learning. In C. Nadeau, K. Newell, G. Roberts, & W. Halliwell (Eds.), *Psychology of motor behavior and sport—1979* (pp. 299–313). Champaign, IL: Human Kinetics.

Herkowitz, J. (1984). Developmentally engineered equipment and playgrounds. In J. R. Thomas (Ed.), *Motor development in childhood and adolescence* (pp. 139–173). Minneapolis, MN: Burgess.

Hutt, C. (1976). Exploration and play in children. In J. S. Bruner, A. Jolly, & K. Sylvia (Eds.), *Play—Its role in development and evaluation* (pp. 202–215). New York: Basic Books.

Langendorfer, S. (February, 1984a). *Aquatic assessment instrument and individualized educational plan*. Paper presented to the Annual Midwest AHPERD Conference, Indianapolis, IN.

Langendorfer, S. (1984b). Health and safety concerns in preschool aquatics, In L. Priest & A. Crowner (Eds.), *Opportunities in Aquatics* (pp. 57–59), Indianapolis, IN: CNCA.

Langendorfer, S. (1985). Health and safety concerns in preschool swimming. *National Aquatics Journal, 1*(3), 8–9.

Langendorfer, S. (1986). Aquatics for the young child: Facts and myths. *Journal of Physical Education, Recreation, and Dance, 57*(8), 61–66.

Langendorfer, S. (1987). Pre-longitudinal screening of overarm striking development performed under two environmental conditions. In J. E. Clark & J. H. Humphrey (Eds.), *Advances in motor development research* (Vol. 1, pp. 17–47). New York: AMS Press.

Langendorfer, S., & Willing, E. (1985). The impact of motor development research upon issues in infant and preschool aquatic development. *National Aquatic Journal, 1*(1), 14–15.

Logsdon, B. J. (1984). Educational gymnastics. In B. J. Logsdon (Ed.), *Physical education for children* (2nd ed., pp. 241–294). Philadelphia: Lea & Febiger.

McGraw, M. B. (1939). Swimming behavior of the human infant. *Journal of Pediatrics, 15*, 485–490.

McGraw, M. B. (1963). *Neuromuscular maturation of the human infant*. New York: Hafner (Originally published: 1943).

McGraw, M. B. (1975). *Growth: A study of Johnny and Jimmy*. New York: Arno (Originally published: 1935).

Miner, M. F. (1980). *Water fun*. Englewood Cliffs, NJ: Prentice-Hall.

Morris, G. S. D. (1976). *How to change the games children play*. Minneapolis, MN: Burgess.

Mossten, M. (1966). *Teaching physical education*. Columbus, OH: C. E. Merrill.

Murray, J. (1981). *Infaquatics*. West Point, NY: Leisure Press.

Newman, V. H. (1983). *Teaching an infant to swim* (2nd ed.). San Diego: Harcourt Brace Jovanovich.

Oka, H., Okamoto, T., Yoshizawa, M., Tokuyama, H., & Kumamoto, M. (1978). Electromyographic and cinematographic study of the flutter kick in infants and children. In J. Terauds & E. W. Bedringfield (Eds.), *International series on sport sciences*. (Vol. 8, pp. 167–172). Baltimore, MD: University Park Press.

Prudden, B. (1974). *Teach your baby to swim*. New York: Dial Press.

Reid, A., & Bruya, L. D. (November, 1984). *Assessment of developmental motor patterns in pre-school aquatics*. Paper presented to the Preschool Aquatics Workshop #3, *Opportunities in Aquatics*, Biennial Conference of the Council for National Cooperation in Aquatics, Fort Worth, TX.

Reid, A., Bruya, L. D., & Langendorfer, S. (April, 1985). *Developmental motor pattern sequences in the aquatics medium: Research findings*. Paper presented to the Centennial

Conference, American Alliance for Health, Physical Education, Recreation, and Dance, Atlanta, GA.

Roberton, M. A. (1977). Stability of stage categorizations across trials: Implications for the "stage theory" of overarm throw development. *Journal of Human Movement Studies, 3*, 49–59.

Roberton, M. A. (1978). Longitudinal evidence for developmental stages in the forceful overarm throw for force. *Journal of Human Movement Studies, 4*, 167–173.

Roberton, M. A., & Halverson, L. E. (1984). *Developing children—Their changing movement*. Philadelphia: Lea & Febiger.

Roberton, M. A., & Langendorfer, S. (1980). Testing motor development sequences across 9-14 years. In C. Nadeau, K. Newell, G. Roberts, W. Halliwell (Eds.), *Psychology of motor behavior and sport—1979* (pp. 269–279). Champaign, IL: Human Kinetics.

Seefeldt, V. (1980). Developmental motor patterns: Implications for elementary school physical education. In C. Nadeau, K. Newell, G. Roberts, W. Halliwell (Eds.), *Psychology of motor behavior and sport—1979* (pp. 314–323). Champaign, IL: Human Kinetics.

Shaw, L. G. (1976). *The playground: The child's creative learning space (MH 20743-04A1)*. Gainsville, FL: The Bureau of Research, College of Architecture, University of Florida.

Thomas, D. G. (1972). *Swimming pool operators handbook*. Washington, D.C.: National Swimming Pool Foundation.

Thomas, D. G. (November, 1976). *Pool chemistry and pre-school swimming programs*. Paper presented to the Council for National Cooperation in Aquatics Preschool Aquatics Workshop, Champaign, IL.

Timmermans, C. (1975). *How to teach your baby to swim*. New York: Stein & Day.

Williams, K. (1980). Developmental characteristics of a forward roll. *Research Quarterly for Exercise and Sport, 51*, 703–713.

INDEX

A

Abduction/adduction, 136
Absolute duration analysis, 6
Action systems, 131–132
Adaptive supportive seating, 25–26
Affective variables, 131
Aging and reaction time, 71–82
Amplitudes of saccadic units, 187
Anticipatory hand orientation, 182
Anticipatory manual adjustments, 182
Aquatic motor development, 219–235
Aquatic skills, 220
Arbib's concept, 170
Articular proprioception, 191
Assessing aquatic motor sequences, 222–223
Assessment of motor development, 28–29

B

Ball color, 205–206
Ball trajectory, 205
Bernsteinian perspective, 158
Bilateral patterns, 146
Biomechanical constraints, 166

C

Calculation of motor time, 74
Children with slow motor development, 23–39
Chloride electrodes, 73
Cocontraction, 51
Cognitive command, 159
Cognitive processor, 158–159
Cognitive style and modeling, 103–14
Compensatory eye movements, 170
Compensatory postural control, 185
Communication skills, 115–126
Concept skills, 117
Conceptual tempo, 103–114
Control of reaching accuracy, 192
Cortical inhibition, 156
Cortical initiation, 157
Cortical supraspinal processes, 156

D

Dekan Automatic Timer, 99

Design copying task, 30–31
Development of object interception, 201–217
Development of postural control in children, 41–69
DIAL test, 115
Direct perception, 156
Discrete feedback process, 166

E

Ecological psychology, 137
Effects of age on reaction time, 71–82
Effects of gymnastic training, 41–69
Electromyographic analysis, 24
Error correction system, 155
Ethology, 134
Eye-hand coordination, 97–100

F

Feedback processes, 152
Fine-grain analysis, 149
Fine motor tasks, 117
Flexion/extension, 136

G

Gibsonian psychology, 137
Gross motor tasks, 117

H

Hand-eye coordination, 146
Head and eye saccadic scanning, 188
Head-eye coordination, 189
Horizontal adduction, 136
Human adult prehension, 168

I

Immature prehension, 190–192
Immature visuomotor system, 188
Impulsive children, 104
Influential environmental factors in catching, 205–207
Interception skill models, 213–215
Interception skills, 202–207
Intermittent feedback, 195
Internal schemas, 168

237

Invariant features, 2

J

Jumping ability in children, 1–22

K

Kinematics, 134
Kinesthetic feedback, 176
Kinesthetic sensitivity, 84
Kinesthetic tuning, 175
Kinetics, 134

L

Lafayette Rotary Pursuit, 97

M

Magnitude of adaption, 154
Manipulative-like action, 148
Matching Familiar Figures Test, 106
Maturation, 130
Mature and immature patterns, 165–199
Mature prehension, 167–168
Medial/lateral rotation, 136
Model for aquatic skill acquisition, 230–231
Model type interaction, 103, 109
Monosynaptic responses, 51–53, 59, 61
Motor schemas, 146
Motor time, 78–79
Movement end location, 83
Movement time, 6
Muscle tone, 27

N

Neonatal reaching, 150
Neurophysiological mechanisms, 157
Nonfixated movement, 152
Normal motor development, 23
Numonic Electronic Digitizer, 85

O

Object/image stimuli, 151
Oculomotor system, 193–194

P

Peabody Developmental Motor Scales, 28
Perceptual Development, 83–96
Perceptual schemas, 168
Postural reflex action, 27–28
Postural support and fine motor control, 23–39
Postural support positions, 29

Predominantly guided reach, 154
Prehensile development, 165–199
Premotor time, 74
Prereaching, 152
Preschool learning, 115–126
Primitive throwers, 136
Proproceptive feedback, 151
Psychophysical factors, 84
Purdue Pegboard, 29–30

R

Radial error, 93
Range of motion, 27
Reaction time, 97–102
Reciprocal inhibition, 174
Rehearsal strategy, 108
Response execution, 101
Response integration, 186

S

Self-concept, 131
Sensory feedback, 156
Sensory-motor reaction, 147
Simple movement recognition, 95
Social play, 116
Social skills, 116
Spatial-temporal tracking, 12
Stimulus input, 101
Subcortical coordination, 189

T

Tactile feedback, 170
Temporal coordination, 168
Temporal parameters in jumping, 1–22
The Weaver's Loom: A Developmental Metaphor, 129–141
Transfer of learning, 98
Two-legged stance pertubations, 64

U

Unilateral arm responses, 145
Unilateral responses, 146

V

Verbal bombardment, 116
Videogame transfer, 97–102
Visual acuity, 28
Visual discrimination problems, 104
Visual fixation, 190

Visual perception, 28
Visual release actions, 183
Visually directed reaching, 143–163
Visually elicited systems, 156
Visually triggered response, 168
Visuomotor coordination, 165

Visuoproprioceptive coordination, 152
Voluntary control of motor behavior, 104

Y

Youth sport competition, 131

2/2000
DVD 2014

DATE DUE